mobile
influence

mobile influence

the new power of the consumer

CHUCK MARTIN

palgrave
macmillan

MOBILE INFLUENCE
Copyright © Chuck Martin, 2013.

First published in 2013 by PALGRAVE MACMILLAN® in the U.S.—a division
of St. Martin's Press LLC, 175 Fifth Avenue, New York, NY 10010.

Where this book is distributed in the UK, Europe and the rest of the world, this
is by Palgrave Macmillan, a division of Macmillan Publishers Limited, registered
in England, company number 785998, of Houndmills, Basingstoke, Hampshire
RG21 6XS.

Palgrave Macmillan is the global academic imprint of the above companies and
has companies and representatives throughout the world.

Palgrave® and Macmillan® are registered trademarks in the United States, the
United Kingdom, Europe and other countries.

ISBN: 978-1-137-27850-0

Library of Congress Cataloging-In-Publication Data

Martin, Chuck, 1949–
    Mobile influence : the new power of the consumer / Chuck Martin.
      pages   cm
    ISBN 978-1-137-27850-0 (alk. paper)
    1. Electronic commerce. 2. Internet marketing. 3. Consumer behavior.
4. Wireless communication systems. I. Title.
HF5548.32.M3736   2013
658.8'72—dc23
                                                                                2012046812

A catalogue record of the book is available from the British Library.

Design by Letra Libre

First edition: June 2013

10 9 8 7 6 5 4 3 2 1

Printed in the United States of America.

To Teri

CONTENTS

ACKNOWLEDGMENTS

Many people helped in so many aspects over the course of the writing of this book and to them I will be forever grateful.

Thank you to all those business leaders involved in various sections of the mobile commerce revolution who took time to share their strategies and insights with me. Many provided candid and detailed assessments of what is working, with lessons learned along the way. These include a range of people, from those leading the mobile charge at well-known brands to the heads of the mobile companies empowering many of them.

Thank you to Karen Wolny, editorial director at Palgrave Macmillan, who instantly and totally got the idea of the book and recognized the magnitude of the coming revolution in shopping behavior. Thank you to Jacquie Flynn, literary agent at Joelle Delbourgo Associates, who is still an editor at heart, for all those many discussions to develop the direction of this book.

Thanks to Cindy O'Brien, director of marketing and publicity at the Mobile Future Institute for advance marketing of the book, especially to the press and national speakers bureaus, as well as for assisting with fact-checking during the editing process. Thanks to Nicole Avedikian, director of digital and research at the Mobile Future Institute, for website and social media marketing relating to the book research and assisting with the organization of the research.

For introductions to executives and mobile innovation in various parts of the world, thanks to all those who helped, including Gordon Lokenberg, noted recruiter in Amsterdam, Diego Fernandez de Cordoba in Panama,

Peter Osborne at Bank of America, and Lihsin Tsai in China. Many thanks to the speakers bureaus around the country who represent me and help me spread the word by placing me in front of so many prestigious audiences.

Thanks to Maarten Lens-FitzGerald, co-founder of Layar, for offering to help create augmented reality "layars" for the front and back covers of this book.

Thanks to Ken Fadner, chairman and publisher of MediaPost, for providing me the opportunity to edit MediaPost's *mCommerce Daily,* write the daily MobileShopTalk column, and for being brand manager of the Mobile Insider Summits and programmer of the mCommerce Summit, where we interact for several days at a time with the leading innovators at brands and mobile companies at the forefront of the mobile revolution. Thanks to Joe Mandese, editor-in-chief of MediaPost, for getting me up to speed to edit *mCommerce Daily* and for sharing continual, astute market insights.

I want to acknowledge the MediaPost team who bring mobile and digital insights to the marketplace through multiple conferences and summits, so credit goes to Rob McEvily, Jeff Loechner, Jon Whitfield, Liam Fleming, Elaine Wong, Seth Oilman, Jonathan McEwan, Junmian Sun, Romeo Bagon, Samantha Bucciero, Mark Kecko, Steve Smith, Persia Tatar, Ryan Loechner, Katie Pearl, Chris Jara, Shanna Rentas, Catalino Rosales, Nathalie Chemaly, Carrie Cummings, Jenny Lee, and the rest of the team.

Most importantly, I want to offer my deepest appreciation and thanks to my family for such total support throughout the entire book process. Whether dealing with the late nights, notes sprawled throughout the kitchen, or the testing of various mobile shopping apps while monitoring shopper behaviors at stores, my family not only indulged me but also tirelessly encouraged me. To Ryan and Chase, our sons and Android wizards in their own right, my sincerest thank you. And lastly, thank you Teri, my wife and lifelong partner, for the continual and unwavering belief, encouragement, support, and love that empowers me to do what I do.

INTRODUCTION

We're in the midst of a revolution in the way people shop, in how they decide to buy, and in all behaviors associated with the entire purchase process. This revolution is being driven by the massive and global adoption of smartphones and tablets, empowering consumers, wherever they are, like never before. This mobile shopping revolution is impacting consumers and retailers of all types and sizes in all locations. With mobile devices, consumers shop constantly and differently.

Mobile shoppers want information sent to their mobile devices based on where they are and what they are doing. They research products on smartphones and tablets before even thinking of heading to the mall or store. They have their phones with them while heading out to shop or just do errands around town. They have smartphones—and many (58 percent)—use them for store-related shopping.[1] Mobile shoppers use their phones as they traverse the aisles, and they are increasingly scanning barcodes as they go. They compare prices through their price-checking apps and ultimately will pay using their phones. After the purchase, they share information about what they bought by texting and sending photos to friends and family.

In the mobile shopping revolution, the mobile-empowered customer, the *m-powered consumer*, is totally in charge. They have new power in the palms of their hands, they are leading marketers on new ways they want to use it, and there are a lot of them. With more than six billion mobile subscriptions globally, the majority of people have a phone (and in many places, they have more than one). Of those phones, more than a billion are smartphones, climbing to more than two billion in 2015.[2] These mobile shoppers are on a new path of purchasing.

Along this new path to purchase are specific times and places marketers can participate in the decision process to exert mobile influence. Throughout this book, you will see how various companies are working to influence behavior during the mobile purchase process. We also discuss some of the mobile industry companies that empower the companies leading the mobile shopping revolution. As you will see, the functions of sellers and customers are being radically transformed throughout the shopping process.

A GLOBAL EFFECT

The shopping transformation is global, with people around the world changing how they shop and buy via mobile devices. While some markets are ahead of others, they are all moving in essentially the same general direction. Some large, very well-known brands are introducing major mobile initiatives on a global scale. The growth potential of reaching mobile shoppers in multiple geographies is huge. Consider these statistics:

- Mobile penetration exceeds the entire population in 106 countries.
- The largest mobile advertising growth is occurring in Europe.
- Worldwide mobile advertising should pass $28 billion by 2016.[3]
- More than half of mobile users in China use mobile wallets.
- Mobile penetration in Latin America is 107 percent of the entire population.
- There will be ten billion mobile connections by 2016.[4]
- Households with Wi-Fi: South Korea, 80 percent; United Kingdom, 73 percent; Germany, 72 percent; France, 71 percent; Japan, 68 percent; Canada, 68 percent.[5]

Mobile apps are also a significant category, no matter the country, with Android and Apple each boasting more than 700,000 available from their respective app stores. With apps, as in mobile websites, comes revenue. For mobile app revenue, the fastest-growing countries for Apple's

App Store are Japan (560 percent of the growth rate in app revenue per market), Russia (115 percent), China (109 percent), and Taiwan (101 percent).[6] The growth in revenue for Google Play in Russia is 250 percent, more than twice the growth rate in the United States.

Slightly different approaches to reaching mobile shoppers are taken based on the country and mobile usage patterns. On a trip to Shanghai, I met with the general managers, directors, and heads of many luxury brands in China, such as Chanel, Land Rover, Mercedes-Benz, Audi, Estée Lauder, Swatch Group, Bulgari, and Hermès. As in other markets, the brand leaders are looking for what they should be doing in mobile and are highly interested in any mobile innovation occurring in the West. Their main focus is on viable mobile business models, ranging from advertising to commerce. The same is true in many parts of Latin America. Most in the audience I addressed in Shanghai said they had a mobile strategy, many for more than a year. Individually, almost half of them said they carried two mobile phones, which is common in executive audiences in the United States and other countries.

In China, unlike in the U.S. market, mobile phones are not subsidized by carriers, leaving consumers to pay the entire cost, which can range from $800 to $900 at the major Apple store in Shanghai. This dynamic provides a self-defined market. As one example of a business taking advantage of the Apple obsession, the three-year-old mobile lifestyle publication *iWeekly* is made available as an app only for iPhones and iPads. While Android leads the operating-system market and Nokia and Samsung lead in hardware sales, *iWeekly* sticks with Apple.

The choice worked, with the app being downloaded more than five million times to become the leading lifestyle app in China, according to Jane Yu, vice president and general manager of *iWeekly,* who notes that it is on 20 percent of all iPhones in China.[7] The reasoning goes that since the devices are bought by the most affluent, they must be the prime target for luxury brands.

The mobile market in China, with a billion mobile connections, resembles that of Latin America, where there are 630 million. But in both markets, two geographies dominate: Brazil and Colombia in Latin America, and Beijing and Shanghai in China.

MOBILE DEVICES RULE

When the internet created online shopping, consumers became more interactive, though marketing messages were still centrally controlled and aimed at large numbers of stationary potential customers. Now, rather than reaching consumers as they passively watch TV in the evening or read a magazine, the mobile device is the conduit to the consumer. Retail revenue is moving to mobile, with more than half of total online retail revenue expected to come from mobile by 2014.[8] The National Retail Federation acknowledged as much by launching the Integrated Mobile Initiative to serve as a source of information about the challenges and opportunities within mobile retailing.

The massive growth in the number of smartphones is well known and visible anywhere you look in the marketplace. Android phones dominate followed by Apple devices, though there are some differences in what happens on each of the two platforms, as you will see later in the book. In just a few years, sales through smartphones are expected to account for 19 percent of total store sales, translating to mobile-influenced sales of $689 billion.[9]

While not as ubiquitous as mobile phones, tablets are also a significant factor in mobile shopping. With their larger screens and in-home portability, they can be used to shop while consumers are watching TV or sitting in the kitchen. This trend will not be lost on marketers, with the number of devices in use estimated to reach 672 million by 2017.[10]

While tablets are being used for product research and price comparisons, they also can be an effective advertising platform for marketers trying to reach mobile shoppers who are at home, couch surfing. London-headquartered M&C Saatchi Mobile found that global spending on tablet advertising has on average led to four times greater conversion than on mobile handset campaigns.[11] When targeting is introduced in combination with creative campaigns, the conversion rate can be up to five to six times higher than mobile, compared to the advertising industry average of two to three times.

Tablet users also tend to use their devices in the living room, more than one in five shop less in physical stores, and more than half buy from their tablets.[12] With $12 billion expected to be spent on mobile Web-search advertising alone by 2017, much of it will migrate to tablets, since consumers are more likely to open search advertising on a tablet than on a PC.

LEARNING WHAT YOU DON'T KNOW

One of the common themes we found throughout the research for this book is that once a company launches mobile initiatives into the marketplace, the more the company finds it doesn't know. Different customer sets behave differently, and until the customer actually sees and uses a company's mobile innovations, the company can't really predict future usage patterns.

Retail can also be somewhat competitive. As a result, some companies do not want to share what they consider to be their secret sauces of mobile. However, once they launch in mobile, their initiatives are instantly visible all over the world. Oftentimes, what brands introduce in mobile is powered by the technology and platforms of mobile industry companies that are also profiled in the book.

In *Mobile Influence,* we attempt to highlight some of the leading thinking from some of the best and brightest in the mobile space as we address the many dynamics associated with mobile shopping.

The chapters in the book each represent one of the areas where marketers can influence mobile shopping behavior. We interviewed and spent time with many mobile industry leaders who shared what they have learned and what is working. We also know many of these industry leaders from regular MediaPost events, most notably the Mobile Insider Summit and the OMMA Mobile conference, both well-known, recurring events in the world of mobile and online media marketing and advertising.

Both domestically and globally, the current and future numbers, percentages, and trends continue to point in the same direction when it comes to mobile shopping behavior. We trust that *Mobile Influence* will shed some light along the path.

one

THE RISE OF THE MOBILE SHOPPER

Mobile is a complete game changer that alters consumer shopping behavior like nothing before it. With mobile, people no longer *go* shopping; they *are* shopping. With mobile, the consumer is more, well, mobile, on the go, always connected, and absorbing information in bite-sized pieces. Mobile shoppers are using their phones and tablets at multiple stages of shopping, before, all the way through, and after the purchase transaction, providing new challenges and opportunities for retailers to influence consumer decision making along the way.

Mobile shopping is different for several reasons. First, it is continuous. Unlike traditional non-mobile shopping, the mobile buying process can happen all the time. Consumers no longer have to be at a physical store or sitting at a computer. They can be researching a purchase while watching TV, on a bus or train, or walking down the street. Mobile shopping is also different because location or proximity to sellers and products can be determined. Someone out and about can, with one or two taps, find the location of something they desire or need based on where they are at the moment. The scope of mobile is also massive. By 2016, the number of mobile Web-connected devices should eclipse the number of people on earth, according to the well-known Cisco Visual Networking Index Global Mobile Data Traffic Forecast.[1] And lastly, mobile shopping is personal, since the device itself is highly personal and communications through the device are inherently one-to-one, whether by voice, text, pictures, or videos.

Indeed, shopping and buying behaviors are being totally transformed by the ability to buy anything at any time from any place. At physical stores, more than half (58 percent) of consumers who own a smartphone have used it for store-related shopping.[2] And more than half (55 percent) of smartphone shoppers have also used their mobile device to check prices as they shop.[3] At the end of 2014, the number of consumers purchasing physical goods remotely from their handsets is expected to reach 580 million.[4] No matter how big the impact mobile is having on shopping behavior, it is only going to get bigger.

THE MOBILE RIPPLE

It is not only physical retail stores of all shapes and sizes that will be impacted. All brands and sellers of products and services will be affected. The implications are significant, since there can be an effect throughout the shopping process that I call the *mobile ripple*. For example, when more ticket sales occur through smartphones and tablets, the mobile ripple is how the sales process affects both the number of ticketing agents needed to sell tickets at a physical event and the printing of tickets as more consumers show codes and receipts on their smartphones as they check in. This is already common at airline security checkpoints, where boarding passes are displayed on smartphones.

The number of tickets delivered to mobile phones worldwide is expected to reach 23 billion by 2016 as mobile users adopt mobile tickets as part of their mobile shopping behavior, according to Juniper Research.[5] These include tickets for sporting events, travel, and entertainment events. By that time, NFC (near field communication) mobile ticket sales will account for more than half of mobile ticket revenue, according to the study, which shows one in eight users in Western Europe using their phones as a contactless metro payment ticket.

NBC Universal's Fandango, which sells movie tickets online, already sells more than a third of its movie tickets via mobile devices, and the app has been downloaded more than 25 million times. The mobile ripple over time can mean fewer theater salespeople along with mobile check-in to get into the show. Airlines are following suit, though they didn't start that way. Initially, many airline mobile apps told you simply when your flight would ideally depart and arrive, and some would let you know if your baggage made the same plane you did. Sell you a ticket? Not so much. But by 2015, 89 percent of airlines plan to be selling tickets via mobile, according to a survey of IT trends in the airline industry by the technology firm SITA, originally known as Société Internationale de Télécommunications Aéronautiques. Notably, United Airlines was early in selling tickets via mobile; its mobile efforts are discussed later in the book. The travel website Expedia expects up to half its U.S. hotel bookings to come from mobile in the near future.

THE MOBILE SHOPPING LIFE CYCLE

The traditional sales funnel is dead. It has been replaced by what I call the *Mobile Shopping Life Cycle*, comprising six specific moments when marketers have the opportunity to impact mobile consumer behavior and purchase decisions. Marketing efforts guided by the traditional sales funnel don't work with mobile because the entire shopping and buying process is iterative rather than serial. In other words, in the old sales funnel, the shopper moved one step at a time toward the purchase and marketers targeted them as they moved closer to making the purchase. With mobile, the process is not in such an organized sequence. The steps of the mobile buying process are happening all the time. But, most importantly, the mobile shopper (*m-shopper*) can be highly influenced during the six distinct moments when they are using their mobile devices on the go. The six stages of the mobile shopping cycle are *influence points*. Once marketers understand these six mobile influence points, they can more effectively target information and marketing messages to reach and influence consumers during the Mobile Shopping Life Cycle.

One of the oldest known traditional buying concepts lays out the traditional stages of the selling process. Known as AIDA, which stands for Attention, Interest, Desire, and Action, the concept provides a way to think about how to interact with customers in the process of a sale. Marketers have to get the attention of the customer before even thinking of convincing him of anything. Then they have to increase interest, perhaps by clearly identifying the product benefits they are trying to sell. Increasing the desire for the product follows by showing how the product may match or satisfy a customer's needs. The last step involves getting the customer to take action, resulting in the sale.

Over time, in the evolution of what became known as the sales funnel or the traditional sales funnel, some of the stages were more defined and refined. They became: awareness, familiarity, consideration, purchase, and loyalty—they still were used as a guideline in how to sway consumers at various stages on the path to purchase. Until recently, consumers were relatively stationary and easy to reach with marketing messages via a centralized, broadcast model. Marketers could reach millions of consumers simultaneously through mass media such as TV or radio.

In the Mobile Shopping Life Cycle, mobile shoppers are active in six phases in the course of an actual purchase. This cycle involves using various aspects of mobile at each phase. At each of these six stages there is the opportunity to sway or influence customer behavior. They are the times, locations, and mind-sets when businesses can interact with mobile-empowered customers to impact the actual purchase. Each of the six

Attention
Interest
Desire
Action

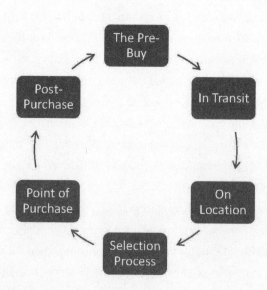

phases will continue to expand as smartphone penetration increases with more consumers joining the ranks of mobile shoppers.

THE MOBILE SHOPPING LIFE CYCLE: THE SIX INFLUENCE POINTS

During the six distinct moments of the Mobile Shopping Life Cycle, marketers have the potential to steer the mobile consumer toward their product and influence shopping behaviors.

1. **THE SETUP: The Pre-Buy.** During this phase the mobile shopper is researching. Consumers use smartphones and tablets to research purchases before they even consider going to the store. Mobile is a pull rather than a push medium. This means that rather than marketers being able to push a message, such as in a TV commercial, to the consumer, they must position information and messages about their products to be pulled by the consumer according to that person's time frame, mind-set, and location.

2. **THE MOVE: In Transit.** This phase occurs when the consumer is on the way to a store or running an errand. With new location-based capabilities, marketers will be able to leverage information, such as smartphone location and speed, to send highly targeted and relevant messages to consumers who have opted in to receive valuable offers. Marketers will have to create value for consumers in order to incentivize them to leave their location turned on in any given app.

3. **THE PUSH: On Location.** This point occurs at a brick-and-mortar store. In the early days of the internet, brick and mortar was a detriment to business, since online-only retailers could sell directly to consumers with fewer associated costs. Some retailers are missing the opportunity to identify and interact with the mobile shopper while they are in the store, while others are leveraging the ability to interact.

4. **THE PLAY: Selection Process.** This is when customers are near the actual product they may be considering buying. With what the mobile industry calls proximity marketing, marketers can

use various technologies to interact in real time with customers with the potential to move to real-time pricing. For example, a number of customers could be walking by a particular product and receive real-time offers, such as a discount on that product. Once a number of those products have been sold and based on inventory and price tracking, the offers could be discontinued as the next group of customers walk by. Consumers are scanning products with their smartphones and being provided with on-the-spot price comparisons with easy-to-use but sophisticated technologies.

5. **THE WRAP: Point of Purchase.** This stage provides the marketer one last chance to sway the buyer. As businesses adopt more mobile self-checkout options and mobile capabilities are embedded into point-of-sale systems, offers and counteroffers can be presented to consumers during the actual buying and checkout process. Companies such as Procter & Gamble and Kraft are in the very early stages of exploring how to insert themselves at this influence point.

6. **THE TAKEAWAY: Post-Purchase.** This occurs after the actual purchase. In this phase consumers exchange photos, videos, and information about their recent purchase via their mobile devices with friends and colleagues, soliciting and receiving feedback. The challenge for marketers is to become part of the conversation at this stage.

Various brands either participate or plan to participate in various parts of the Mobile Shopping Life Cycle, which we detail in later chapters. Some companies either are or will be active at all six influence points, while others are active in only a limited number of them. In some cases, a mobile shopper can be influenced to jump from one stage of the cycle directly to the actual purchase phase or point of purchase, which we also detail later.

DRIVERS OF MOBILE INFLUENCE

There are two categories of companies that cause and drive mobile influence. I call these two types of businesses *captains of mobile influence* and

facilitators of mobile influence. The captains of mobile influence are tho_
companies that truly get mobile and are deploying mobile initiatives, some
on a global basis. The facilitators of mobile influence are those companies
that enable and in many cases power the captains of mobile influence.

There are a number of captains of mobile influence, those companies
that understand and embrace the transformative nature of mobile. They
are well past the early research and development (R&D) and experimental
stage and now see mobile as core in all they do. For these companies, mobile is not an afterthought or something they add to an already-conceived
marketing plan. It is integral. These are the companies that embrace innovation from companies in the mobile industry and, with open eyes
and a willingness to fail, try new approaches to influencing behavior. The
captains of mobile influence continually seek best-in-breed mobile technologies and approaches, striving to provide increased value to mobile
shoppers throughout the Mobile Shopping Life Cycle.

In addition to the captains of mobile influence, there is a substantial
and robust mobile industry that powers much of the mobile activity that
customers see and experience. These are the facilitators of mobile influence and many of these companies are hardly household names, though
many are well known by the leaders directing the mobile strategies at some
of the best-known companies in the world, many of them captains of mobile influence. We call these mobile industry companies that make mobile
happen facilitators of mobile influence, since it is their technology or service that underlies much of the mobile and tablet activity today.

Some of these facilitators of mobile influence are led by former heads
of internet start-ups from the internet boom years, and others are led by
young entrepreneurs with new and innovative ideas. Some of them are
very well funded, some are making lots of money, and others are struggling to succeed. Many have talented staff members at all levels of their
ranks, and they generally all are moving full steam ahead. The facilitators
of mobile influence can be located anywhere geographically, and they are
scattered all over the United States.

Although these companies are commonly referred to as mobile start-
ups, many of them have been doing what they do for a number of years.
Sometimes they are called start-ups because they just got discovered by a

company that finally needed that particular mobile function and never had a need to search for companies that could provide it until now. In all cases, the goal of these facilitators is to power and empower other companies to succeed in the word of mobile. All the mobile companies involved in any type of selling or transacting fall into one of the six influence points, and some, as you will see later in the book, are active in many or all of the six stages.

Throughout the book we identify the captains of mobile influence and the facilitators of mobile influence and attempt to show what they do and, in many cases, how they do it.

BRANDS MOVING TO MOBILE

Mondelez International comprises the global snacking and food brands of the former Kraft Foods Inc. and was officially created in late 2012. With about 100,000 employees around the world and estimated annual revenue of $36 billion, Mondelez represents some of the best-known brands and products in the world, including Nabisco, Cadbury, Oreo, Trident, Halls, Chips Ahoy, Milka, and Tang, to name a few. The company is also one of the captains of mobile influence.

Some of the brands leading with mobile innovation are large and global, like Mondelez, which does not see its size as a disadvantage. "I actually do not subscribe to slow and lumbering," says Bonin Bough, vice president of global media and consumer engagement at Mondelez International.[6] "I actually believe that if you look at our company, maybe there is a bit more paperwork necessary than for a smaller organization, but if you look at the rate at which we can effect change in reality, I can create platforms that have millions of users overnight."

Just because a company is large, with established processes in place, doesn't mean it can't also be relatively nimble in mobile. However, a company does need a corporate recognition of the significance of mobile and the leadership commitment to allocate significant resources. Mondelez approaches the mobile marketplace with a clear vision of the importance of mobile. "We are the world's largest start-up," says Bough. "We have a single mantra, which is about speed. Beat the market, beat the thinking, beat the profitability. I actually think that you will see that what used to be looked at as big, lumbering organizations will now be looked at as levers to change the world. The difference is that scale. I can operate at scale in a way that most organizations can't. We are one of the largest food companies in the world, and that comes with a scale that allows you to put things into the marketplace."

The captains of mobile influence tend to take both a short- and long-term view of the implications of a world gone mobile. They tend to look beyond incremental change and slow growth, leaning toward rapidly keeping pace with their customers. "We are looking to shift 10 percent of all media spending globally into mobile with a focus on how do we make sure we are where the consumer is," says Bough. (The typical level of advertising spending on mobile is less than 1 percent, as detailed later in the book.)

"It requires being a part of an organization that has great leadership," says Bough. "My leadership said yep, put it into the market. Do it quick, do it fast, do it often.

"If you believe, like I do, that every single package in your grocery store will be connected to the internet at some point," says Bough, "then the beauty of the future is, and it is just a matter of when, and I see the future in the next five years. As a result of that we might be the largest technology company. You might be talking to the head of global media for the largest technology company in the world in the next five years because we will have connected packaging in the marketplace. I do not subscribe to the sense that big organizations are slow. I believe that big organizations are levers for transformation in the future."

One of the easier steps that brands can take to create mobile influence is to move more advertising dollars into mobile experiences for the shopper. Current advertising budgets for TV, print, and online media can be many millions of dollars a year at a large brand. Mondelez looks beyond traditional advertising as it attempts to move with its mobile customers. According to Bough:

> There are four key areas where mobile specifically can help us globally. First is video equivalency. So we know that more and more people are watching on television or consuming content, 23 percent of media is consumed on a mobile device, and we know they are consuming

video content, and quite frankly, all types of content on this device. So how do we build a reach? How do we maximize the reach of our communications by making sure that we have a focus on, in this case, video equivalency? So how do we make sure that we are looking at screens as a platform versus as an individual first screen, second screen, third screen. How do we look at screen-based media?

The second piece really is about increasing engagement. While the first one was about reach, this is about engagement. In a world where people are continuously becoming distracted or disconnected from their viewing experience, you watch TV and the moment a commercial comes on you use the DVR or you look down at your phone. How do we create complementary engagement that can actually increase the effectiveness of our largest investment? How do we create second-screen experiences? How do we take advantage of the emerging behavior that is social chatter?

The second big bucket that has two pieces is really about driving purchases. The first is around impulse. We know that mobile devices are at scale. There are seven billion people in the world and 5.1 billion of them have a cell phone and only four billion have a toothbrush. Mobile is clearly a scale platform and there are scaled media opportunities.

What's more interesting is there are opportunities closer to the journey, closer to our products. You wake up in the morning and check your phone—there is opportunity for top-of-mind awareness. You start your commute; this is opportunity for top-of-mind awareness. While you are on the journey toward the point where you might purchase, you get off. Here is another opportunity for top-of-mind awareness. By the way, you are probably walking by some kind of retailer that sells one of our products. There is a huge opportunity for that: how we start to look at media channels and the impulse channel.

There are a number of ways to reach the consumer. I think the first tip of the spear in terms of beginning to show results and get organizations focused on it will be shifting advertising dollars, because that is the most flexible part of the marketing cycle.

All the other stuff you are going to attach—applications development, content creation, and all those kind of things—requires a lot more work for most organizations. From a macro perspective of organizations, the spear will be shifting ad dollars. If you look at the internet, there was a lot of that from the tip of the spear. But ultimately, it's about content experiences. Those content experiences can happen on the big platforms that people use their mobile phones for, like Facebook and Twitter.

How are you thinking about the different types of mobile community management? Community management built for mobile devices. Whether it's changing the size of the images you post, knowing nobody will watch a two-minute video anymore, creating links that drive to something that leverages the power of the phone, like the location, or any of those kind of things, and potentially even developing apps or experiences that people engage in. All three of those will be important parts of the equation. The first piece will probably be the tip of the spear that you'll see most marketers move to the fastest in term of volume of actual spending.

The last piece is mobile at retail. What are the new opportunities for us inside of the retail environment? What are the new transformations we have to bring to the way we think about the shopper experience? What are the ways we think about our packaging as it relates to our mobile phone?

Unlocking of the content, engaging with the package and the device, and engaging with health information, recipes, or companion purchases. All of those things become a real skill set that is necessary to win as you look at the future of the consumer and retail. And even more than that you could become the deciding factor as to if someone buys you or not.

Or, even scarier, the phone could be the point of wallet. So as things like NFC and wallet come online, I could be tapping my phone to purchase and then I have to deal with couponing, discounting, and all those type of things. But I also have to deal with the fact that the person might have an automated shopping list in their phone and getting into the shopping list is probably one of the most difficult things that we've seen when we look at players that try to approach us directly, like Amazon. All of a sudden, the problem that we are having in the e-com world becomes magnified in the mobile com world when it comes to retailer experience. Those are really the four buckets that we are looking at strategically across the landscape.

Bough looks at the consequences of a company like Mondelez *not* moving to mobile.

"You have to ask yourself about risk," says Bough. "What does the word 'risk' mean? I've been in a lot of meetings lately and the word 'risk,' they keep telling agencies you have to be willing to take risks. I just don't understand what you mean by risk. There are just countless brands inside an organization that look just like ours that were billion-dollar brands that are now nonexistent because people did par for the course. Is risk going where you know the consumer is going, where you know the future is going, or is risk not doing it and having it done to you? I guess it just requires a new thought process around what risk is. And the beauty, I think, as a business culture is that we have been moving towards this anyways. It is just those who can accelerate that trend and build the culture inside the organization that are ultimately going to win.

"We're also trying to launch the world's largest mobile panel. Why wouldn't I do it? So what's a risk? If you read card-level data and panel data and you believe that's telling you the picture of your consumer, you are fooling yourself. Because how many convenience stores do you go in with a loyalty card? None. How many millennials do you know that are actually doing that panel data, scanning of the products? None. So all of a sudden you have a blind spot around an entire group of people and an entire purchase point. What is more risk? Not knowing what their behavior is or not knowing what you did in the past is safe? I don't know."

Like other captains of mobile influence, Mondelez is involved in multiple areas of mobile. "We are at the infancy stage with this stuff," says Bough. "We are doing NFC stuff, doing wallet stuff, I'm doing stuff with Catalina. At the end of the day if you sit down with any other organization what they can tell you directly about where the future is going with this stuff—not much.

I can sit down and give you a plethora and talk to you about NFC and what has worked and what hasn't, what type of content people engage with, having engaged with shelf talkers, I can tell you that stuff. Very few organizations can provide that level of conceptual thinking and actual operationalization of that. And why wouldn't I want to do that? I can give direction as we move forward with these things. And not all of them are going to win."

Each of the stages of the Mobile Shopping Life Cycle will evolve and mature over time. They also can develop slightly differently, depending on the country and mobile culture. "What I would say is the bigger win is outside of the U.S. and that is what I think organizations are failing to realize more than anything," says Bough. "That it's interesting here and it feels like it works, but the other markets are where people are skipping. All of the knowledge base that you have about digital media buying on desktop, all that stuff is a waste now because most people are skipping over other developing markets. You cannot rely on your digital center of excellence and how they used to think when you enter into the new world. I am so focused on winning mobile battles in those other markets."

THE MOBILE FUTURE OF MONDELEZ

As part of its commitment to its mobile future, in late 2012 Mondelez launched an initiative it named Mobile Futures, with the intent of collaborating with start-up companies innovating in mobile. The idea was to pair Mondelez brands with select companies to accelerate and scale existing mobile innovations as well as incubate new mobile ventures, each in a three-month period.

In his previous position as director of digital and social media at PepsiCo, Bough spearheaded a similar program called the PepsiCo 10, a process that encouraged employees to seek ideas being driven by promising start-ups. Entrepreneurs could submit an online application in one of four categories: mobile marketing, place-based and retail experiential marketing, social media, or digital video and gaming. All the proposals were evaluated based on how they could impact brands.

In the PepsiCo program, the start-ups had to have been in technology for less than two years, raised up to $2 million, or had revenue of $250,000. The company started with 500 applicants, which were ultimately narrowed to 20, all of which, over two days, presented to brand managers at PepsiCo headquarters. Ten were selected and then paired with PepsiCo brands to launch pilot projects. Of the ten selected, five focused on using mobile.

In the Mondelez program, the first phase focuses on understanding and embracing the start-up entrepreneurial spirit. The start-ups chosen get to work one-on-one with Mondelez brands like Oreo, Trident, Sour Patch, and belVita, to scale and activate pilots into market within 90 days. The process becomes a two-way street, as the brands spend a week working alongside their start-ups, immersing the company's marketers in that culture. The brands also create and incubate completely new mobile ventures, and at the end of the program, Mondelez pitches the new venture concepts to angel investors and venture capitalists in hopes of securing seed funding. Bough says:

> We can help to continue to put the fuel necessary to help entrepreneurial ideas fit into the marketplace quickly and have scale. If you look at how this program is set up, it is all about at scale. We brought the partners that are going to help us put things to scale into the marketplace. We got a social TV idea and were aligning it across Viacom. We brought AT&T, clearly mobile, but how do we get those mobile ideas out at scale? We got retailers, how do we get those into the retail marketplace quickly? That is the level of scale that we can bring to the table that no others can.
>
> We know that there is a future of mobile that we are either going to have imposed upon us or we will be a part of shaping it. We also know that there is a ton of innovation that comes from us internally and there is a ton of innovation coming from the outside. So we created a platform for us to engage with entrepreneurs that are shaping the future of mobile. We really want to do it at a pace that looks exactly like their pace. The key mechanism organizing principle underneath mobile futures is build the future in 90 days. It's about pace, about speed, about flexibility, it's about agility. It's about thinking and acting not only like an entrepreneur but also like an intrepreneur.
>
> The first stage is open call. Give the start-up three criteria: social TV, mobile retail, and location. We find the brand that can partner

with that start-up and put a pilot into the marketplace within 90 days. During that phase one of our team members will actually go and sit with the start-up so they have an acculturation experience. They will become close and pretty much live and breathe the thinking around that start-up. Then we will pass them and take what they have learned and put it into thinking closer to the problems that we have with our business.

The second phase is about taking our start-up, which now will be operating more as a mentor because we've already launched the pilot, so we go into small limited mentor phase. For one week, we fly our folks and the start-up mentor out to the advance research institute in California and task them with building a venture on their own. They then have one week to create a new venture, a venture that they see as addressing one of our business challenges that has to be built on mobile. For the next 90 days we incubate a couple of ones that we think have the best opportunity. We actually put them into the market. We are trying to launch our own ventures into the market during that phase two. The goal is, if P&G was about to reinvent the soap opera and put a piece of our own content, our own mechanism into the marketplace, why can't we do that in the marketplace? But also how can we continue to drive the thinking and cultural change that will be necessary for us to win in a future that is defined by mobile? The first phase is about supporting entrepreneurs and the second is about creating intrepreneurs and encouraging our folks to think like start-ups in the mobile space. At the end of the day, the best way to predict the future is to invent it. And so we firmly believe that. That culture transformation is what we are driving after.

The Mondelez program is much more focused than the PepsiCo 10 challenge that preceded it and includes refinements based on past lessons. "This is all mobile," says Bough. "At the end of the day, it's not about a successful pilot, it's not about a new venture, it's about transforming the culture. Transforming the minds of our marketers so they can think every day and everything that they do how to be mobile forward."

One of the leading mobile marketing organizations is also involved in the mobile future initiative. "This initiative demonstrates to the world the level of mobile innovation and scale that can be delivered through an organization of Mondelez International's size," says Greg Stuart, CEO of the Mobile Marketing Association, which assisted Mondelez with the program.[7] "The value of mobile as a communication channel can no longer be challenged with mobile offering endless opportunities for brands to connect with consumers in a more powerful and personalized way."

Early in 2013, Mondelez selected the nine start-up companies to work with: Lisnr (Cincinnati), ROXIMITY (Denver), Waze (Palo Alto), Shelby.tv (New York), Dailybreak (Boston), inMarket (Venice), Endorse (San Mateo), Kiip (San Francisco), and Banjo (Redwood City).

Captains of mobile influence tend to be more forward thinking about the impact of mobile on their brands. They also are proactive about seeking mobile innovations and solutions from the facilitators of mobile influence. And most importantly, they continually monitor and watch for signs of behavior in their mobile shoppers.

BEHAVIOR OF THE MOBILE SHOPPER

Much as online shopping transformed purchase behaviors, mobile shopping is even more transformational, for several reasons. While not everyone in the world had or has a personal computer with internet access, there are more than six billion mobile subscribers, more than five times the number of PCs in the world. And while online shoppers typically do it from their desktop or laptop, mobile shoppers do it everywhere. Moreover, mobile purchasing can be executed at any time, since mobile shoppers almost always have their phones and they are likely on. Tablets also have opened the door to even more remote browsing, price checking, and purchasing.

There are numerous research studies identifying how many people use phones to shop, how many scan products, how many look up store information, and all other mobile activities. While some of the results in percentages may vary, the studies all show generally the same trends and patterns: mobile and tablets are on the rise in a wide range of categories and activities. The most significant consistent finding is that smartphone and tablet owners are very active in using their devices.

For example, 64 percent of tablet owners and more than half (55 percent) of smartphone owners in the United States check their bank account balances on their devices, according to research from GfK, one of the world's leading research companies, which conducts research in more than 100 countries.[8] More than half (52 percent) of tablet owners and more than a third (39 percent) of smartphone owners make payments or transfers for a bank account on their mobile devices.

Overall buying activity on tablets and smartphones is almost the same, with 40 percent of tablet owners and 38 percent of smartphone owners purchasing something remotely. When it comes to using their device to help with shopping, tablet owners are highly active, with 58 percent engaged in the activity. Smartphone and tablet owners purchase from a range of categories, with consumer electronics leading the way and auto purchasing at the low end (see Table 1.1).

There also are demographic differences. Sixty-seven percent of smartphone owners 18 to 34 years old use their smartphones to shop, while 44 percent of those 35 years old and above do the same. Tablets follow a similar pattern, with 27 percent of those 18 to 34 using them to shop, compared to 17 percent of tablet owners 35 and older. A higher percentage of younger mobile shoppers are more active on social networks, are less loyal to retailers, desire customization, and are more loyal to those allowing input (see Table 1.2).

table 1.1

CATEGORIES OF MOBILE/TABLET SHOPPING

Consumer electronics	40%
Clothing	33%
Food/beverage	27%
Health/beauty	23%
Mobile phone	21%
Home improvement	18%
Lawn/garden	15%
Auto	14%

table 1.2

SHOPPING BY AGE

	18–34	35+
Using social networks to shop	58%	35%
Less loyal to retailers (shop around)	51%	46%
Like website tracking in return for customization	43%	27%
More loyal to those letting me input	47%	43%

As they shop, mobile consumers are using their phones and tablets to seek value, gain information, conduct transactions, use social media, and use location technology. For example, a large number of them (89 percent) are seeking value, with more than half (52 percent) comparing prices and 44 percent trying to find a coupon. The second most popular category is to gain information, with 59 percent using their device to locate a store, more than half (52 percent) to check product availability, and about half (49 percent) to search for information or reviews. Mobile activity is highly integrated with the entire shopping process.

RETAIL AND THE MOBILE SHOPPER

Many retailers are paying close attention to evolving mobile consumer behavior, and for good reason. Four out of every five smartphone users—86 million people—accessed retail content on their device in one month alone. Amazon was the number-one retailer, visited by 50 million people in one month alone. Apple had 18 million mobile visitors, Walmart 16 million, Target 10 million, and Best Buy 7 million, according to comScore (see Table 1.3).[9]

Male and female smartphone users represent nearly equal proportions of retail category visitors, but females account for a higher share of retail destinations at 56 percent of retail minutes on smartphones. The study also shows that 71 percent of smartphone retail visitors are less than 45 years old. One third of smartphone owners visiting retail stores had annual incomes of more than $100,000 (see Table 1.4).

table 1.3

VISITORS BY RETAILER

Retailer	Unique Visitors (in millions)
Amazon	50
eBay	33
Apple	18
Walmart	16
Target	10
Best Buy	7
Ticketmaster	6
CVS	4
The Home Depot	4
Blockbuster	4
Barnes & Noble	4
Walgreens	4
Limited Brands	3
Lowe's	3
Etsy	3

table 1.4

PERCENTAGE OF SMARTPHONE VISITORS

Male	51%
Female	49%
Age	
18–24	19%
25–34	29%
35–44	23%
45–54	16%
55–64	10%
65+	4%
Income	
<$25K	12%
$25K–<$40K	9%
$40K–<$60K	11%
$60K–<$75K	20%
$75K–<$100K	16%
$100K+	33%

THE RISING EXPECTATIONS OF THE MOBILE SHOPPER

Mobile is causing some of the roles of buyers and sellers to evolve, with each gaining new responsibilities in the shopping process. During simpler times, shoppers could do their research at home before heading to the mall or store. They could search online or pore through newspapers and magazines. They also could end up shopping for nothing in particular and decide on an impulse purchase.

The behaviors were relatively simple and predictable. Marketers could reach these future buyers through ads in various vehicles and at various times, such as prime time. The shopping process was serial, with research followed by the shop and buy. The shopping-buying process is now being blurred by consumers armed with smartphones and tablets searching, researching, sharing, and shopping all the time and in all locations.

Throughout the Mobile Shopping Life Cycle, the functions of customers and sellers are being transformed. The definitions of the roles of each in the shopping process in various categories are emerging.

> **Proactive research.** Consumers are searching and researching on mobile devices on the fly as well as during the much-talked-about multiscreen sessions. They also are researching in the store and on the way to the store, some all the way to the buy. Mobile is a pull, not a push, medium. Customers want to pull information from the business to them on their time frame, based on where they are and what they're doing. Marketers must be prepared to answer questions on the customer's schedule.

> **Product content.** Consumers want more content and context around the products they seek to buy, and they want on-the-spot product information. Shoppers want and expect to get more information than is often provided with the product itself. They know how to text and can receive videos on their phones. Some companies have figured this out. For example, the Intel mobile website provides a few quick questions that can be answered in well under a minute to produce the proposed computer

specs with suggestions of which Intel processor would be best. Marketers are using *geofencing,* which creates a virtual perimeter of any chosen range around any location, to better serve more relevant information based on a mobile shopper's location.

In-store scanning. Better phone cameras are making barcode scanning by shoppers easier and faster. Scanning provides them with competitive pricing from other stores and online. While some retailers (such as Nordstrom) have their own proprietary barcodes and others (such as Target) look to have suppliers use codes unique to them, mobile consumers want to know the context of their current buy. Is it a fair price, higher or lower than a competitor, or is it unique to that store, such as a Staples-branded item at that store?

Price match. Consumers, understandably, want to get the best value, which is often perceived as a product at the best price. Mobile shoppers now have access to a range of pricing information in real time. Retailers will have to weigh the risks and benefits according to their own metrics and balance sheets. For example, on one visit to a Dick's Sporting Goods store, I scanned an item to purchase and found it for 30 percent less at another physical retailer within reasonable driving distance. The clerk asked the manager on duty if they would match the price and she replied, "Absolutely not." The other retailer offered one-click purchase, so the decision to purchase elsewhere was facilitated.

Inventory transparency. Mobile shoppers expect to be able to see if a product is in stock. Many retailers have provided this capability online for years. But mobile adds another dimension, since the customer's location needs to be factored in. The mobile consumer wants to know the nearest location that has the product now. Some companies jumped on this early. For example, Citi last year teamed with Best Buy to make the entire Best Buy inventory viewable from the Citi ThankYou app.[10] The

Citi Rewards card holder could check inventory, scan an item in a Best Buy, purchase the item with points via mobile, and pick up the item at checkout a few minutes later, bypassing any store associates in the process.

And this is just the early stages of the mobile revolution at retail and in shopping behavior. The mobile shopper is active and using a mobile device in new and innovative ways, looking for brands and marketers that are accommodating to them.

ALWAYS SHOPPING

Mobile influence involves so much more than just creating advertising for mobile shoppers. It involves crafting highly relevant messages that are highly targeted and personalized. It is not a one-size-fits-all approach.

Founded in Miami in 1988, Crispin Porter + Bogusky, known as CP+B, is a full-service, integrated advertising agency. It has 800 employees in offices in London; Göteborg, Sweden; Miami; Boulder; and Santa Monica. Its clients include Old Navy, Best Buy, and American Express. The agency promotes itself as specializing in making brands famous, turning them around, and generating outrageous business results. Its focus is on solving business challenges rather than just making ads, and it is one of the many facilitators of mobile influence. It also is heavily involved with innovations at retail.

"The thing that makes mobile retail exciting is that for the first time ever we can really market to an individual in the right context, the right place, and the right time," says Angel Anderson, experience director at CP+B.[11] "When they are passing by our products, we can reach out to them through geofencing, we can send push notifications to them to let them know about a deal, or let them know that a particular item is on special."

Many mobile influence facilitating companies have focused on aggregating various mobile technologies and capabilities and honing them to effectively serve mobile shoppers, always with an eye toward the future.

"We can use technology like the iOS Passbook, where not only can we message you when you're passing our location but we can also remind you when you're passing our competitor's location because you can geofence a

Passbook location to up to ten different locations," says Anderson, who has more than ten years' experience humanizing digital products and services for clients. "So it gives us a bit of a playful edge to tweak the competition as well."

Mobile is even transforming the way people think about shopping. With mobile and tablets, time and location become less of a factor, making the shopping process an all-the-time event.

"People are using geo-location and time-based alerts and being able to have that kind of contextual relationship," says Anderson. "What it has done is shifted the way we think about shopping. We used to say, 'I am going shopping.' Now, when we talk about something that we're going to buy, we say, 'I *am* shopping.' 'I'm shopping for a new car,' 'I'm shopping for a dress to wear for a wedding.' Not 'I am going shopping.' What that speaks to is this notion that we are always shopping.

"There is less need to go to a store, but you may spend the time on a mobile phone browsing through a couple of different sites looking at cocktail dresses. Then you might go online at work and take a peek at something a friend sent and later go home and while you're watching TV you see a dress on a character and you might look that up on your iPad. Now I have used three different devices. And it's not that I am using a mobile device or using a laptop. *I* am mobile. Because I am mobile I am ping-ponging between all these access points in my shopping experience. I am shopping across them. It's top of mind so that when I see something in the store I bookmark it in my mind. So it's this shift away from shopping as an event to shopping as an always-happening thing. Kind of like how we are with the internet now—this always-on mentality. You don't go onto the internet anymore, you are just connected."

Like some other leading-edge agencies, CP+B has used various known mobile components and services for its clients. This approach tends to leverage the creativity, services, and platforms of others and package them to be most appropriate for its particular customers. For example, CP+B wanted to leverage location knowledge with Old Navy, one of its clients.

"One of the things we have done is utilize Foursquare for check-ins and offer specials," says Anderson. "That is a known thing, everyone is doing that. Old Navy was the number-one Foursquare check-in in the retail category. When you think of an Old Navy customer you may not think of them as super technology savvy, but they are when it comes to shopping. They take on any behavior that is going to help them win their shopping game. There are things like shopkick where you can visit different stores to earn points. Recently in one of our research phases we talked to a woman who every day on the way to work and on the way back goes into the mall and goes to the stores to get all her points that are redeemable for things.

"So we're using points-based rewards, Foursquare check-ins, and we're taking advantage of Passbook. As soon as Google Wallet evolves to store coupons we'll probably be doing a similar geofencing technique where not only do you have the coupon saved in your wallet, but it also reminds you to use it when you're passing the product or the store.

"Tagging a product to alert someone walking by is a little bit trickier. That requires even tighter collaboration with the clients' IT [information technology] system and their technology department. It is something that we are moving towards but it's a challenge because it's not something most clients are set up to handle yet. We're helping clients get there because our competitors are jumping on this."

The facilitators of mobile influence keep pushing the envelope, which is necessary just to keep up with many of the evolving mobile behaviors. Consumers continually look to mobile to make things in their lives easier, better, cheaper, and even more fun. Agencies like CP+B are always looking at what is being done across entire categories, especially in matching shoppers to precise products based on location.

"Target is a really great example," says Anderson. "When you do a barcode scan on a Target product it will pull up exactly that product and you can find out if it's available at the other side of the city, and you can go there, and it will navigate you toward the product. That speaks to some back-end data they have been storing on this stuff and they're now surfacing it and making it public. The challenge for Old Navy and other retailers is that they may not have that data to access. It is something we are working towards, getting you specifically to that product, but we are taking steps towards that.

"Customers absolutely want this. It is that expectation that we now have with this always-on culture. Information is out there and people should be able to find it without struggling. Back in the day if a person couldn't use a piece of technology or find information they'd say, 'I'm not good with computers.' Nobody says that now. They just say, 'This piece of crap phone doesn't work,' or 'Ugh, I can't use Yahoo! search because it sucks.' They will just switch to something better. They no longer internalize the failings and shortcomings of technology. They realize what is bad design and they will switch to something that's better."

The opportunity for businesses is to introduce or manage capabilities for mobile shoppers that give them more control over the process. This could mean being more transparent and finding new pieces of information to associate with products that may not yet have been previously considered.

"I would love to see our clients' customers feeling really empowered," says Anderson. "I would love to see them feeling that the information we give them is super personalized to them. Right now we're in a world that in most places you can scan a barcode and get a price comparison and that's great so you can find where the product is offered cheapest, but I'd like to see more of a rich experience about what is right for me, not just what's less expensive.

"Right now I'm shopping for a car. Price is something that is interesting to me, but fuel efficiency is much more important to me. The recyclability of the car itself is also a factor. How many of the parts can be recycled and how much will end up in landfills? When I go shopping I want to be able to scan the barcode on the car decal and find out not just the Carfax and history of the car but how much of the car is recyclable? What is the *true* fuel economy according to drivers? I don't want it from the manufacturer.

"That's where I would like to see things going with retail and clothing. I want information that is relevant to me. With clothing it's all about fit. We heard this from real customers when we did research with Old Navy. People who are not in the design world, not technologists, not working in this realm at all, fantasize about being able to upload 3D models of their bodies to see how clothes are going to look on them and know exactly what product will give them the best figure.

"Old Navy's tag line is 'come fun, come all.' It's a very inclusive brand. There are products for men and products for women, but the primary customer is a young woman who is probably a mother, probably a wife, and she is shopping for the whole family. She is definitely mobile. We have to make sure we are on top of this. She's a very mobile-savvy shopper, surprisingly.

"We are embracing this mobile technique and design process because we're seeing the trend in our customers. The mobile majority's tipping point will be in 2014. Our customers are tracking slightly ahead of that. We think we will get there in 2013 because we've seen an exponential uptick in our mobile visits. We are seeing a 50/50 split between iPhone and Android, so it's not just early adopters in iPhone."

MOBILE ALIGNMENT

Part of the approach of *Mobile Influence* is to ensure alignment of mobile initiatives with all other channels within a company. While mobile activities logically started as R&D at many companies that wanted to experiment, the next phase requires moving mobile out of its silo. Captain-of-mobile-influence companies don't look at mobile strategy as a bolt-on to another channel but rather as part of the overall integrated approach.

Andrew "Drew" Koven, who was in the process of joining Guess as vice president of e-commerce at the time of this writing, is part of a team that includes IT, retail store operations, and marketing and that is charting the company's mobile and digital course.[12] Koven is hardly new to mobile. In the earlier days of mobile, he was president of e-commerce and customer experience at Steve Madden Ltd. While there, he strongly promoted the culture of fashion companies doing business as a fully integrated multichannel enterprise, with the customer at the center of the model. He is also experienced in the digital interactive world, having held the positions of chief of marketing and digital at Melissa & Doug, vice president of business development and customer relationship management at ShopLink, a pioneer in the online grocery shopping business, and chief marketing officer of FreshDirect in 1999.

Koven's role at Guess is to oversee e-commerce, digital marketing, and customer service for the company, including leading a team to manage multiple brands and websites. He is charged with helping to develop the longer-term strategies and how digital influences the business at large. Says Koven:

Mobile is becoming a brand's centerpiece because the consumer has unprecedented access to information, the ability to share, and the tools to drive it. My involvement at Guess will be centered on exceptional customer experience and working with my partners to ensure its delivery.

Several top-tier brands have current mobile capabilities that are in alignment with this philosophy. I've always looked at e-Commerce, digital and mobile as channels that directly engage consumers. The key to success is to extend all of one's best practices in a high-touch retail store environment to a self and/or collaboratively served digital one. In short, live your brand!

Speaking as both a brand advocate and a consumer, mobile supports the need for absolute transparency. It puts the consumer's needs front and center. Time will ultimately tell, but from my experience it is fair to say that in order for a brand to compete effectively, it cannot be sharp in one channel and less so in another for very long. But it's not easy. It takes a lot of work by several departments to get it right and keep it right.

Once again from my experience, you have to contemplate and plan to make everything work together in a seamless way. This requires patience, focus and keeping an open mind. In a multi-channel environment, things can and do change very quickly. A company that has its own stores, wholesale partners, websites, partners that have their own stores and digital businesses and more, all pose the need for strategic thinking and timely action.

Marketing, Retail Store Operations and IT teams need to be involved with messaging, execution and system integration respectively. The biggest change from my early days in mobile versus today's state is that all parties share a cultural readiness to participate in a multichannel world, which is terrific!

So for me it's about having the teams together and constantly aligning as a part of the strategic planning and execution process. Not to oversimplify the point, this takes a lot of work on the part of very busy people.

I am careful not to draw a marked distinction from the importance of information architecture and the overall presentational standpoint between mobile and desktop. I've observed that the best always focus on ease of use aligned with brand and aesthetics. My experiences and positions are drawn from a consumer experience point of view.

I think it used to be that consumers fell into two camps; I shop in store or I shop online. Now it's I shop in store using online, i.e., mobile that leverages the digital universe. Everything is complementary today, which enables the consumer, his or her peers and brand/business to partner together in decision making. When you add the whole social component to it where you can push out things and get instant feedback, well it not only gets more powerful, but it can also be a lot of fun.

One of the reasons why I got into mobile so early and behind it so aggressively is because I never looked at it as separate or distinct from other retail channels. I always looked at it as a natural part of how people research, communicate and buy. I never looked at it and said this is a separate channel. I never embraced the divide between a website and a store and have always maintained the need for cross departmental collaboration and innovation. Everything starts with an idea.

The philosophical question that I always challenge myself and others with is, "Why would I do it exceptionally well in one channel and not in another? Stated another way, why would I do it one way for this consumer and another way for that one?" So if I have a store with really great product and presentation, I think that I should maintain that across all of my channels whether digital, stores, wholesale partners, etc. and I look at everything as a continuum. I don't get caught up creatively, intellectually or emotionally in the "this channel that channel play" if you will. Everyone wins when the consumer does.

Eighty-five to ninety percent of business is still done in a retail store. As multichannel retailers charged with managing brands and customer relationships we need to make sure wherever we are seen, whatever information consumers need to access, however they choose to shop and whatever tools they choose to use, all are all really sharp.

Businesses that link mobile approaches to holistic marketing plans have an advantage in the Mobile Shopping Life Cycle. As more shoppers move between and among their different screens, whether TV, PC, tablet, or smartphone, companies need to provide a similar positive experience and value.

GLOBAL MOBILE

Much more than TVs or even PCs, mobile is a global phenomenon. People in some countries who never had access to the internet due to lack of a computer are gaining access via mobile. The sheer number of phones— more than six billion global subscriptions and still climbing—provides a larger footprint and opportunity for many marketers. Consider these statistics:

- More than two billion people globally use the internet.
- In developing countries, only 20 percent of the inhabitants have internet access.
- Seventy percent of total households in developed countries have internet access, and in Iceland, the Netherlands, Norway, and Sweden more than 90 percent of the population is online.
- In one year alone, 142 million mobile subscriptions were added in India, twice as many as in Africa and more than in the Arab states and Europe combined.[13]
- Countries where mobile cellular penetration increased the most are Brazil, Costa Rica, and Kazakhstan.
- Developing countries account for more than 80 percent of new mobile subscriptions.

The captains of mobile influence understand the significance of these statistics and many look at global mobile initiatives. Cell-phone penetration exceeds the entire population in more than 100 countries (see Appendix).

The growing number of mobile devices will also be gaining access and using higher speeds, with some markets growing faster than others. Mobile operators are seeing mobile broadband as their fastest-growing revenue stream, according to Infonetics Research, which forecasts revenue of $976 billion by 2016, with the majority coming from mobile broadband.[14] This means mobile consumers will have and use faster services, with about 40 percent of mobile subscribers globally having mobile broadband by 2016. The highest growth areas are Asia Pacific and Latin America, while Europe, Africa, and the Middle East are showing a slight decline, according to Infonetics.

MOBILE POWER USERS LEAD THE WAY

When people buy a new TV, they typically are replacing one they've had for some time, in many cases a very long time. They likely buy a high-definition set, and can't wait to get it out of the box and instantly receive a dramatically improved television-viewing experience. As a result, many of these consumers are so satisfied with the improvement they don't take the next step and subscribe to a high-definition service from their cable or satellite provider. The new set is such a dramatic improvement they may never realize that adding high-definition service would make it exponentially better.

Mobile follows this model to some degree, with some of the new smartphones not yet being fully utilized. Moving from a typical old-school phone to a state-of-the-art Android or Apple phone can seem like such a dramatic move forward that some new owners don't yet capitalize on the new handheld power they possess.

However, there's a flip side to this. There are a number of consumers who, at their gut level, understand the newfound mobile empowerment and move forward to use it in innovative and productive ways. This is a category of mobile user different from the rest. These are the mobile power users. They are the ones from whom others will learn as they see them doing more with their mobile device than "normal" users. Power users are willing to enthusiastically share their mobile knowledge with most anyone interested.

It's not all that difficult to identify mobile power users, since they're often heavily engaged with their mobile phone, and not just for texting. For example, at one MediaPost OMMA conference in New York, many mobile power users gathered to hear keynote presentations and panel discussions on a range of subjects, including mobile, video, and social media.

"I don't use anything else and I have no land line," says power user Mark Hodson, who works for a marketing platform company. "Because I travel and work remotely, it's this thing or nothing," he says about his iPhone 4. His loaded apps include Kayak, SPG, Yelp, ESPN, PGA, AA, Instagram, Groupon, ShopSavvy, and QR Reader, among many others.

Another mobile power user, Joe Caruso, a sales director, uses a large number of apps from his iPhone 4S, including Facebook, LinkedIn, ESPN, and Yahoo! Sports, in addition to a number of sales and expense-reporting applications. He also uses his phone as a remote for his TV via Verizon and as the navigation device in his car.

"The level of interaction I have with my phone is complete, with digital media, photos, and music," says Caruso, who is continually looking for things to replace by using his phone, such as for banking and video viewing.

Power users are leading the way in mobile and pushing the limits. They are more than early adopters of technology, since they are not so much gadget nerds as value conscious. They look for mobile to make their lives easier, more efficient, and more portable.

Mobile power users can be found in any demographic, and if you are reading this book, you likely either are one or know one or more.

So how do you know? Well, you might be a mobile power user if:

- You routinely use your phone to find places and things around you.
- Attending a conference, you live Tweet from your smartphone even though your laptop is in your bag.
- You have both the SoundHound and the Shazam apps to be sure you can identify any song you hear anytime.
- You figured out how to do the workaround to get Google Wallet loaded and functioning on your Android with Ice Cream Sandwich (and, of course, know what Ice Cream Sandwich is).
- Your utilities include a speedometer app, such as Ulysse Speedometer or Speed-o-Meter, and a flashlight such as TeslaLED (Android) or Flashlight (iPhone).
- Your 2D barcode readers include ScanLife and SnapTag Reader—and you use them.

- You routinely price check in stores using ShopSavvy, Red Laser, or Amazon's Price Check without giving it a second thought.
- You use your phone for navigation.
- Your primary weather-checking device is your phone.
- You have at least three airline apps and three hotel apps and are registered at all.
- If you travel, you regularly use travel apps such as OnTheFly, Kayak, AutoPilot, or Flight Sites while in transit.
- You regularly use check-in apps, such as Foursquare for location and shopkick for rewards.
- You are self-equipped to use mobile payments such as Square, MoneySend, Google Wallet, or Serve and are just waiting for the market to catch up.
- You have your phone synced to your computer and/or your other mobile phone and are comfortable with syncing apps such as SugarSync or Dropbox.
- Your reward card numbers all are in your phone in Key Ring or CardStar.
- You program your DVR remotely from your phone.

While this is not an entire list, you get the idea. Mobile power users are the mobile elite. They are at the forefront of the mobile revolution and will shine the light forward for the mobile industry.

Whether you're a power or casual mobile user, the impact on shopping behavior around the world will be significant. As more advanced mobile capabilities are introduced by smartphone and tablet makers and more shoppers start to use more features of their powerful handheld devices, marketers will face more opportunities to reach the buyers in all six phases of the Mobile Shopping Life Cycle. The first stage of that cycle is during the pre-buying process before the mobile shopper even goes to the store, which we will discuss in the next chapter.

two

THE SETUP

the pre-buy

MARKETING TO THE MOBILE MIND-SET

The timing of an actual purchase no longer takes place at only one time or one location but rather all the time and at all locations. Executing an actual purchase where money changes hands becomes only one of the events in the Mobile Shopping Life Cycle. During the pre-buy, consumers are tapping in and out of mobile on a continual basis, whether at home, the office, or anywhere in between. They also are being influenced by others in the post-purchase phase of the cycle, which we discuss in a later chapter.

Before heading to the mall, mobile shoppers are using their devices to research items, look for sales, and compare pricing, among other things. When they get to the store on location, they continue to use those devices. At the pre-buy phase of the Mobile Shopping Life Cycle, consumers are open to suggestions and considerations, both directly from brands and marketers and also from peers. This is the first step in the cycle where marketers need to put their best foot forward; companies not involved in reaching consumers during this phase risk being left out of the entire new shopping cycle.

This stage of the cycle is the research and identification time where the consumer uses a mobile phone or tablet to help identify the what and the where of a potential purchase. Mobile-empowered consumers tap into companies' mobile websites for pricing and availability and check with friends through social networks and texting. Influence points for brands and marketers include mobile advertising, mobile websites, product and inventory information, immediate feedback mechanisms, and mobile coupons. More and more consumers are researching the purchase via mobile early in the purchase decision process, with the percentages increasing each year as more people get smartphones and tablets.

There are times during the pre-buy that a mobile consumer conducts research for a later purchase. They may be researching an expensive item, such as a car, major appliance, or new computer. But there are other times during the pre-buy that the consumer decides to make a purchase on the spot from a mobile device. Any marketer not actively involved during this stage of the Mobile Shopping Life Cycle takes a risk that their product or service will not be seen and therefore not be considered.

REACHING THE PRE-BUYER

Checking for sales with a smartphone is the most common mobile activity before going to a store, according to MarketLive, with 42 percent of shoppers checking for sales and specials and almost as many (41 percent) looking for competitive pricing at Amazon.[1] The least common activities were reserving a product for pickup at the retail location and checking inventory of a product of interest before making a visit to the store (see Table 2.1).

Mobile Advertising

Being visible at the pre-buy stage is much like being visible on the Web. However, internet advertising can be more visible because of the larger screen, allowing a better fit for advertising within the context of the product or website being viewed. The small screens of mobile devices, especially smartphones, are a limiting factor for large-scale advertising. But screen

table 2.1

BEFORE VISITING A STORE, LIKELY ACTIVITIES

Check for sales, specials	42%
Look for competitive pricing on Amazon	41%
Look up store information	37%
Browse an online store for product	37%
Look for competitive price outside Amazon	35%
Check for product ratings, reviews	33%
Look for competitive price on shop engines	30%
Look up price on retailer website	30%
Check inventory of product of interest	28%
Reserve product for pickup at retail	22%

size is not the only reason restraining mobile advertising from breaking through. Mobile consumers are not clamoring for more ads on their phones, but advertising that brings value is another story.

When mobile ads are highly targeted and used in the context of what the consumer is doing, they can be perceived as content, at least from a consumer's perspective. When advertising on the internet started, it was very small. Over time, it grew to more than $30 billion a year. As it relates to advertising, mobile is about where the Web was in its early days: starting small, with huge projections ahead. One of the main reasons mobile advertising will be so big is the sheer number of people with phones. Moreover, usage is up close and personal, providing great potential for personalized marketing messages.

The relatively slow growth of mobile advertising has to do with the amount of resources businesses are allocating to mobile as part of their marketing budgets. One major advertising spending study led by the Mobile Marketing Association analyzed the return on investment of mobile based on actual market cost, current mobile effectiveness impact, U.S. smartphone penetration, and phone usage considering reach and frequency.[2] The study concluded that the optimal level of spending on mobile advertising for U.S. marketers should be 7 percent of the budget allocation, compared to the current budget of less than 1 percent.

Viewed another way, almost 100 percent of a company's customers generally are using mobile phones and less than 1 percent of its marketing budget is allocated to mobile marketing. Mobile marketing and advertising is projected to have double-digit growth every year through 2016, reaching U.S. spending of $17 billion, according to the highly respected media research firm PQ Media.[3] The largest mobile spending by then will be on marketing apps, mobile coupons, streaming video, and mobile search, according to the study. With the number of mobile users of the internet expecting to soon pass PC users, worldwide mobile advertising is expected to reach more than $28 billion by 2016.[4]

Not only is mobile usage up close and personal, but much of the advertising delivered to mobile devices will be sent in relation to the location of the person at the time. Local businesses often desire to reach mobile consumers who are nearby. By 2016, local mobile advertising, a subset of all U.S. mobile advertising, will reach $5.8 billion.[5]

Major online platforms, watching their users migrate to mobile devices, are logically following the eyeballs with advertising. For example, after Facebook saw its massive user base switching to mobile devices, it focused its efforts on mobile advertising. Within six months of ramping up its mobile ad business, almost 15 percent of Facebook's ad revenue was coming from mobile.[6]

On a global basis, the effectiveness of mobile advertising varies by market and also by device. Running on many different phones from different manufacturers, Android is the dominant platform around the world, followed by Apple. However, that does not necessarily mean that Android phones dominate in advertising effectiveness in all regions of the world. There also are differences in advertising reach based on various categories, such as entertainment and travel. No matter the region, marketers will continue to increase efforts to reach mobile shoppers in an attempt to influence purchase behavior. One of the moments to reach the mobile shopper by advertising is during the pre-buy stage of the Mobile Shopping Life Cycle.

Global Mobile Advertising

Since people everywhere have mobile devices and marketers tend to send their messaging to where the people are, it follows that advertising is moving to mobile. Brands and agencies often use advertising platforms to get the right ads to the right people in any given market. One such platform is London-based Adfonic, which sends more than 100 billion advertising messages a month to mobile devices around the world. The company has offices in Madrid, Munich, New York, Paris, San Francisco, and Singapore and reaches about 250 million different mobile users each month with more than 6,000 monthly advertising campaigns. The company developed performance metrics to gauge what works and closely tracks results by geography.

Mobile ads for style and fashion shown on news sites can increase by eightfold the number of ads viewed, and technology campaigns shown to males can increase uplift by 164 percent, according to Adfonic research.[7] The study, the Global AdMetrics Report, is based on 79 billion mobile ads from thousands of mobile advertising campaigns running across almost 15,000 mobile websites and apps. The largest mobile advertising growth is in Europe, with 23 billion ads, passing those sent in North America. Android phones see the largest share of advertising in North America, Europe, Asia, and Africa while Apple devices lead in South America (see Table 2.2).

Significantly more ads are sent to mobile phones than to tablets, with phones accounting for 91 percent of ads sent, according to the Adfonic study. Entertainment, media, and technology audiences combined account for two-thirds (67 percent) of the amount of money spent on mobile by advertisers. Results are measured by consumers opening the mobile ads, and entertainment and media had a success rate 260 percent above the average, with consumers keen to install media-related apps. Business and

table 2.2

MOBILE ADVERTISING BY DEVICE

	Android	Apple
North America	63%	30%
Europe	43%	34%
Asia	40%	38%
South America	30%	34%
Africa	14%	11%

finance and retail both bring results 130 percent above the average, and style and fashion campaigns deliver 62 percent above average. Overall mobile ad spending around the world is led by entertainment and media, with the lowest amount of spending on lifestyle and health advertising (see Table 2.3).

Advertising by category differs based on geography in the Adfonic study. For example, in North America the largest advertising is in entertainment and media, while the top vertical in South America is technology and telecoms (see Table 2.4).

Success by vertical by region, measured by the number of people who click on the mobile ads, varies significantly by region. The most successful verticals in Europe are consumer packaged goods and retail, with a 31 percent higher click-through rate on ads than other regions. In North America, the technology and telecoms category generates a 37 percent click-through rate. In Asia, automotive leads the other categories, generating a success rate of 85 percent.

Advertising to mobile shoppers in these countries will have to be done with care, since 38 percent of those in a study conducted by Accenture consider ad banners annoying, with just as many finding mobile advertising through texting to be irritating.[8] However, two-thirds (66 percent) felt favorably toward information on coupons and promotions, with almost half (46 percent) viewing it as informative and 20 percent as amusing. This highlights the need for marketers to reach the mobile shopper with the

table 2.3

MOBILE AD SPENDING BY CATEGORY

Entertainment & media	39%
Technology & telecoms	28%
Business & finance	8%
News & education	6%
CPG (consumer packaged goods) & retail	6%
Social & dating	5%
Automotive	3%
Travel	2%
Lifestyle & health	2%

table 2.4

TOP VERTICAL MOBILE AD CATEGORIES: BY REGION

North America

Entertainment & media	45%
Technology & telecoms	21%
News & education	18%
CPG & retail	6%

Europe

Entertainment & media	35%
Technology & telecoms	24%
Business & finance	12%
Social & dating	9%

Asia

Entertainment & media	45%
Technology & telecoms	34%
Business & finance	6%
Lifestyle & health	3%

South America

Technology & telecoms	50%
Entertainment & media	36%
News & education	4%
Social & dating	4%

best messages, which can be more effective when delivered considering location and context, which we discuss later.

Mobile Internet

Advertising to mobile devices can be highly targeted to consumers around the world, but there is another factor of mobile influence that may be overlooked by some marketers, which is how mobile consumers are tapping into the internet.

In some countries, internet access will be primarily by mobile phone, and since there are substantially more mobile phones than there are PCs globally, some people will access the world of the internet for the first time and only by mobile phone. Outside the United States and South America (especially Brazil) have the highest number of users accessing the internet on mobile devices, while France, Germany, and Finland have the fewest, based on research from Accenture.[9] The Mobile Web Watch study was conducted across 13 countries in Europe, Latin America, and Africa. Some of the findings regarding those who access the internet via mobile device:

- 69 percent of all internet users accessed it through a mobile device.
- 61 percent access the internet via smartphone.
- 22 percent access the internet via tablet.
- 73 percent of males and 66 percent of women access the internet via mobile.
- 58 percent access for personal matters, 20 percent for work-related matters.
- 45 percent of those above 50 years old use the mobile internet.
- 62 percent accessed online communities such as Facebook.
- 46 percent conducted a bank transaction via mobile device.
- 71 percent downloaded programs or apps via mobile.
- 51 percent downloaded or viewed short videos.
- 70 percent have concerns over data security.
- 78 percent are interested in cloud consumer services.
- 87 percent are interested in premium technical services.

Mobile shopping is already happening to some degree in Europe, Latin America, and South Africa, with more than half (55 percent) already buying tickets for events such as concerts, cinema, and theater. Almost half (46 percent) buy train and airline tickets via mobile device, and more than a third (39 percent) buy clothes or shoes. More than a third (37 percent) purchase other consumer goods from their smartphone or tablet, and more than one in five (22 percent) buy goods or groceries that way.

As in other markets, tablet usage is growing and opening new markets for mobile influence. The devices are used across all age groups, with the highest usage among those 14 to 39 years old. More than half of tablet owners access the internet at least once a day, and almost a third (30 percent) use them several times a day. The majority (66 percent) of tablet-owner activity revolves around downloading and viewing short videos that run for fewer than five minutes, though more than half (52 percent) also watch movies, TV, or longer video clips. And as with mobile shoppers elsewhere, many of them (61 percent) check prices, one of the primary functions during the pre-buy.

Mobile Email

Ever since the early mobile days of the first BlackBerrys, people have been enamored of being able to send and receive email by mobile phone. Mobile email is a function that frees consumers from their desktop computer and from reading email at a specific location. What some marketers may be missing, though, is the degree to which mobile shoppers can be reached via email. Email marketing to consumers on PCs has been well established over the years, just like physical direct mail in the years before that. But each new delivery mechanism typically dramatically changes the one before it, even if not initially. Email specifically directed to mobile devices is yet one more way to reach both the on-the-go and the on-the-couch consumer to exert mobile influence. Just as SMS and MMS are viewed as messaging between the brand or company and the consumer, so too is email.

In countries other than the United States, receiving and sending emails continues to be the most common way to access the internet, with 70 percent using email programs installed on their mobile device or by the website of an email provider (60 percent), according to the Accenture study discussed earlier.

Marketing and advertising to the mobile shopper does not always have to take the form of traditional advertising, whether by a mobile banner ad or various forms of in-app advertising. Since mobile is not a "traditional" medium in terms of screen size and how it is used, multiple marketing methods should be used to ensure effective messaging at all stages of the Mobile Shopping Life Cycle. Sending email marketing messages to mobile consumers can be more effective if you know what happens to those emails after they are sent.

An email marketing message can be most effective when it is opened, of course, and even more effective if it causes engagement. However, not all email messages sent to all mobile devices are received in the same way.

Emails opened on phones outpace those opened on tablets by about three to one, according to the Mobile Email Opens Report by Knotice.[10] The six-month study, based on more than 800 million emails sent across eleven industry segments, found that mobile phones accounted for 26 percent of all email opens and tablets for 10 percent.

The open rates by smartphone device were found to be different, with a much higher percentage being opened on iPhone (20 percent) than on Android (6 percent). The study also found an increasing number of consumers opening emails on phones and fewer on desktops, with more than a third (36 percent) opening email on mobile and 64 percent being opened on desktop. Android and Apple devices together accounted for 99 percent of all mobile email opens. That translates into the requirement that marketing target those two devices to market to the mobile mind-set via email.

Mobile email open rates by industry are another important gauge for reaching mobile shoppers. The top categories for open rates in the study were consumer services and financial services and B2B ad associations (see Table 2.5).

This table indicates that about a third of emails sent within the top categories are opened on mobile devices. Categories of open rates that saw significant increases from the previous quarter were consumer products, retail, and consumer services. There is another important measurement marketers use to tell whether the consumers who have opened an email on their mobile device take any action. This is whether the consumer clicked

table 2.5

MOBILE EMAIL OPENS BY INDUSTRY

Consumer services	34%
Financial services	33%
Cable & telecom	26%
Entertainment	26%
Hospitality	24%
Retail	24%
Consumer products	23%
Education	23%
Association	17%
B2B	14%

table 2.6

EMAIL CLICKS ACTIVITY ON PHONE

Financial services	15%
Consumer products	12%
Hospitality	10%
Association	9%
Retail	8%
Entertainment	7%
Cable & telecom	6%
Consumer services	6%
B2B	4%
Education	2%

on a link in the email for additional information or on an offer after opening the original email. It is a way for marketers to measure the general effectiveness of the content in the email. For example, if a large percentage of recipients open an email on their mobile device and then take no action, the marketing message may not have been a success.

The Knotice study projects the mobile email open rates across industries will move from 36 percent to well beyond 50 percent for most marketers in short order. Marketers attempting to reach the mobile shopper should take this into account, since Knotice points out that most brands included in the study were not actively optimizing their programs for designing emails with mobile users in mind. Mobile email recipients will soon be the dominant audience for opening emails. One apparel retailer in the study found that more than 60 percent of its email opens were on mobile devices and that its traditional desktop design approach did not work for mobile screens.

Immediacy of the Message

There is a pattern of when emails are opened on mobile devices, with the share of email opens spiking during the evening, late night, and early morning hours, according to the Knotice study. Email opens on mobile devices are also heavily concentrated within the first three hours following email delivery, falling off quickly after that. Email engagement via mobile is significantly higher in the first 90 minutes. This means marketers should use their particular customer data to establish the best time for their emails.

Another mobile marketing factor is what consumers do after opening the email, in addition to whether they click on the message inside. For email messages from the retail industry to consumers, once an email is opened, no matter on what device, it is unlikely to be opened again. The common assertion that people use their mobile phone inbox as a filter and save emails to revisit later on their PC just is not happening in a big way. Almost all (98 percent) email is opened exclusively on one device. In retail, 21 percent of all email is opened on a mobile device. If the retail marketer did not create a compelling subject line and deliver the right offer, the window to the mobile consumer can be totally missed.

WHAT PEOPLE WILL BUY VIA MOBILE

In addition to reaching mobile shoppers early in the Mobile Shopping Life Cycle by advertising, there are times when consumers will show what they want by their actions, sometimes to the surprise of the brand or marketer. While a marketer might be using a mobile advertising approach to reach potential customers in the pre-buy phase, the customers may conduct the actual buying on their own without being prompted. As you will see throughout the book, there are no limits to what consumers will purchase via their mobile devices. Part of the reason for this is that smartphones and tablets can be used to perform essentially the same actions as on a computer, so many consumers naturally use their mobile devices as computers.

It is obvious that some things are a better fit with certain screens. For example, movies look better on a movie-theater screen, a television series may be more pleasant on a large-screen TV, and spreadsheets are easier to work with on a PC screen. It's intuitive to consider that filling out lengthy applications also would be better suited for PC screens rather than the smaller screens (and keyboards) of mobile phones. But in the Mobile Shopping Life Cycle, there is room for activity in virtually any category, at any time, and sometimes when not expected. After all, how much data would a consumer be willing to enter through a smartphone? It turns out that many people will enter a lot—as one company surprisingly found out, they will even fill out lengthy loan applications on mobile phones.

CUNA Mutual Group, a financial services provider that produces retirement and investment products, launched a loan application website called loanliner.com, marketed to credit unions in 2000, well before the mobile revolution. Credit unions throughout the United States then marketed the loans to their members, using the loanliner.com platform. But ten years after launching the site, CUNA Mutual was totally surprised to find that thousands of loan applications were coming from mobile devices. It was counterintuitive to think that consumers would go through all the data-entry steps, page by page, and apply for loans from their phones.

The company decided it had to customize its process for smartphones and tablets, since customers were using their phones to access the loan application forms at the traditional website—hardly an optimum experience. The online loan process had been designed to be used from a computer, but customers were using their phone despite the arduous process. While CUNA Mutual initially expected its customers to be using their mobile devices in the pre-buy as a research tool, they found that customers were converting that phase into the actual transaction phase.

Like many others in the world of mobile, the business faced the choice of whether to create an app or a mobile website to serve its mobile customers. Since CUNA Mutual is a compliance company and credit union loan applications are highly regulated, the company took the mobile Web route, launching in mid-2011. This allowed always-updated disclosures—much more difficult than it sounds—to be displayed to loan applicants of the 552 credit unions that have access to what is known as loanliner.com with Smartphone Loans. As loan applicants move through the mobile loan process, a series of screens, each with different disclosures of information, appears based on their previous and current input.

Building the process for the mobile loan application was complex. "The most difficult part to solve was the display of the mandatory disclosures associated with the promotion of our credit protection products," says John Putman, director of lending business systems at CUNA Mutual Group. "It was necessary and important for us to find ways to display these disclosures on devices with very small screens so that the user understands the voluntary nature of the coverages, understands that they can change coverage options, they understand that election has no impact on whether the loan is granted, and that they very clearly understand the cost of the coverages. Once we perfected this disclosure process, and did it in a very simple and understandable way, our credit union subscribers and their members benefited greatly."

In addition to finding more people using the mobile method since the start, CUNA Mutual found that the mobile loans were effective. They found that those filling out the loan forms on a mobile phone were more likely to finish the process compared to those using a computer on the traditional website. "The average loan has a 42 percent completion rate, while mobile had a 49 percent completion rate," says Putman.[11] The net result of more people finishing their loan applications through their smartphones than computers was that it ultimately produced more revenue for the loan originator or credit union. Depending on the credit union, some of the information within the loan application self-populates or is automatically filled in as the loan process moves along, all with the obvious security in place.

"It is very clear from our Smartphone Loans tracking results that mobile users, on average, are a bit younger and have high expectations related to the user experience," says Putman. "Based on what we've seen so far, we've hit the mark." Here is some of what CUNA Mutual found from the mobile loan process:

- The average age of the loan applicant from desktops was 40 years old; from smartphones it was 31 years old.
- The average loan amount via PC was $17,000; from smartphones it was $10,000. (Putman suggests that the lower age demographic may be borrowing less since they have less income than their senior counterparts, and so may opt for a less expensive car to borrow for, as one example.)
- There were initially 50 loans a day via smartphones at launch in July 2011. That number is now around 166 mobile applications a day.

- More than 43,437 loan applications have been submitted from the Smartphone Loans version since launch.
- Slightly more loan applications come from iPhones than Android phones, with 58 percent from iOS and 42 percent from Android.
- Of the loan requests coming through Apple devices, 51 percent come from iPhones and 49 percent from iPads.

Next up for the mobile loan process of CUNA Mutual is developing an iPhone and Android app that ties into the mobile Web. "The mobile Web does not give access to the camera or GPS," says Putman. He sees the potential scenario of a credit union member driving into a car lot and spending a certain amount of time there, then being pushed a message saying they're preapproved for a loan, information that could be readily available through the system. The idea is to more tightly link the purchase and loan process so that, at least conceptually, while a person is shopping, they can borrow on the spot. This is another way to link together multiple phases of the Mobile Shopping Life Cycle, with potential influence at the pre-buy, on location, and at point of purchase.

That the masses of consumers will fill out lengthy forms or apply for loans via smartphones may not be intuitive or even on the drawing boards for some. But if there is a way for something to be moved to mobile so that the consumer can do it while on the go and on his or her time frame, the chances are high the mobile consumer will move to it. The smart businesses will be on the lookout for that movement and follow them.

The move to mobile by CUNA Mutual customers was initially unexpected, but once the company identified and accommodated it, the mobile platform grew even faster. "What surprises us the most is the extremely rapid and continuous growth in the overall use of mobile devices, along with the comfort owners have with using these devices for just about everything, including financial transactions," says Putman. "My personal belief is that this is likely due to a whole generation having grown up with these extremely powerful handheld computers called smartphones, and using them for many of the things that had been previously reserved for traditional laptop and desktop computers."

The growth of the mobile loan platform of CUNA Mutual more than doubly outpaces the growth of the process on computers. The company also found that those completing loan applications on smartphones and tablets were younger than those completing them on computers (see Table 2.7).

table 2.7

LOAN APPLICATIONS BY DEVICE

Loan Application Increase Year over Year by Device	
PC	110%
Smartphone	264%
Tablet	385%
Average Age by Device	
PC	40
Smartphone	31
Tablet	38
Median Age by Device	
PC	29
Smartphone	25
Tablet	27

"From the perspective of our company, whose core products are sold during a loan event, we're seeing tremendous success in the acceptance of our insurance coverages that credit unions promote within our Smartphone Loans product," says Putman.

MANAGING THE CHANNELS OF THE PRE-BUY

In many cases, mobile consumers are doing their work on a tablet or smartphone from home, and researching travel is no exception. After Continental Airlines and United Airlines merged, the combined airline took steps to ensure that the source of all the information presented was the same, no matter the device from which it was viewed.

"We pulled a team together and started developing business requirements and technology requirements," says Jeff Ulrich, senior manager of emerging technology at United Airlines.[12] "It was originally programmed and has launched on the Continental side, with the United data entered after the merger."

One of the challenges of businesses with large and fast-flowing data feeds is to make sure all entry points used by consumers have the same information all the time. "We feed from the same services that the Web uses for our mobile channel," says Ulrich, who initially was with Continental. "So all our inventory is current and up to date."

United determined it was critical for all its channels to tie back together and transfer the same data across all the channels, ultimately feeding on the same back-end Web services. As is typical with many large enterprises, United started with what it was doing on the Web and simply extended that to mobile. And as many other large organizations learned, United realized that mobile consumers want and demand more than what is provided on the Web. Says Ulrich:

> We already had all the website operational and mobile was just an extension. We saw the continued growth and popularity of mobile as well as customers using the mobile website at airports and it became more apparent that we had to have an app.
>
> There's going to continue to be a shift towards mobile and more time specific information. Meaning that as people get closer to the time of their flights they may want to purchase or change flights or make updates to their travel information. In our case that's where the shift is going to be. I think planning and long term still takes a lot of place before, but mobile I think it's going to be closer to the flight.
>
> You see it now when you're riding home on the train and you're shopping for upcoming trips on the weekend or several weeks out. It's a great place to shop. Many customers purchase on mobile and that's going to continue to expand as more people get comfortable with it.
>
> We continually get their [the consumers'] feedback and we're continually looking for new features to add to mobile to make it more useful for our customers. It's interesting because if you think back just five years ago we all had flip phones and feature phones. Five

years' time, that's how quickly that changed, so we can't even predict what's going to happen in three to five years from now. It's just constantly keeping your eyes on the horizon.

We have monthly content and feature updates to things that need to be fixed, added, tweaked, corrected, those sorts of things.

We're constantly getting feedback from customers about what they want. They want more information, they want more tools, they want it to tie in closer to their contacts, and to their calendar. They just want it simpler.

A mobile site makes you focus on what is important versus a website.

For the app it's just making it tighter and trying to find features that integrate the phone, making it more specific to the device. The mobile Web allows us to capture the other devices that we are not app specific.

Many people use the mobile Web, but it's shifting. I'm amazed at the times I have been at the airport and seen somebody using a mobile boarding pass when they've obviously checked in through the Web and the boarding pass is rotating because the screen doesn't lock and they're not using the app, even though they're on an iPhone. I want to run over and tell them how much better the experience is on the app.

It's also about marketing strategies and getting the word out. There are so many apps out there and we get our loyal base, our Mileage Plus members and people that fly with us all the time. But there's a huge segment out there that aren't really tied to any airlines, so as a customer, I'm not necessarily going to download your specific app because I'm flying with you one time this year. For those customers the mobile Web makes sense.

What United and other large brands have found is that once they launch into the world of mobile, their customer behavior will help point out the next direction. That could be faster apps, better mobile Web experiences, or new features never before considered. For United, the early research efforts, whether at home on a smartphone or tablet, can end with a purchase from a different location. Without noting and participating in the early stage of the pre-buy, a company can very easily miss being part of the Mobile Shopping Life Cycle.

THE ANTICIPATED BUY

There are different activities within the pre-buy, some dealing with non-physical goods, such as loans by CUNA Mutual, or the selling of travel, such as airline tickets by United. There is more to this phase, however, than simply conducting early research for a down-the-road purchase. Some businesses in the pre-buy provide product information and create anticipation for the transaction.

Each day at 11 A.M., Boston-based Rue La La launches a curated boutique filled with special offers for women's and men's fashion, as well as other items, including for home or children. Rue La La is for members only and each new daily store remains open for only 48 hours. "We sell all of the stock we have until it is sold out or until it turns over two days later," says Tom Weisend, vice president of user experience at Rue La La.[13] "We are turning over the store a complete 100 percent every 48 hours."

Commonly referred to as Rue, the company introduces several hundred new products each day. Until moving to mobile, some potential of any pre-buy was limited by requiring the consumer to be tethered to a PC to make the purchase. With the limited quantity of some items, this could mean missing out on desired products in the flash sales when items sold out quickly after the launch time.

To create anticipation in the pre-buy, Rue provides a preview of the boutiques scheduled for launch the next day at 11 A.M. For example, on one day upcoming boutiques featured products from Seiko, Maison Chic, Court of Versailles, Celine, Versace, Time for Sweets, and Europe2You. The app allows the shopper to check a box at any of the desired upcoming boutiques to be sent a reminder when the sale starts. With mobile, it doesn't matter where the shopper is located when they receive the reminder, since they can one-touch buy from a mobile device.

Rue La La started as a traditional Web-only shopping platform. "Our first phase was building a brand and getting people to like and support the brand, which I think we did fairly successfully and fairly quickly," says Weisend. "What mobile has done is it made our immediacy a driving force so that our brand is now still about 11 o'clock and always, when we're launching it, you want to get in before it is sold out. What mobile has done is it allows people to embrace that as opposed to saying, 'I'm never at my desk at 11 o'clock and I'm not going to bother because I am always just disappointed.' We would hear that and people would say, 'By the time I get there all the good stuff is sold out because I was at a meeting or whatever.' What smartphones and tablets and even our mobile Web have done is allow people to re-embrace and become re-addicted to Rue La La because it is available anywhere if they're on one of the devices. And that has really been a game changer for us and the adoption that we have seen is tremendous. More than one in three items in Rue La La are coming through a mobile device. And we didn't even really have mobile to speak of a few years ago."

Rue initially launched a mobile website in late 2009 so that anyone with a smartphone could at least buy something from their mobile device. The goal at that time was simply to facilitate a method for a potential buyer to see a picture of a product and order it from their phone. Some early adopters used the mobile site for purchases, but it did not achieve a mass scale. However, the first foray into mobile did provide a platform to test and learn, one of the number-one rules for mobile marketing.

"I was doing usability testing in spring of 2010 and one of the participants was a Harvard Law student," says Weisend. "She said that before our mobile Web, she did not take 11 o'clock classes. Then we introduced mobile Web and now she could look at the stuff in her contract law class, her 11 o'clock class. I remember thinking that is amazing. There is an opportunity there and I never want her to be my contract lawyer because she's buying shoes and not listening to the professor. So there is the good and bad, but I think that was an example of really sticking our toe in the water and finding that the current was really swift."

ADDING MOBILE RESOURCES

In the middle of 2010, Rue launched apps both for iPhone and iPad, and increased the resources behind its mobile business. Since then, hundreds of thousands of people have downloaded the app. Like many other businesses, Rue found that once mobile capabilities are aligned with customer needs, the mobile customers follow. Another mistake marketers commonly make is not to consider mobile first. "For a long time mobile was an afterthought," says Weisend. "We thought we would make a functionality change to the site and say, 'Oh, we have to do that on mobile too, we'll get to that.' Now we don't make the functionality change unless it is universal. In some cases, we do mobile-only functions."

Shortly after its iPhone and iPad launch, Rue's mobile business accelerated, most notably on the iPad, primarily since there were not a large number of shopping apps for the iPad at launch. "Within weeks, our percentages went into the double digits and then went high into the teens," says Weisend. "I think what caused that was that our model is so perfectly aligned with being there at the right time, regardless of how you get there. We created an experience that felt seamless with the website, which was the huge driver, and still is the bulk. We wanted to make it so you could have a totally mobile relationship with Rue La La and still be a successful member, feel good about it, feel that the brand is there, understand what Rue La La is all about, invite your friends, do all of the behaviors that we encourage our members to do, and never have to look at the website if you don't want to. It was all about aligning our brand and our experience with the mobile device.

"We have a stake in the ground with mobile that we are never are going to do something just because a smartphone or tablet can do something. If it doesn't contribute back to the actual Rue experience we're not going to do that. We're not looking to win an award in a creative competition as much as we're trying to make the experience as best as it can possibly be for our users. What we're finding is we are doing a little bit of both."

Every day Rue usually lists at least ten different brands or boutiques in addition to an offer that is more local. It also has "today's fix," an attractively priced single item that has color or style variation. It could be a bracelet or pair of shoes, for example. The mobile shopper in the pre-buy phase can quickly move to the transaction phase starting at the precise time of 11 A.M. They also can check what items will go on sale the next day and then use a mobile device for advance research on those items from other sellers. Meanwhile, Rue continues to closely watch its mobile shopping numbers and behaviors. Says Weisend:

> We continue to make changes. We have new releases, bug fixes, and all of that. We found that our members totally embraced the app and our mobile retail. Not only did they regularly use it, they craved it, they returned to it and spent more time. We're finding out, not just Rue but everybody, that people are spending more time on the iPad than the site or on a smartphone. They are browsing more, reading more, considering more, and enjoying the experience that much more. Their average order value is higher on a tablet, though not necessarily buying more. Some of our higher-end luxury goods and higher-end experiences are more apt to buy on tablets than on smartphones.
>
> About 35 percent of our mobile sales are on mobile Web and 65 percent are on the app. For the first time in one month, the iPad was consistently a higher percentage of those sales than the iPhone. And it has been pretty consistent as the iPad is slightly inching the iPhone.
>
> We are seeing behaviors between iPhone and Android as the same. Adoption we are way, way, way in the iOS. We have low adoption on Android. We have two theories on that; neither of them is scientifically proved. One is that people that are drawn to a new way of shopping, which really the private sales base is still a new way of shopping although people have been on it for five years or so, are more likely to be in line with the iOS platform and more likely to be iOS adopters. The other thing is we are very heavily female. iOS is much more friendly to females and more adopted by females than Android has been.
>
> We're closing in on 40 percent mobile and it is continually adopting. Within ten days of iOS6 and the iPhone 5 being launched we had almost 70 percent of our total app users updated to iOS6. I think that is an indication that people are very aware of what is going on technologically but also what is going on with Rue and how to get the best experience out of that.
>
> We have already had individual days where mobile was 52 percent of our sales. I think that consistently within 2014 mobile will be more than 50 percent of our sales.

In terms of usage, we are finding it is mostly out of home, whether that be at work or at a coffee shop, but out of home. In the evening, when people are spending time on their iPad, that is another thing. We are finding again at 11 o'clock we had hundreds of thousands of people there and at five in the afternoon it was hundreds of people because everyone came in for that rush. What we're finding now is the iPad has given us a whole new day part in the evening where people are spending time. Our traffic has dramatically increased and it's almost 100 percent due to iPad usage.

We are finding that people who want to shop at home or on the couch when they are their willing to see what we still have, what brands we have, what's coming next. They can spend some time looking at all of our previews and even though it is going to be at 11 o'clock tomorrow I can still have my phone with me because I know I love Puma or cashmere or something like that.

We're not seeing a huge variance in Monday through Friday versus Saturday and Sunday versus what we usually see. We're selling $12,000 bags on the weekends that are really helping to drive traffic. We do see that for some reason on Tuesday we tend to have a dip on mobile use and we have no hypothesis as to why that is. If you look across a year's data, Tuesday seems to be slightly lighter. In some days it might actually dip into the high 20 percents, whereas the rest of the week it will push into the low- to mid-40s.

What has surprised me is the loyalty to iOS. We launched our Android app four months after the iOS app and it is a good app, but we have not had the adoption. I also am surprised by how loyal people are to Rue across devices. We will see people who might place something in their cart on a desktop, come back and buy it two hours later if it's still here, on their phone if they are considering or something and how people are very comfortable going across. If they are in the office on Monday and they use their desktop, then they are on the road Thursday and they use their iPad. The experience for them is seamless. They don't think of it like we do, which is "Oh, they bought that on a desktop, they bought that on their phone." They think of it as "I bought it from Rue." I think that is a pleasant surprise for us because it means that we created the experience in a way that is consistent for them and makes them comfortable that Rue is Rue is Rue and they aren't going to get substandard product, service, or experience because they chose to do something one place versus the other.

We work to create a new way of bringing surprise and delight to what has become a very mundane experience of shopping online.

Whether working in the area of anticipating the buy like Rue La La, dealing with customers who want to apply for loans via mobile like CUNA Mutual Group, or tracking the mobile behaviors of airline travelers like United Air Lines, the pre-buy stage of the Mobile Shopping Life Cycle is one of the first stages of opportunity to influence the mobile shopper. After that stage, they are on the move, which we discuss in the next chapter.

three

THE MOVE

in transit

MOVING WITH THE ON-THE-GO CUSTOMER

It used to be that when a consumer was on the go or making her way to the store, she was essentially detached from the purchasing process. The consumer at home or at the office could research what to buy through online research, visiting company and product websites, and leafing through newspapers and magazines. But once the consumer left that activity, she became disconnected from the purchase process while traveling to the mall or store.

The good news for marketers during those pre-mobile days was that there were a clear and finite number of ways and times to reach the consumer. These included prime-time television commercials, radio spots, and advertising through newspapers and magazines. As consumers migrated online, advertising followed. With global advertising spending at more than $450 billion a year, a piece of that transferred to online advertising, which continues to grow. But all that TV, print, and online advertising can reach customers only when they are at their physical devices. This could be in the evening for someone watching TV, in the morning for anyone who might still read a printed newspaper before going to work, or during a leisurely magazine read, perhaps during some weekend relaxation. The marketer also could reach online consumers as they search and surf through websites during the course of their day, either at home or at the office. But in all these cases, the consumer is, literally, not mobile.

Smartphones and tablets change that. Marketers now can reach mobile consumers *in transit,* between the buying research phase and the purchase itself. While it is intuitive to expect that mobile customers would use their devices close to the actual time of a purchase, they also use them while in transit. On the way to the store, 50 percent of smartphone owners use their phones, providing yet another opportunity to reach the shopper during the in-transit phase of the Mobile Shopping Life Cycle.[1]

SEEKERS AND CRUISERS

Mobile consumers always have at their fingertips the power to find and buy just about anything at any time. They can buy from where they are, either through their phone directly or from the brick-and-mortar location in which they stand. However, the situation and mind-set of mobile consumers can differ. There are two different characteristics of the in-transit consumer, making them what I call either a *seeker* or a *cruiser.*

A seeker is a customer who is destination bound with a specific purchase intent in mind. This is the shopper who has done all the research and is now headed to the store. A seeker is more focused on the trip to purchase and the product or service to be bought. Seekers have:

- **Entered the post-research phase.** They have done their homework on a product. They may have seen a TV commercial for a product and then conducted their own research online and/ or likely on a tablet or smartphone.
- **Made up their mind.** After conducting their own research, some to a higher degree than others, this consumer decides on the product. The product decision can range from pretty sure what they are going to buy to definitely deciding what they will buy, but in all cases they are more than 50 percent sure.

- **Determined destination.** After settling on the product, the seeker decides where they intend to buy. Factors considered are price, availability, and location, such as distance from home or how difficult it is to get to the location.
- **Shared intent.** After choosing a product and destination, the seeker is likely to text or call someone else and let them know where they plan to go and what they plan to buy.

A cruiser is a consumer roaming with no specific purchase intent in mind. The m-powered consumer is in motion and equipped to buy but not necessarily focused on it. This could be a casual shopper meandering through a mall or even a person going through their daily activities, which include purchasing at sporadic times of the day. Characteristics of a cruiser:

- **In the continual research phase.** This consumer is not looking to purchase anything in particular at the moment, though they may end up making a spontaneous purchase. They may see something at a store that catches their eye and may use their phone for a quick Web search to find more details on a product.
- **Flexible on location.** This consumer is on the move and wandering among or between various tasks. The cruiser may be driving to or from work, dropping off the children at school, heading to the gym, walking through the mall, or going to the bank.
- **Open to suggestions.** The cruiser may receive an email or text message from a friend or family member making a suggestion based on the cruiser's location, which they readily make available. The proximity to a particular store or product makes the suggestion more relevant.
- **Shared intent.** Sharing location and intent is common for this consumer. They may call or text a friend or family member, post what they're doing on Facebook, or check in via mobile so their friends can see where they are.

Mobile consumers are at times seekers and at other times cruisers, depending on the day, the time, or the situation. In either case, marketers can still reach out to both seekers and cruisers during the in-transit phase of the Mobile Shopping Life Cycle, though the approach may vary. To reach the seeker, a brand or marketer should also have been active during the previous phase of the buying cycle, the pre-buy. The seeker can be reached during the in-transit stage by identifying earlier interactions with the company and reaching out to continue the conversation. Perhaps the shopper did product comparisons on their smartphone. That would have been an opportunity to incent the shopper to provide at least their contact information in trade for an offer, for example. If they are already a rewards or loyalty member, that information can also be leveraged.

COUPONS, THE ULTIMATE LOCATION DRIVERS

A key way to use mobile influence over both seekers and cruisers is through the use of what I call *location drivers*. These are actions or offers that cause a person to go to a location. The most common tool of this type is the mobile coupon. Although some businesses tend to frown upon using coupons since they discount what could be bottom-line revenue, from the mobile shopper standpoint, they work. Coupons persuade both seekers and cruisers to go to a store or location, and they are becoming even more prevalent on mobile devices. By 2016, the total redemption of mobile coupons globally is expected to top $43 billion.[2]

Mobile coupons have come a long way. Rather than sending masses of coupons printed in daily newspapers or freestanding inserts, marketers can send specific coupons to in-transit consumers to influence where they go. Mobile shoppers can opt in to certain coupon offers, such as those offered by Target. By joining the Target mobile coupon program, the consumer receives a text message with a link to several coupons every couple of weeks. A few days before the deals are to expire, Target sends a gentle reminder text message with another link to the coupons. To redeem the coupons, the consumer simply shows the coupon code on their phone and the cashier scans it. Some other examples include:

- **Coupons.com.** From the website of the same name, a wide range of hundreds of coupons are offered and sorted by category. You can open a free account, and then after a coupon is selected it gets added to the card. The coupons, from a range of items like coffee, cereal, soup, magazines, and juice, can be "clipped," and once your selection is complete, you hit print and the coupons are printed (presuming you have a networked printer nearby). Coupons can also be selected and easily emailed to someone else.
- **Valpak.** Another major coupon supplier that contains some larger offers, such as $15 off a massage, $20 off a month of fitness classes, and a car wash for $10. Contains offers from other large companies, such as an offer to save $500 on custom roofing by Sears.
- **The Coupons App.** Offers discounts based on your location, which your phone automatically knows. These range from 51 percent off a steak dinner to a free dance training class. Also lists deals sorted by categories.

In addition to using coupons to drive seekers and cruisers to locations, various other mobile approaches can be used, such as geofences, automated technologies that surround locations and trigger mobile messages as customers come within a certain distance of the geofence (assuming, of course, that they agreed in advance to receive such messages). The challenge during in-transit is hitting a roaming target, especially in the case of cruisers. In the non-mobile world, traditional large brands, such as Macy's and Saks Fifth Avenue, create elaborate window displays to attract passersby. Businesses can now add sophisticated mobile-enabled marketing to the mix. The opportunity is to provide relevant information to lead a person to a particular product or service. This is the time when the mobile consumer is on the go or on the way to the store, which could be an immediate directional activity or one after running an errand. For the destination-bound individual, the marketing opportunity is to reinforce or even modify purchase intent before arrival at the destination.

The concept of in-transit marketing involves reaching mobile customers on the go with offerings that exert mobile influence. Since the mobile consumer uses a phone throughout the day, marketers have multiple opportunities to influence purchase decisions at random. For example, to monitor its behind-the-ear thermometer, Vicks used Google hyperlocal targeting to send ads to mobile phones of mothers located in areas experiencing high incidence of the flu and within a couple of miles from a store that sells the thermometer. Marketers use advertising and offers based on the proximity of the consumer to the retail outlet using location-based technologies.

THE CHECK-IN

While you're at any given location, mobile makes it easy to let others know you're there. There are two major methods. The on-location consumer can use their phones to post what they're doing through services like Facebook and Twitter. The other method is to check in, using a service like Foursquare. While some users might feel self-conscious having others know where they are by checking in, others readily check in at many locations. With specific check-in services, the only people notified of the check-in are generally those the individual has accepted as friends on the particular services.

In the earlier days of mobile, checking in was less frequent than today, primarily because there are now so many more smartphones and people using them providing more opportunities to broadcast when arriving at a location. The challenge for marketers has been how to capitalize on the location-based check-in. One of the earlier ways for local establishments to reach on-location shoppers was to advertise or offer special deals based on a person's location, but not necessarily based on what they were doing at the time. For example, a restaurant could have an offer displayed when someone checked in with a few blocks, hoping they would be persuaded to drop by to claim the offer. Innovative marketers and mobile industry companies have since developed methods to take this to the next level.

MOBILE CONTEXT IS KING

The power of using mobile check-ins as a trigger for marketing or advertising messages is the high degree of potential relevance to the person based on where they are and what they're doing. Rather than general advertising based on particular websites or apps being viewed, the mobile shopper can receive highly targeted and personalized messages based on what they essentially just said. For example, if a person broadcasts to their mobile world that they just entered Macy's looking for a new blender, they could instantly be sent a suggestion via Twitter to check out a new model by Cuisinart.

This is what I call *contextual mobile marketing*. It is the focus on marketing to mobile customers by sending relevant messages based on the context of where the person is and what they are doing. Rather than creating essentially broadcast messages and sending them indiscriminately to mobile shoppers, which would be content without necessary relevance, contextual mobile marketing involves targeting specific people with personalized messages created for the individual at a specific time and location.

One facilitator of mobile influence that has created a platform to execute such a process is LocalResponse in New York. The business tracks all public posts and check-ins from platforms including Twitter, Foursquare, GetGlue, Miso, Foodspotting, and Instagram. LocalResponse registers the activity, whether it's from a location-based service or social network where people are publicly posting either the check-in or the sentiment itself.

The company works with clients across multiple categories—including electronics, consumer packaged goods (CPG), health and beauty, quick-service restaurants (QSR), automotive, entertainment, and retail—and it counts among its clients Coca-Cola, Kraft, McDonald's, Audi, Volvo, General Motors, Verizon, Walgreens, H&M, K-Mart, and Sears.

"We're a B2B ad network, for lack of a better term," says Kathy Leake, president of LocalResponse. "We realized that the data is incredibly valuable to marketers."

As an example of contextual mobile marketing, LocalResponse zeros in on data related to intent, which is based on a number of factors. Once intent is determined, specific marketing messages are sent to the individual on location. Says Leake:

Originally we started the company just on check-ins. We were looking at two types of check-ins, one is using location-based services like Foursquare, which we call an explicit check-in. Explicit check-in is someone using a location-based service to check in to a location. An implicit check-in, which is actually the majority of our data, is someone broadcasting their location over Twitter. What we see is an increasing number of people broadcasting where they are without using a location-based service. So people are saying, "I'm at Macy's" over Twitter versus using Foursquare to do it.

It's publicly expressed intent. They could be using a location-based service like Foursquare to check in to a location, they could be broadcasting their location over Twitter, or they could be expressing relevant sentiment publicly that might relate to a particular marketer's campaign. For example, if someone were to say, "I need new jeans," that sentiment is relevant to our Levi's client. So we essentially turn all that intent data into targetable impressions.

We analyze all of this data and then serve advertising in a number of different ways in response to that data. One is a direct-response type of ad, where we're responding within Twitter via an @ mention to someone who expressed or broadcasted a check-in. If someone were to check in to a standalone Levi's store through our platform, Levi's would respond back to that consumer in real time via mobile. It's happening in less than five seconds. An @ mention, which is a direct one-to-one communication, would go back to that consumer from Levi's, and usually it's some kind of teaser copy like "Thanks for stopping into the store today, here is 20 percent off your purchase, click here for more details." An @ mention is essentially 140 characters, so it needs to be short. At the end of that copy is a link where we drive people to a mobile landing page where the call to action and the offer live. The other way we deliver ads is through display. Again, the client determines the targeting parameters and then we serve both mobile banners and desktop display in response to that.

In the direct response to an @ mention, the direct one-to-one communication, we see about 40 to 60 percent of people click through to the mobile landing page. So it's a huge engagement. I really think that is because it is so contextual to the end user. If you check in to Macy's, Macy's speaks back to you and essentially rewards that check-in. You are really thrilled. It's contextual. You're broadcasting that you are at Macy's, you're publicly declaring you're a brand advocate by broadcasting your location. I really think that's why we're seeing that level of engagement.

We're capturing the 60 percent of people who publicly post or broadcast their check-in. So 60 percent of people who use these platforms, whether it's a location-based service or social network like Instagram, 60 percent of those people do link their account to Twitter.

What we've done is taken this tremendous change in behavior and social media and the fact that people are broadcasting their location for the very first time in history. Checking in is almost like taking a megaphone and screaming that you are at Macy's. This hasn't been done before. Previously, marketers weren't speaking back to those people. Those check-ins were met with an empty, deaf response. Today, we're able to turn all that publicly expressed intent into a valuable impression for marketers to respond back. People expect to receive some sort of communication from their particular location or establishment.

Because we've been aggregating all of this data we've never been dependent on the growth of pure-play, location-based services. The campaigns usually comprise both broadcast location as well as relevant sentiment. And that was really born out of client demand, the sentiment piece. Clients would inevitably say, "Can you also target people publicly expressing intent that makes sense for my campaign?" So for K-Mart, it's people expressing that they're looking for back-to-school clothes or shopping for back-to-school clothes. That publicly expressed intent is valuable to them.

LocalResponse is finding an increasing number of brands directly involved in mobile. "Over time I've seen that change quite a bit. Instead of having mobile just being this ugly stepchild in marketing, they're hiring people to own mobile as a channel," says Leake. "Of course, that happened on the ad agency side a while ago. So it's nice to see that the agency has a counterpart on the client side. So for us, it's either coming from mobile, both the client side and agency side, social or just media. It comes from digital media in general."

When the on-location consumer digitally announces their location, the direct-response product is in real time, which occurs over mobile while someone is standing at a point of sale (POS), since it is known that they are in the store. The mobile display and desktop happen within 24 hours of the publicly broadcasted intent, making it more of a re-targeting play than the real-time offer. Leake says their clients tend to do a combination of the two.

Of the LocalResponse activity, the direct-response component comprises 40 to 60 percent clickthrough and on-display advertising sees a 0.7 to 0.9 click-through rate. "If you look at traditional mobile display, which is about 0.1, we're still outperforming seven to nine times on mobile display," says Leake. "I think the differentiating factor is the intent being expressed. We're not guessing about what people are looking to do and we're not guessing where they are. It's very declarative. There's data that sits behind if we serve someone an ad or not. We're not making any assumptions about that person or where they are or what they're looking for."

LocalResponse deals only with public data and provides a way for anyone to opt out. The mobile shopper gets either the @ mention over Twitter in real time or a banner ad displayed on mobile or desktop, depending on how the retailer or brand wants to execute the campaign. The @ mention to the consumer comes from the brand to which the person broadcast their location. So if you check in to K-Mart, K-Mart sends you an @ mention back. The messages provide a way for brands to communicate with people the way they communicate over Twitter.

When businesses use the LocalResponse platform, the consumer messaging is automated after the brand establishes the parameters, at which point LocalResponse sets up the campaign. If a marketing campaign is of the customer-service type, some brands that have social media managers or agencies that own the customer service can manage consumer responses manually, sending personal messages as desired. Conversely, it could be a marketing campaign that automates responses to data that a company previously ignored.

"The retailers love it because it shows them the scale of what's happening, as well," says Leake. "The fact that people are doing this in increasing numbers, whether it's an implicit check-in or explicit check-in, the fact that people are broadcasting their location in increasing numbers, is what's really interesting to them."

THE RETAIL CHECK-IN

The opportunity for retailers is to be aware of mobile shoppers checking in so they can influence them based on their current presence, since they are in all likelihood there to buy, or at least to shop and consider a purchase. But checking in is not evenly distributed across the board.

When it comes to mobile check-ins at major retailers, there are some notable differences. The largest percentage of retail check-ins are at Walmart, with 38 percent of all retail check-ins. The second-largest check-in location is Target, followed by Costco, Best Buy, Walgreens, Home Depot, CVS, Lowe's, Safeway, and Kroger (see Table 3.1). Men also tend to check in more than women, with more than half (54 percent) of check-ins from men and less than half (46 percent) from women.

There also are differences in check-ins based on the day of the week, with Saturday being the largest check-in day, followed by Friday and then

table 3.1

RETAIL LOCATION CHECK-INS

Walmart	38%
Target	15%
Costco	9%
Best Buy	7%
Walgreens	6%
Home Depot	6%
CVS	5%
Lowe's	5%
Safeway	4%
Kroger	4%

Check-ins by Gender

Retailer	Male	Female
Best Buy	67%	33%
Lowe's	65%	35%
Home Depot	62%	38%
Safeway	58%	42%
Costco	58%	42%
Kroger	58%	42%
Walgreens	54%	46%
CVS	52%	48%
Walmart	51%	49%
Target	47%	53%

THE VALUE OF CHECKING IN (OR NOT)

The quest for value via mobile check-in continues, though somewhat in a land of extremes. At one extreme are those who view checking in to locations as totally pointless. At the other end are those who will check in everywhere they go.

For example, Ryan and Chris, two friends I know in their early twenties and both recent MBA grads, compete with each other for points on Foursquare. At times the competition to "out-check-in" each other gets the better of them. "Sometimes I check in even when I don't want anyone to know where I am," says Chris. "I want the points."

With Foursquare, when a person checks in more than others at a location, the person is bestowed the title of mayor of that location. "For the first time, I was the mayor of my gym, but then I went away for a few days and found I was now four days away from being mayor," says Ryan. The two friends even have guilt-ridden check-ins, all in search of points. "I check in all the time at the bagel shop and fear my friends think I'm eating bagels all the time, but I'm actually having fruit smoothies," says Chris. "But I want the points."

Another driver of checking in is so that friends can see where their friends are, a value besides the points. "You don't have to notify a whole bunch of people when you're going somewhere," says Ryan. But at least the mobile marketplace is witnessing experiments, some of which will work and others not.

For example, in its early experiments with check-ins, Starbucks offered a deal through Foursquare. For Starbucks mayors, the chain offered a discount on a Frappuccino drink. The obvious problem was that if the mayor—arguably one of a Starbucks store's most loyal customers—did not like or drink Frappuccino, the offer was of little value. However, after that experiment Starbucks moved to accepting payments by scanning mobile phone codes in the Starbucks app. The quick mobile checkout with automatic account reconciliation added value to the Starbucks experience.

American Express created a program with Foursquare whereby check-ins at certain locations and paying with an American Express credit card trigger a credit to your account. In one case, a synced AmEx card at Best Buy would provide a $20 credit for a $200 Best Buy purchase, and in another a breakfast at a certain restaurant would give a rebate of $10. This approach bypasses the local-establishment

> personnel training issue, since the cashiers or store personnel don't even have to be aware of the program for it to work for the mobile customer.
>
> While there will be those who will never check in because they see the process as worthless, there are others who will always check in. Within the two extremes of those who will not check in no matter what and those who will always check in no matter what lies the opportunity.

Sunday. LocalResponse data show that at Costco visitors use Instagram more than any other platform to check in. By gender, the top check-in locations for males are Best Buy, Lowe's, and Home Depot, while the top check-in locations for females are Target, Walmart, and CVS (see Table 3.1).

BEYOND THE MOBILE CHECK-IN

There is little doubt of the importance of location awareness in a world gone mobile. As digitally enabled customers walk around car dealerships, shopping malls, and local retailers, they use their smartphones to check the latest information and make sure they're getting the best deal, all in real time. Many businesses figured out that reaching customers based on proximity to their location can bring them more business. To adapt to mobile shoppers at the in-transit stage of the Mobile Shopping Life Cycle means determining where the person is physically located and also where their interest at the moment is focused.

While there are still issues with point-of-sale systems integrating with loyalty programs and mobile shoppers, many businesses are headed in the right direction. But in addition to shoppers proactively pulling information to them, there is a certain amount of information consumers are willing to share with the business. For example, some customers will share their location in trade for a special offer from a business near where they are.

Tasti D-Lite, the dairy-based, soft-serve frozen dessert company that started in New York before spreading nationally, was an early pioneer in mobile check-in, with POS and rewards program integration. The Tasti

D-Lite approach provides a good road map of how to align mobile, online, and in-store experience, and it learned much along the way.

In 2009, the company was well established with mobile couponing on Twitter, which caught the attention of Foursquare, then a young mobile check-in app company. Tasti D-Lite worked with Foursquare and pioneered the check-in specials, which let businesses promote an offer to potential customers based on their location. "They called us up, so we started working with Foursquare to start figuring out how businesses could use them to interact by targeting people based on their proximity to our physical location, which at the time was revolutionary," says BJ Emerson, vice president of technology at Tasti D-Lite and Planet Smoothie.[3] "There was no other way at the time to measure the physical foot in the door. So you had this new metric now that you can do all kinds of things with and provide some context around location. Everyone was really excited about the whole check-in process, but over time every new mobile application is adding that powerful ingredient of location."

The company found that user-generated content around its products naturally moved to mobile as customers were attaching tips or surprises to locations, such as secret items not listed on the menu. Over time, Tasti D-Lite identified additional social networking behaviors of its customers in transit and moved its approach along with them. Says Emerson:

> As easy as you can tag a person in a picture you can add the location through GPS or through the carrier. Along with the content for your post or status update, you are layering in the location element. We are starting to see that everywhere as new social networks or applications doing the same thing are gaining popularity. While Foursquare is primarily location centered or venue centric, you now have applications like Instagram, which are image-centric. So now we are capturing an image which is the focal point of the conversation and then we can tag things like location, people, along with the status update, comment, or review. Other applications are starting to tag things with emotion. We're starting to use these technologies to communicate in different dimensions around different physical and virtual objects.

With check-in or location tagging becoming mainstream, interesting things are happening as more apps are enabling connections to Twitter, which makes them public.

One of the things we do at Tasti D-Lite is look at all the public content on Twitter and check to see where the content originates from. It might be a Foursquare check-in at a Tasti D-Lite location, a Yelp review or other post that was pushed automatically to Twitter. We find many Instagram photos the same way. So as marketers we can say, "what are our opportunities to interact as a business on that platform or within that community?" The links within the tweets tell us where we need to look. Foursquare for example will have a link to the venue where the user checked-in at. The Instagram tweet will have a link to the picture that was taken. To a marketer, this should be valuable business intelligence.

All of this is for effective mobile marketing. Searching for your location or brand name on Twitter is a great way to discover what mobile apps consumers are interacting with.

We want to be where our customers are interacting. Joining those mobile and social communities allows us to interact, create and curate content around the brand. Ultimately we are able to create touch points with existing customers and reach new ones as well. In our case we find many great photos being shared as customers are enjoying their Tasti D-Lite usually when they are still within one of our locations. I am usually the one that breaks the ground on new social networks and then it just becomes part of the social media efforts internally. In a franchise environment, local owners can interact directly and use the tools to interact or create campaigns that reach new people based on their proximity. Each market can be different however and some mobile apps are more popular in different areas of the country. What we see in New York City is a little different than in Cary, North Carolina. You'll only know what is popular by keeping a close ear to the ground.

One example would be our Planet Smoothie in Cary, North Carolina. We acquired the Planet Smoothie franchise chain some time ago which has around one hundred locations. The owner started to see high schoolers coming in to Planet Smoothie using Instagram on their mobile phones to share photos with friends. The location now manages their own Instagram account and can "like" and comment on photos shared by customers. When customers are passionate about a product or brand, they are generally appreciative of the time we take to interact and support them. We rarely have a negative response because we are careful to participate in the spirit of the community. There is a right way to do it and a wrong way. The right way would be to focus on the customer and the emotional connection they have with the product and get out of the way. You really don't need to sell them. Promote them and encourage them and their decision. If they have questions about nutrition or locations, you want to be there to provide good information and exclusive offers from time to time.

As long as the consumer is in control of the experience and marketers are providing sufficient value, we are going to continue to see greater adoption and interaction around these technologies. I think it is important to focus not on the technology itself but on the behavior of customers. This will be different for any given brand and in different parts of the country and certainly the world. All of this starts with listening.

Beyond understanding that customers are going about with the Internet in their pocket, reviewing, rating and sharing their experiences in real-time with the world, we need to appreciate the dynamics that exist within the applications. While many have for years pursued mere transactional loyalty, others are starting to understand that these tools can be used to foster emotional loyalty. We can choose to simply follow the digital bread crumbs that customers leave behind but there is a greater opportunity here. Capturing the heart of the mobile consumer means recognizing, rewarding and supporting what they love about your product.

HOUSE BUYING VIA MOBILE

Some things simply work better on mobile, especially as companies create products or services specifically for mobile devices. The same was true at the beginning of the commercial internet, as businesses such as Amazon and YouTube were born to take full advantage of the medium. Not only were entities such as those created for the Web, they did not exist outside it. The same is true for mobile.

There are two types of digital platforms around mobile, those that are known as *pure play* and those that are *traditional.* Pure-play mobile are those entities created exclusively for and residing only in the mobile world. An example of pure-play mobile is a location-based service such as Foursquare or Poynt, which lives only in mobile. In many ways, a pure-play mobile effort can be more effective since it can take full advantage of smartphone and tablet technologies like location and portability.

Then there are the traditional entities that transfer what they were doing in the previous digital world of the Web to mobile, such as Weather. com, Facebook, Twitter, and any number of news and content sites. In many cases, the move to mobile was simply a logical location-based extension of what was being done on the Web.

However, there is a third hybrid category, businesses that started online and were doing relatively fine but for which mobile was game changing. By expanding to mobile platforms and capitalizing on the built-in capabilities of smartphones and tablets, some companies find their product or service becomes exponentially more useful and relevant. One such business is the Seattle-based company Zillow.

Mobile opened the doors to the buying and selling of a wide range of products and services large and small. Like many other categories, looking for houses for sale was doing fine with consumers skimming through newspapers and realtor websites. In early 2006, Zillow launched online to enhance and advance the house-hunting process. It has grown to more than 550 employees with offices in San Francisco, Chicago, and New York. Its advertising network, the Yahoo!-Zillow Real Estate Network, is the largest real estate network on the Web and is the number-one real estate brand in all of the top 20 local markets in the United States.

The company created a real estate information marketplace, featuring information about all homes, not just those on the market, real estate listings, rental listings, and mortgages through its website, Zillow.com.

Consumers could use the site to find estimated home values, houses for sale and rent, and quickly connect with local real estate agents. Target Zillow users include homeowners, buyers, sellers, real estate agents, renters, and landlords. The company's stated mission is to empower consumers with information and tools to make smart decisions about homes, real estate, and mortgages.

Mobile totally transformed the Zillow business. It launched its first app for iPhones in 2009, two years before the company went public. It followed by introducing the app on every major mobile platform, including Android (smartphones and tablets), Kindle Fire, BlackBerry, iOS (iPad and iPhone), and Windows Phone 7. With real estate being inherently mobile, within three years of Zillow's first app, the number of homes viewed on mobile devices passed the number viewed from personal computers. By late 2012, more than one billion homes had been viewed on Zillow apps since the beginning of the year.

"Real estate was a category really built and tailor made for mobile," says Jeremy Wacksman, vice president of consumer marketing and mobile at Zillow.[4] "It's inherently a mobile experience. Once people could get Zillow on their smartphone, we really saw our business take off." And take off it did:

- By December 2012, there were 33 million unique users of its mobile apps, with year-over-year growth of 47 percent.
- By late 2012, Zillow's suite of apps comprised 22 different apps, including real estate, dedicated rental and rental professional apps (Zillow Rentals), dedicated mortgage apps (Zillow Mortgage Marketplace apps), and the Buyfolio and Hotpads apps.
- By the end of 2010, six homes per second were being viewed through its mobile apps. By the last quarter of 2012, 62 homes per second were being viewed.
- In one month alone, 166 million homes were viewed through Zillow's mobile app, or 22 homes per second.
- More than 45 percent of Zillow's overall traffic across all categories comes from a mobile device. On weekends, it's more than 55 percent.

- People used the Zillow mobile mortgage calculator about 10 million times since bringing Zillow Mortgage Marketplace to mobile in June 2011.

The mobile stats tell only part of the story. What Zillow tapped into was the newfound ability to move with the on-the-go consumer. Rather than conducting research before heading out to look at houses, shoppers could now drive through relevant neighborhoods, see a sign that a house was for sale, and get immediate and detailed information on the property through the app. Zillow's traditional online model was turned on its head as shopping for a home became an on-site, always-on experience. Says Wacksman:

When we first saw Zillow explode on mobile we really saw it transform from a nine-to-five shopping experience from a PC to a 24/7 shopping experience. People could get updates and listing and information whenever they wanted as opposed to when they sat down at their desktop.

The other trend was that the use case changed a bit. We have always been a research tool and a shopping comparison, but now we're an on-demand one. So when you're out at curbside and want to check surrounding neighborhoods or you want to get more information on a home before you go into it, we are a shop-along tool for the buyer or renter. We have become the price checkout for the curb.

We already tipped to mobile in terms of homes viewed. Even early in 2012 we were seeing more home views on mobile and tablets than on traditional PCs and laptops.

It's hard to determine where it's going to go, but if you think about the growth rate a year ago at this time we were at 21 homes viewed per second on mobile, so it has more than tripled in a year. That growth rate is what caused it to tip, and I don't see that going away. I think more of our real estate consumption will continue to move toward mobile devices.

In addition to targeting people house hunting, the company created a set of apps for rental agents and property managers, allowing them to access their property management systems from smartphones. Operating what has become the most popular suite of mobile real estate apps across platforms, Zillow started to see different consumer behaviors between its traditional usage patterns and those on mobile. It also saw some differences based on what mobile device was being used. Says Wacksman:

> Real estate is a category that is a little less traditional to begin with. It's a very long shopping cycle and you're doing research and trying to find the perfect home over a period of months. What mobile has done in our category is make that a more on-demand, always-on experience. With our mobile users we see a higher visit-per-user engagement level with our app. We also see that they're more transaction ready.
>
> Our mobile users are three times more likely to contact an agent about a property than our traditional desktop and laptop users. They're consuming whenever and whatever they want on their device. They're contacting more often because they are on demand. It's because the focus of those using Zillow on a mobile device are using it as a primary shopping tool and in an on-demand fashion. So if they're out and see a house that they like they can contact someone about that house right then and there. If you are at work on a Thursday and see a new listing pop up, you'll flag it for yourself and say, "Oh, I have got to check this out, maybe I'll look at it tonight or drive by when I can." The idea that you can pull up information in the context of shopping makes it more shopper focused or transaction ready.
>
> There is a heavy incremental audience on mobile that hadn't found us before, but a lot of people are using it multiplatform. We track contact from consumers to agents, which is a good demand signal for transaction activity. The fact that people are three times more likely to make contact on a mobile device—that is an indicator of a higher transaction and ready audience.
>
> The apps are a combination of getting Zillow to the different platforms, tablet optimized versus smartphone optimized, and we have apps that are optimized for a single purpose. For example, we

have a mortgages app for iPhone, iPad, and Android and rentals app specific to the rental industry for iPhone and Android.

There has been such a rapid adoption of both platforms. We see iPads being different from iPhone and different from Android. They're all very big and important platforms for us and all are growing rapidly with consumers adopting them en masse.

The iPhone and Android phones are a price-comparison shopping tool in our category. Not that tablet isn't, but the iPhone is really the most pure form of that. Our category can be so research focused, which is why the tablet fits in so nicely.

We see the tablet as a hybrid between the desktop PC and the phone. It's more on-demand and has higher consumption patterns, but its time-of-day usage is a lot like desktop. It's a little heavier on nights and weekends and it's a little lower on the GPS usage than the manual search usage. So it's a hybrid; the desktop is most traditional, the phone is the most on-demand location, and the tablet is in the middle.

What we do track is how often shoppers are using the GPS to do a search versus how often they enter a search manually. As you would expect, GPS usage is high in terms of iPhone and Android. People say, "I want to search towns nearby," or "I want to look at something close to where I am standing," and that's lower on the iPad.

Mobile has become a powerful tool for companies like Zillow and it is a disrupting factor for the home-buying process. While some mobile capabilities such as last-minute booking are not relevant for buying a house, the instant access to information based on the potential buyer's location relative to a house for sale totally transforms the dynamics of the process. "You aren't going to buy a house in less time, but you're able to see a house faster and get the information about the house faster," says Wacksman. "That's why it's really huge for us, because we're in the business of getting that information to consumers so they can make a decision as opposed to if they actually sign on the dotted line. In our funnel that is where the disruption is happening."

Zillow makes its money from advertising, such as ads from mortgage lenders and real estate agents that appear during consumer visits, so increased mobile visits and activity can increase potential reach.

"Having more on-demand tools to put the consumer in charge was accelerated with mobile," says Wacksman. "We're all about empowering the consumer with the best tools to make a good real estate decision, and putting that on your phone just increases that empowerment over what a traditional laptop/desktop could do. Real estate is a shopping cycle that was already being augmented by technology. It's not a traditional funnel and is a multimonth shopping process."

CARS BY MOBILE

Then there are cars to be bought via mobile. For example, Cars.com was initially founded in 1997 as a joint venture of various newspaper companies to combat the loss of newspaper classified advertising. After mobile came along the company launched an iPhone and then an Android app targeted to active car shoppers with mobile, who typically view more pages than those on the website.

I bought a car exclusively through the Cars.com app, conducting all research and using location technology, bypassing much of the car-buying hassle. No newspaper ads, no blind visits to car dealerships, and not even Craigslist. I would search the Cars.com app for cars based on my location, see Kelley Blue Book used-car values and receive free Carfax reports via the app. I could see all the car details with multiple photos with the one-tap click to call or email. When I visited dealers, I usually had more knowledge of the car than did any given salesperson and at times even had lower pricing in the app, since that data was updated more frequently than the prices on windshields in the car lots.

It turns out that many cars are being purchased by mobile device. EBay sells well over 3,500 cars a week via mobile device and more than nine million car parts and accessories via mobile.[5] The eBay mobile app has been downloaded more than 90 million times, so plenty of people have the capability in their hands to buy a car, with the mobile ripple being the impact on car dealerships and car salespeople. As with many of the examples in this book, mobile shopping is not only a U.S. phenomenon, it is world-wide. In the United Kingdom, smartphone users are buying exclusive cars, including Porsches and Land Rovers, with a tap of the finger. In that market, 45,000 cars were sold via smartphone within a three-month period.[6] If something can be bought, it ultimately will be bought on a mobile device.

MOBILE GAS

While some purchases such as houses are large and are bought over a period of time, the in-transit stage of the Mobile Shopping Life Cycle also relates to smaller and more immediate purchases.

GasBuddy was founded in Brooklyn Park, Minnesota, more than a dozen years ago as a collection of websites to give people a way to find and share gas-pricing information. By entering their zip code at the GasBuddy website, consumers could find gas prices at stations within the zip code. It was useful if you were searching for gas prices before leaving home. Over the years, it built a modest following while only on the Web. However, mobile takes services like GasBuddy to a whole new level. By adding location while in transit, the program because exponentially more valuable to literally mobile consumers.

"When you need to buy gas, you're typically in your vehicle," says Jason Toews, who cofounded GasBuddy simply to help motorists find the cheapest local gas prices.[7] The app has been downloaded about 24 million times, and 60 percent of GasBuddy usage is now from mobile, says Toews. He notes that many still use the website because "only half the country has a smartphone."

With a computer background, Toews and team connected some automated data feeds from gas stations to the GasBuddy system to ensure real-time pricing. They then built a mass of 243 local gas websites that carried the local gas price information. "It splits our traffic 243 ways," says Toews. The sites are advertising supported. "Ads pay the bills," says Toews. "We're totally independent and neutral. We don't consult for big oil on anything."

The majority of gas price information comes from an army of what Toews calls *spotters,* about six million people who tap in gas prices from their local stations. Another way to look at it is that the content is provided by the customers. "Some do it once a month, some do it daily," he says. "People feel they're making a difference and helping each other."

GasBuddy is one of those in-transit businesses that were doing fine on the Web but that became more relevant and substantially more useful to consumers actively using them in the field when they expanded to mobile. "We grew organically," says Toews. "A lot of people didn't know about us." That was before they went mobile.

BUYING ON THE FLY

During the in-transit phase of the Mobile Shopping Life Cycle, timing in relation to the purchase can play a significant role, although more in some industries than in others. As in the case of Rue La La discussed in an earlier chapter, mobile customers crave using their phones for activities even if a business has not yet planned for it. By default, many mobile shoppers use their phones to access a company's traditional website. And as we heard from companies during the research on this book, the deeper companies get into creating mobile solutions for their customers, the more they learn and the more they determine there is much yet to learn in the evolving mobile marketplace.

Alaska Airlines is one of the many companies that saw mobile activity happening in its channel even before it promoted it. "What's amazing to me is that we had a lot of purchases happening via smartphones before even developing a smartphone-optimized purchasing solution," says Curtis Kopf, managing director of e-commerce and innovation at Alaska Airlines.[8] "People were purchasing on a desktop site using a smartphone, which shows how badly customers want to buy things on the phone."

Kopf, who worked at Amazon in the United Kingdom when it launched there in 1998 and moved to Seattle in 2000, sees similarities between mobile and the early days of the Web. "It reminds me a lot of being at Amazon at the start of e-commerce," says Kopf. "I don't think anyone would have predicted what's happened over the last 15 years. And to me mobile is very comparable to that. We're just learning, and I feel like we know about one percent of what we're going know. What we do know is that a surprisingly high percentage of our purchases are coming from mobile."

Alaska Airlines found that mobile purchasing grew exponentially with the majority of the purchases coming from tablets, mostly iPads. They also found that purchases from smartphones occur closer to the date of departure, a pattern found by other airlines as well. "That makes sense when you consider that is very likely a person who is sitting at the airport, or in a hotel, or on the road who wants to change a flight or add another leg," says Kopf. "Two or three years ago they would have had to go back and pick up the phone and call or wait till the next time they got to a computer. Now they can just do it."

The late buy or last-minute purchase within the in-transit phase of the purchase cycle has significant marketing implications. "As the percentage of purchases on mobile devices double and triples, which it will, a huge percentage of those purchases on smartphones are going to be last minute. So then you start to think about how you're going to change how you market to those customers. What kind of information do you provide to those customers? We'll look at that very carefully and build our approach based off what customers are doing."

Since digital marketing is part of Kopf's group at Alaska Airlines, he needs to focus on how to market to that last-minute in-transit customer. "We're looking at it literally on a daily basis, what are people doing," says Kopf. "What are the purchase patterns? We have customer satisfaction surveys. What are they happy about? And we're literally looking at that every day. So that's where it starts. But then from there, once you observe, 'Wow, there's a high percentage of last-minute purchases,' then it becomes a discussion with the marketing team." Kopf defined a series of questions to be asked as part of a pattern:

- What do you guys think about this?
- What's interesting to you?
- What opportunities are there?
- Are there opportunities to fill those remaining open seats on the flight?

- Those three or four extra seats that are still open at the last minute?
- What customer problems can we solve? What business problems can we solve?

Kopf also recalls some lessons he learned from his stint at Amazon, much of them involving customer focus and customer service, for which Amazon is well known. Says Kopf:

I started with Amazon in '98 and learned a lot that's guided everything I've done ever since then in my career. There were a lot of great things that Amazon did, but two fundamental ones: Number one. Always start with the customer. What is the customer trying to do? Where is there a gap in the customer experience? Where is there a gap that could be better? The Kindle is a good example of that. I finish reading a book, I want a new one. I used to have to order it and wait or drive to a bookstore. Now I can lie in bed, I finished a book, click, click, click, I have a new book. There's a gap in customer experience that has been closed.

So one guide will be where are there gaps in the customer experience that we can fill with this. So that's number one. Start with the customer. What are they trying to do? What problems are they trying to solve?

And then secondly is look at the data. Look at the facts. And one of the things I learned at Amazon is always start with what you know. The facts may not give you all the answers. If you just looked at the facts, Amazon probably never would have developed the Kindle. I'm not sure you could leap from an analysis to "We should have a Kindle." I'm not sure that if you just looked at metrics, Apple would have developed the iPhone.

So there's still a leap you need to make, but look at the data. And I think in mobile we are seeing dramatic changes month by month. By comparison, an e-commerce business, it's mature. You see very consistent trends. We're back to 1998–99, where the data is changing significantly every month. Even faster than e-commerce. Our

e-commerce team, which is probably typical of a company that is doing a pretty good job at it, does releases every two weeks. Iterative
releases. We get customer feedback, we discover a friction point. I
mean, we can do it faster than that, but our regular cadence is every
two weeks the website is getting better.

With the way we're developing mobile, the apps we have today,
is we do two-week sprints. We use agile as our methodology. So that
literally means that every two weeks we have new code, a prototype,
we take it out to our boardroom, which is our club in the airport. We
ask customers if they sit down with us and we walk them through it
and get their feedback and go right back into development.

Alaska as a brand is very fortunate in that when we say, "Hey"—I
mean this is literally how my team does some of its research, part of
our team is sitting in the conference room in the boardroom—"any
of you are interested? We'll give you free coffee"—or whatever it is we
give them—"if you're willing to spend 20 minutes with us." Customers gladly come sit down with us and we walk them through it. And
we find things that, you know, jeez, that design is not as intuitive as
we thought—okay, now we're going back into development for two
weeks. That's different from what we've done before. That is because
of mobile.

A lot of people call it agile development. You could call it iterative development. I think there's a general trend with really smart
technology companies to move fast, to do what we call iterative development. And that could be your website, that could be anything.
I think any smart digital and e-commerce team is doing continuous
testing. That's another piece of it, continuous testing.

We have tests running every day where we are saying A, B, C, D,
or E? It could be colors of a font. It could be that we just completed a
test on the checkout path. Taking a page out, changing that page, get
the data and change it.

I'll tell you one learning Alaska had that a lot of companies had.
Alaska started with mobile several years ago. In the travel industry,
we were one of the airline industry's first to come out. We did a kind
of write once deploy many approach and it didn't tailor the app to

the platform as well as it should. iPhone has its own set of design guidelines and look and feel. If you want to be successful you need a map to that. So we kind of took a do it once, out to many and in a way that we couldn't make rapid changes. That was learning number one.

About 18 months ago when I started at Alaska we literally started from scratch. I would say that's very typical of anyone who is in mobile. We went back to the drawing board with a focus that was much more tailoring your app to this device and the Android app to that platform. And the site to the site.

Other things that we've learned, there's a lot of just very small design things. As much as you user test, you still cannot anticipate all the friction points that are going to happen. The real test is when the customer is sitting at a noisy airport with a million distractions trying to check in, trying to get flight information.

We know going in we're going to do the best we can but we absolutely know it could be tiny things—"Well, I didn't realize that when I clicked that button it drops down," and so there's a lot of small things that we continue to tweak. You learn that from the customer. You are absolutely unequivocally never done.

It's the same principle. I think the only difference, as some of the speakers said, mobile is growing and the penetration is happening even faster than e-commerce. I think that just means you have to move faster. And I think that another factor that's unique to mobile is there's a lot of data out there and the attention spans when someone is on one of these is much, much shorter. So there are stats out there and you could find them about, of all the apps a consumer downloads there's only a tiny percentage that they end up using regularly.

So you get one shot. The customer opens up your app—it's not intuitive, they don't get it, that's it, you're done. You've lost your opportunity. That customer may never go back to your app again. So I think the onus, or the bar for getting it right, is even higher.

At some point it will be as big of a revenue channel as the desktop website. I don't know when that tipping point will be. Mobile will continue to be a way to provide a lot information to customers that they can't get today. I think that when NFC happens, there's a lot of debate out there about when that's going to happen. You can go to Asia and parts of Europe today and they're in the future. They're where we're going to be in three years. An example with NFC is that there will be a point when a customer will walk into the airport and we'll know they're there. If they're a mileage plan member, they won't even have to check in. They maybe checked in just by walking into the airport. They may be able to do a lot of things they do today with pieces of paper just by walking by a stand or something with no staff and just waving their device. So I think that's one of the things that's going to change.

All of us are realizing that as an airline, I know in a given day a customer might be on their PC on a desktop site and then a few hours later they might be on our app or mobile website with this. A few hours later they might be at our airport with our kiosk.

We have a lot of screens, and we need to think of them holistically. Being consistent, but then tailoring the experience to what a customer wants to do with this.

While the in-transit phase of the Mobile Shopping Life Cycle deals with reaching the mobile consumer while moving and on the go, there is another opportunity to interact with them once they get where they are going, which we discuss in the next chapter.

four

THE PUSH

on location

THE NEW VALUE OF BRICK AND MORTAR

During the early days of the internet, having a physical store was considered to be a detriment to business. In many ways, having a building to showcase and sell products, with all the associated costs, was a liability. Why go to Borders to buy a book when you could have one easily shipped to your home from Amazon, in most cases tax free? Now Borders is gone and Amazon has moved from selling only books to just about everything.

With the internet, location was less relevant since the online shopper could have anything delivered. There was no way for a physical retailer to capitalize on the online shopping behavior since the consumer typically used their computer at home or work to order from online retailers. All major retailers ultimately entered the same online arena with websites of their own, often with substantially more online products than those available at their physical locations. However, the advantage still fell to online-only retailers, since they had fewer cost burdens of real estate and on-site staffing.

Mobile yet again changes the buying-selling dynamics, with physical location becoming a critical component in the Mobile Shopping Life

Cycle. With mobile, location and location-based services become a core function in almost every aspect of the purchase decision for both cruisers and seekers.

Now retailers can identify and market directly to mobile shoppers while in their physical stores, since location technology is built into smartphones, enabling savvy businesses to identify those shoppers, provide value to them, and entice them to make their purchases there. Leveraging location and location information provides businesses the opportunity to reach the mobile consumer as they walk the aisles in a physical store. This doesn't necessarily mean sales associates will be running up to shoppers when they see them using their phones while they shop. There are sophisticated mobile technologies that continually increase the effectiveness of reaching consumers by using information related to location.

There are essentially two forms of location identification. There is the actual mobile technology, such as GPS, that identifies the location of the phone both in the abstract and also in relation to other things, such as stores, restaurants, or products. There is also the direct activity by the consumer, who self-identifies to small or large groups of people where he or she is at any given moment.

The on-location time is when customers are in or at the destination in which they intend, are likely, or can be persuaded to buy. This is where location-based marketing and location-based services come into play. With location-based marketing, marketers attempt to attract customers to their facility by sending mobile offers based on the location of the customer in relation to the store. For example, shoppers on the second floor of a Singapore shopping center might receive offers only from retailers located on the second floor, since the marketer can tell the height of the phone to determine the floor on which the shopper is walking. Brick and mortar becomes an asset when the mobile shopper can be identified and acknowledged.

There are many mobile tools being used to influence mobile behaviors at this stage, including text-to offers, mobile check-ins, real-time bidding, momentary offerings, and various location-based incentives and offers. This is the stage when what I call *location magnets* such as mall-mapping services and location-based offers are used to increase the amount of time the shopper stays at the location.

Location-based services, in which mobile customers converse with each other about purchase decisions and check-in services, provide marketers with additional opportunities to become part of the discussion and influence the purchase decision. This fact has not been lost on brands. One study by the Chief Marketing Officer (CMO) Council found that 49 percent of marketers believe mobile will help influence customer interactions by providing a more personalized and relevant experience.[1] According to the study, marketers found that personalization and an increase in engagement lead to new avenues of engagement that will prove to be a competitive advantage for the brand. Marketers are looking for this edge through value-added services, and 34 percent of marketers in the study see the ability to increase frequency of communications as a key way that mobile can influence consumers.

MOBILE BEHAVIORS ON LOCATION

There are a variety of activities for which mobile shoppers use their devices on location and a range of research findings about those behaviors, though many of the general patterns are the same in the various studies. Mobile is projected to influence 17 to 21 percent of total retail purchases by 2016, adding up to an impact valued at $628 billion to $752 billion, according to Deloitte Digital.[2] While in stores, 58 percent of smartphone owners use their phones for in-store shopping, with almost half (49 percent) shopping in electronics and about one in five (19 percent) in convenience stores and gas stations (see Table 4.1). Once the behavior of mobile shopping on location starts, it doesn't stop, with more than 50 percent of smartphone owners' shopping trips involving mobile use in store, depending on the category, according to the Deloitte study. Smartphone use for in-store shopping increases by 40 percent after the first six months of getting the device.

On-location use of a smartphone is more likely to be by someone between the ages of 24 and 34, since more of that age group own and use

table 4.1

SMARTPHONE IN-STORE USAGE BY CATEGORY*

Electronics/appliances	49%
GM (general merchandise) /department store	46%
Clothing/footwear	38%
Food/beverage	35%
Books & music	33%
Home improvement/garden	31%
Sporting goods/toys	30%
Health/personal care/drug	27%
Furniture/home furnishings	24%
Misc., including office supplies	22%
Convenience/gas stations	29%

*Based on Deloitte study involving smartphone owners who have used a smartphone to shop.

their smartphone while shopping in a retail store. Retailers whose main objective is to use mobile to drive customers to their websites in hopes of boosting online revenue may miss the larger picture and opportunity in on-location mobile influence.

Another reason to interact with mobile customers on location is that usage can translate into sales and revenue. More than a third (34 percent) of smartphone shoppers who used their phones on their previous shopping trip used a retailer's mobile app or website, reports Deloitte. The majority (85 percent) of them actually made a purchase that day, compared to 64 percent who did not use the retailer's app or website.

When they get to the store, mobile shoppers are also active in using external sources they tap into from their phones. When on location, the top smartphone activity is looking for competitive pricing at Amazon while in the physical store, according to MarketLive.[3] This means that even if retailers are not aware of Amazon's pricing of products they carry, many mobile shoppers in their stores are finding out, likely before they make the final purchase decision. The shoppers are also looking for promotional coupons for redemption at the store. Brick-and-mortar retailers may be happy to hear that the least common in-store smartphone activity is making a purchase from another retailer from their phone, according to the MarketLive study (see Table 4.2).

table 4.2

LIKELY IN-STORE SMARTPHONE ACTIVITY

Look for competitive pricing from Amazon	31%
Access coupons for redemption at store	31%
Look for competitive prices on online retailers	27%
Check for product ratings and reviews	26%
Look on retailer's website for product info	25%
Purchase product from retailer website	24%
Scan barcodes to compare prices	24%
Check in to receive reward points for visiting	22%
Make a purchase on phone from another retailer	19%

The most common mobile activities are redeeming coupons during an in-store purchase and researching gifts on the phone before the store visit, according to MarketLive. The smallest percentage of mobile shoppers purchase gifts as a result of a text message from a retailer and researching gifts on a tablet during a store visit (see Table 4.3).

table 4.3

HOW LIKELY TO INTERACT WITH MOBILE DEVICE

Redeem coupon during in-store purchase	43%
Research gifts on mobile before store visit	29%
Research gifts on mobile during store visit	28%
Redeem coupons when making mobile purchase	25%
Research gifts on tablet before store visit	25%
Purchase gifts on a tablet	22%
Purchase gifts from mobile phone	20%
Research gifts on tablet while in store	18%
Purchase gifts as result of retailer text message	18%

THE DREADED SHOWROOMING

As smartphone technology advanced over the last few years and consumers became more comfortable using their phones in all aspects of life, it was only a matter of time before savvy shoppers figured out ways to get the best deals. They could find a store that carried the product, perhaps get a demonstration from a sales associate or at least see and try the product, and then use their phone to find a better deal on that product elsewhere. The process, commonly known in the retail industry as *showrooming,* is when a customer browses at a physical retailer but then buys via mobile either online or from a competing store. The shopper is just using the retailer's facility and inventory as a place to check out products.

The smartphone has transformed what consumers can do in a store. They can use the phone to scan product barcodes, compare prices, take and send product photos to others, text for advice, read product reviews, look at the retailer's website offerings, and view products at online retailers. Smartphone owners also are likely to have their phones with them while they shop, more than during any other activity, according to the Vibes Mobile Consumer Report (see Table 4.4).[4]

With more than 80 percent of smartphone shoppers roaming the aisles armed with essentially a small but powerful computer, some retailers are concerned, to state the case lightly. "Showrooming tends to have this negative connotation," says Jack Philbin, cofounder, president, and CEO of Vibes.[5] "The industry is sending up a red flag and a big alarm signal for retailers about how Amazon is going to crush you, and people are using your store to browse—but then buy online. That's technically true, but there is so much more consumers are doing than just that."

However, the advantage the brick-and-mortar retailer has is that the shopper is on location, even if only walking the aisles comparing prices. Every smartphone shopper in the store is a potential buyer at that moment.

table 4.4

PERCENT OF THE TIME PHONE IS ALWAYS/
OFTEN WITHIN ARM'S REACH

While shopping	82%
Working	74%
Watching TV	65%
Sleeping	55%
During meals	44%
Exercising	38%
Showering	11%

table 4.5

ACTIVITIES OF SMARTPHONE OWNERS WHILE IN STORE

Compared competitor's site	33%
Looked up product review	31%
Scanned a QR (quick response) code for info	27%
Researched store's site	20%
Used company's app	17%
Sent text for info	10%

And the Vibes research found that activities of the smartphone consumer in the store vary (see Table 4.5).

There are two types of activities by smartphone shoppers in the store—comparison shopping and research. A third of those comparison shopping compare a competitor's website, and 20 percent view products on the store's site. Shoppers conducting research tend to look up product reviews and are looking for additional information about a product. In-store signage promoting text messaging is one way for retailers to make it easier for shoppers to receive additional product information, as discussed later in this chapter. The other obvious way to assist smartphone shoppers is to provide in-store Wi-Fi. Consumers who want additional product information on the spot can easily become frustrated by poor mobile signals, and you can end up losing a customer even if you have the best product offering.

Mobile can be used to help customers while they shop by providing information that, at the very least, makes the consumer feel more positive about their purchase (see Table 4.6). "Showrooming is about people feeling

table 4.6

KEY RESULTS AFTER SMARTPHONE OWNERS SCAN/ TEXT FOR PRODUCT INFO

Feel better about my purchase	48%
I was dissuaded from making a purchase	15%
Made a purchase I hadn't planned to	14%
The info didn't have an impact	13%

more confident as shoppers," says Philbin. "It goes back to basic human behavior. You want to make sure you're making a good decision. For retailers, this quest for shopper confidence is really a competitive weapon and mobile marketing should lead the charge."

Almost half of smartphone shoppers who scan or text for product information feel better about their purchase, and only a small percentage of the consumers were not impacted by information they received, based on the Vibes study.

Showroom shoppers also exhibit somewhat different mobile behavior. For example, the majority (57 percent) of showroom shoppers redeem mobile coupons, while more than a third (39 percent) of smartphone owners do the same. While almost three-quarters (70 percent) of showroom shoppers would use NFC (near field communication) for a purchase, fewer than half (48 percent) of smartphone owners would.

A deal is more likely to appeal to showroom shoppers, with more than half redeeming mobile coupons and half sharing their location for a deal. The showroom shopper also is active engaging with marketers.

Showroom shoppers also can be turned away by marketers based on what they are sent and the volume of messaging. The number-one reason that showroom shoppers unsubscribe is the volume of messages they get (see Table 4.7).

KEEPING SHOWROOMERS IN THE STORE

Once showroomers are on location, keeping them there can present an opportunity for brands and retailers. There are a number of factors that

table 4.7

TOP REASONS FOR SHOWROOM SHOPPERS UNSUBSCRIBING

Too many messages or updates	86%
Information wasn't relevant to me	76%
Coupons/incentives were not good enough	51%
The messages were untimely	44%
I couldn't personalize information received	23%

can influence the behavior of showroomers. While customers would rather have a product immediately, a small price difference found elsewhere using a mobile device is enough to make them leave and buy elsewhere.

When the online price is just 2.5 percent lower than the in-store price, almost half (45 percent) of customers say they would leave the store to buy online, based on a GroupM Next study.[6] When the discount increased to 5 percent, 60 percent of customers say they would leave. At a 20 percent discount level, a small minority of shoppers (13 percent) would stay in the store. Based on price, the majority of showroomers would leave if the difference was more than $5. The GroupM Next study shows that if a brick-and-mortar store can stay within 5 percent of the online price, nearly half the potential showroomers will decide to complete their purchase in the store. This means savvy retailers need to continually be aware of the pricing of their products compared to the same products online.

The profile of typical overall showroomers is that they are younger, primarily female, frequent online buyers, and have a lower income. The GroupM Next study shows that about 10 percent of purchasers complete the purchase in store no matter what discount is offered elsewhere. The opportunity is in the next 10 percent, who can be swayed to stay in the store. The study determined the characteristics of the group to target, called the marginal showroomer (see Table 4.8).

Showroomer behavior can also be impacted by salespeople, with 13 percent of those who interact with a sales associate more likely to purchase in store.

table 4.8

PROFILE OF MARGINAL SHOWROOMER

Gender	90%+ male
Average age	52
Median income	$60,000
Some college	98%
Buy online once/month	55%
Buy online once/week	21%
Buy online more than once/week	11%

RETAIL READY FOR REVERSE SHOWROOMING?

Many retailers have become all too familiar with showrooming, and the obvious response is for retailers to attempt to interact with consumers as they scan and shop, whether through technologies like geofences or plain human observation by sales associates. That would be *counter-showrooming.*

But what if retailers could find a way to incent shoppers to scan products in their stores to promote sales of those products to others not in the store? This would be true *reverse showrooming,* using the showrooms of retailers to sell their products to people not on location.

A consumer-to-consumer online shopping start-up is heading in that direction. Shop My Label, billing itself as "an online community that supports and facilitates peer-to-peer sales," launched starting with fashion and beauty products. The idea is that a consumer opens a free account to create their online shop. They select items from participating retailers to "stock" their shops. The shop owner then shares information about their store with their friends through their social networks. When their friends or anyone else buys from their online store, they receive up to 10 percent commissions on each sale.

The individual stores are positioned to be marketed to each other, mainly through Facebook, the primary sign-in method to create a storefront. "We're a social company," says Dearrick Knupp, founder and chief product officer of Shop My Label.[7] Knupp is situated with more than a dozen employees working upstairs in a building in New York only a few blocks from the original Foursquare headquarters.

The company has signed dozens of retail partners, including Saks, Delia's, Avenue, Armani Exchange, and Vince Camuto. And those retailers should be happy, since the items sold at the personal shops will be at full retail.

The edge for the personal shop owner is that they can create an outfit by mixing and matching from a number of stores and brands, giving the buyer a one-stop-shopping experience with payment and free shipping being aggregated. "We're driving full price sales, so free shipping was a necessity," says Knupp. He adds that part of the marketing partnerships with the retailers is that they market Shop My Label to their customers.

Shop My Label has inventory data feeds from the retailers, which Knupp says was far more difficult than anticipated. "Retailer integration is not easy," he says. "And fashion is tough. We have to integrate 45,000 products just from Saks.com and we have to manage 700,000 SKUs." Prices from the retailers are updated daily.

The first clue of the potential mobile future of Shop My Label was that the company named as its chief operating officer Boris Fridman, mobile pioneer and former CEO of Crisp Wireless (now Crisp Media). The intent is for Shop My Label to scale gradually and then add mobile as the second phase, says Knupp.

With mobile, consumers with storefronts could potentially visit physical stores and scan products to have them automatically entered onto their personal store. They then would have a firsthand database of the products they viewed and scanned, giving them more detailed information to add to their marketing to their Facebook friends. This is essentially peer-to-peer selling with the premise of sellers and buyers engaging with one another while using the Shop My Label platform.

The mobile consumer becomes a repackager of sorts, an advance scout who can see and feel the products before autoselecting for their personal storefronts. Of course the challenge for the retailers at the customer level will be to figure whether the scanning shopper is doing so to use them, by showrooming, or help them, by reverse showrooming.

EXTENDING MOBILE INFLUENCE TO THE STORE

Retailers of all sizes and locations are facing new behaviors from mobile shoppers and finding new ways to influence them. In the Netherlands, there are more phones than people. With mobile phone penetration at 115 percent of the population of about 17 million, retailers there face challenges and opportunities dealing with mobile shoppers on location.[8] As the largest and one of the oldest department store chains in the Netherlands, V&D determined to find ways to exert mobile influence.

V&D, named after its two founders, Vroom and Dreesmann, was founded in 1887 and over its 125 years has grown to more than 10,000 employees in 62 locations throughout the Netherlands and the launch of the webshop in 2008 with more than 700 brands online. The chain prides itself on its service and has won numerous awards for most trusted brand in the department store category in the Netherlands. The consumer move to mobile allowed V&D another opportunity to take advantage of its location and VD.nl, where more than two million people a week shop.

"We are an old brand but we are getting younger every day," says Brent Van Rossem, brands director of V&D.[9] "We are trying to get ahead of the curve with our mobile strategy compared to other traditional retailers. I must say that we are building our online credentials faster and faster at the moment, and there are a lot of exciting things going around here within our general strategy."

The Mobile Shopping Life Cycle is essentially the same in all countries, though not all countries are exactly in sync in each of the stages. For example, in some markets smartphone penetration is lower than in others, pricing for data plans is different, and location-based technologies are being used differently.

"The speed of the mobile revolution developing in the United States is enormous, but it is even faster in the Netherlands," says Van Rossem. "In the United States 50 percent have smartphones, but in the Netherlands it is almost 60 percent of the population already. That development and combination with record developments of online shopping in the Netherlands made us launch the mobile version of our website m.vd.nl six months sooner so that it could be accessed from a smartphone and a tablet."

As soon as it launched its mobile versions, V&D customers started interacting with the chain while on the go. "About 2 percent of online sales are already coming from the mobile website," says Noël Manning, manager of e-commerce at V&D.[10] "We also have an optimized version for tablet customers, increasing rapidly with almost 10 percent of online sales now coming from the tablet version. We see the share of sales triple from the previous year. We are seeing people actually shop on the tablet version using the mobile version."

The V&D approach is to link all its shopping channels together, providing access to consumers no matter how they prefer to shop. The chain also found that consumers research products before coming to the stores, so it trains its salespeople to knowledgeably assist those shoppers. "Consumers are more and more open to shop across channels and even in stores more and more customers are asking the staff if we still have this product available online," says Van Rossem. "And, of course, the staff checks if it is available online. The consumer base is developing faster and we now can invest further in having screens at the point of sale where shoppers can find items that we are out of style or size in a store."

Another way that V&D leverages its brick-and-mortar location is by offering assistance to in-store customers to find products not in the physical store. Sales associates use tablets or other screens in the store that provide access to V&D's online showcase. "When customers get in store they are open to extending their shopping experience wider than just what we have in stock in the store," says Manning.

The approach of V&D is to make the shopping experience with them seamless, no matter if it is in store, online, mobile, or on a tablet. This approach tends to avoid showrooming, since the customer is assisted through the digital assets of the store that extend beyond on-site inventory. And in true on-location fashion, a consumer may have come to the store because of a mobile purchase, but V&D then looks to influence the shopper while on the premises.

"We have our 'omni channel strategy,'" says Manning. "Within the omni channel strategy we try to make sure that our customers don't experience a difference within our channels. For example, if you order online at home you can click and order and collect it at the store. Then, when you are in the store collecting the item, we try to make you spend more money in the store. We are more and more trying to support the needs of our customers that are already there and store staff is trained and we are getting better and better. For example, our customer-service areas are fully trained."

While V&D is not using location-based technologies, it has a tablet and a smartphone app for both Android and iPhone that it uses to promote merchandise and share promotions and new products. It also is equipped for payments so that customers can pay via PayPal among other payment options. Most store managers carry tablets to assist in-store customers with finding V&D's products online. As in other markets, there are numerous online-only sellers that lack the ability to leverage brick-and-mortar assets and mobile shoppers on location. This has not gone unnoticed at V&D, which tightly links its online and offline sales.

"Seventy percent of online sales are shipped to homes, 30 percent of sales are picked up in store, and 70 percent of all returns are returned to the store," says Van Rossem. "This is important because it creates traffic in stores so they return a product and then buy something else. A number of pure players market extensively their free delivery to stores. We do free delivery to homes above 75 euro and to stores, and people are in shopping centers frequently."

V&D is bullish on the future of mobile in the Netherlands and is preparing accordingly. "It's going to be big," says Van Rossem. "We see more and more introductions of apps into the market that offer different competitors in one app and those that can be different location based. We connect socially like Facebook, Twitter, and Pinterest. We believe that that can add hugely to our customer base."

"The smartphone will become more and more the central device that people will use, and conversion will grow," says Manning. "Payments through smartphone will grow and become easier in coming years."

Other retailers who have not already done so would be well advised to follow the lead of V&D's linking its digital and physical channels together. In the Mobile Shopping Life Cycle, the time spent in a store is only part of the process, not necessarily the end game. In addition to buying at physical stores, mobile shoppers also go there to research and even compare prices of items at different stores and online sellers. Retailers such as Best Buy have systems in place for consumers to order via mobile or online and have the items delivered to the store for customer pickup. The incentive for the consumer is to avoid shipping charges and, as in the case of V&D, the advantage for the retailers is they guarantee a store visit by a shopper, giving the store a chance to leverage their brick-and-mortar facilities.

BIG TICKET ITEMS

In addition to the many items in department stores like V&D, there is an opportunity to connect with mobile shoppers looking for big ticket items within the Mobile Shopping Life Cycle. One of the facilitators of mobile influence that helps leading brands connect with mobile shoppers is Arc Worldwide, the global marketing services arm of Leo Burnett.

When it comes to more expensive goods, some on-location shoppers have a general idea of what they're looking for but may seek real-time advice, especially before spending large sums of money. "Mobile hits certain touch points of a customer journey," says Molly Garris, digital strategy director and mobile practice lead at Leo Burnett and Arc Worldwide.[11] "There used to be a really defined path to purchase, but now it's completely changed with so many on-demand channels that are available to shoppers."

For example, early in the shopping process for a computer, a consumer may not even realize they want to purchase something. Their current PC may be slow starting, getting old, and not compatible with newer software. "That's where above-the-line media like TV and print will start to seed it in their mind, while mobile will play a role when they are physically in the store and looking for more information like rating and reviews," says Garris. "They're looking for a non-biased source to help them pick a new computer. That's where mobile can play a really interesting role. It's to help them with these decisions or provide information that maybe they don't feel comfortable asking a sales representative who may be incentivized to push them to a certain brand."

A mobile shopper at Best Buy can scan the QR (quick response) codes on three different products and compare the features side by side. "Channels like television, print, and radio can create general awareness, but when it comes down to the drilled down details, people are searching for those quick bits of information using their mobile phones."

Mobile also has a role in-store for consumers looking for large household appliances. Says Garris:

With the product lines of Whirlpool, we found that customers only shop for appliances every seven years. The brand wouldn't necessarily benefit from sustaining a mobile app because consumers may not be shopping very often. However, where mobile plays a role is getting shoppers to the store and providing them with relevant information to influence their purchase decision.

We conducted mobile shopping research and found that with higher ticket items like appliances or cars, people want to actually go to the store. They don't want to buy it right off their phone. They need to go and touch the door and understand the capacity size by looking at it. We already know that they are going to go to the store to do those things but being there with that information to help them make that purchase, whether it's what kind of warranties are available, what kind of service and deliveries are available, what are the color option? That is where mobile can really help and play a role.

For Whirlpool, we created a mobile optimized site. We ensured it would complement a mobile search strategy so that when people are looking up appliances we can direct them to this shopping tool that helps them understand the different features, side-by-side product comparisons, product reviews, and buying guide. The purpose was to make the appliance shopping process easier and more seamless.

We think of the shopper journey from "I don't know that I even need this product" to "I've bought the product and need to service it." We look for those touch points throughout the entire journey. Where we think mobile plays the strongest role. For higher ticket items, we think this is when people are in the store touching and feeling these items, when they're right about to pull the trigger.

Appliances and high ticket goods are different than what we see with CPG, clothing, and other categories. Consumers may not perform as much online research in advance of going shopping. When they get to the shelf they're not pulling out their mobile phones to research this brand of brown sugar vs. the other brands. Rather, it's more about accessing deals, loyalty apps, or list-making apps. Because mobile shopping behaviors are so varied across product categories, we are challenged to set different mobile strategies based on the type of good the person is shopping for. The only mobile shopping behavior we saw transcend across all product categories was using coupons and offers, whether they came from a specific app or from an email that the shopper received.

SMS ON LOCATION

As anyone observing mobile behavior knows, texting is alive and well, especially among teens. Seventy-five percent of all teens text, with older teens, those 14 to 17 years old, sending and receiving about 3,000 messages a month, according to the Pew Research Center.[12] But teens are not alone in sending and receiving text messages, as SMS messaging remains a large and effective means to achieve mobile influence, especially for mobile shoppers. In Canada alone, more than 268 million text messages a day are sent.[13]

A third of consumers use text messaging constantly throughout the day, with fewer (29 percent) using email, according to the Channel Preference Survey by ExactTarget.[14] Many of these can be messages intended to influence buying behavior, well before a person enters a store. The preferences in how consumers receive messages have changed over the last few years, with the choice of getting them by email down from 66 percent in 2008 to 45 percent recently. Text messaging had the opposite trend, increasing from 16 percent five years ago to 36 percent more recently. This makes it appear that email is out and text messaging is in.

SMS messages can reach almost all phones and can be a relatively low cost of mobile marketing. For example, in the United Kingdom, a bundle of 1,000 text messages costs about eight cents (in U.S. currency), dropping to about five cents for a larger number sent.[15] Overall mobile messaging, including SMS, MMS, instant messages, and email, is projected to reach 28 trillion a year by 2017, with the largest amount of revenue coming from SMS and MMS.[16] Globally, SMS traffic alone is expected to hit nine trillion messages by 2016.[17]

Even though it is decades old, SMS is still so effective and popular because almost anyone can receive a text message. Brands of many types are finding ways to use SMS on location to exert mobile influence. One of the facilitators of mobile influence in this arena is SMS leader Hipcricket, headquartered in New York, with operations in Seattle, Dallas, Chicago, Atlanta, Los Angeles, San Francisco, and Miami. Hipcricket's clients include Macy's, MillerCoors, Nestlé, Clear Channel, and Ford.

Unlike an individual sending a text message to another person, SMS marketing has become highly sophisticated. Customers can be targeted by a range of ways, such as location, demographics, and time of day. There also are rules and procedures that must be followed in SMS marketing, such as getting explicit opt-in from mobile subscribers, since sending messages to random phone users without their permission is spam. Ethical mobile marketers follow the rules and guidelines issued by the Mobile Marketing Association.

You likely have seen some SMS marketing programs. You may have seen an offer in a store, for example, that if you text "offer" to 48938 you will be entered into a contest. The series of numbers, or in some cases a brand or product name, is known as a short code. When you send the text message, you may receive an offer or other incentive with an invitation to opt in for future benefits. Every SMS from brands and marketers carries along with it the easy ability for the consumer to opt out of the messages. Hipcricket, the mobile marketing and advertising company, is the North American market leader when it comes to short codes, provisioning more than anyone else on behalf of brands.

SMS MOBILE INFLUENCE

One of the primary objectives in marketing by auto manufacturers is to cause potential car buyers to contact their local dealer, or, better yet, to visit the dealership. For car dealers, on location is everything, so whatever can be done to get people to locations will create money with bottom-line potential. Before launching a marketing campaign using SMS, Ford had not added a call to action on its TV and print ads, even though the company is one the heaviest advertisers in the world through traditional media. Initially, it simply did not include mobile, which changed with the addition of SMS.

Ford's primary advertising purpose was to create leads that turned into sales, and it decided to do this through TV commercials and print campaigns, which called for SMS. The company wanted to strategically place a call to action in national newspapers such as *USA Today* and TV programs including *NASCAR RaceDay* and *Law & Order*. The SMS part of the advertising message was a success because it opened the door for Ford to engage interactively with potential customers.

"If you wanted to know the local offer for the Ford Focus you would text in your local zip code and you would get the number that would say, okay, it is 2.9 percent or whatever the going rate was in your particular area because there was a variation depending on your location," says Jeff Hasen, chief marketing officer of Hipcricket, which deployed the program.[18] "People responded back, turning passive into interactive folks engaging with traditional media. They were sitting with a tablet or sitting with a phone and they are engaging."

The campaign showed that SMS worked, providing high conversion rates and leads to local dealers. The easy interaction of texting from home while watching a commercial caused a solid response rate.

"We had folks who texted in their zip code and got the local offer and then because they engaged with us we were able to give them one additional message, and that was 'Would you like to be contacted by a Ford dealer in your area?'" says Hasen. "And if they would, we gave them a keyword to text back in.

"Of all the things I want to do tomorrow, if I made a list that is a mile long I would never put I want to be contacted by a car dealer. It is just one of those situations that you go through every few years or whatever your interval is and you are happy when you are done. But remarkably, 15.4 percent of people who took the first step, which was to give the zip code, took the second step to be contacted by the local dealer, which was gold for Ford. We gave the local dealers the information and they would contact the consumer within minutes. They would call them. It is the same objective as it always was, to get somebody to come down to the dealership."

One of the added benefits of the SMS responses is that potential customers easily self-identify themselves as more likely to be in the market at the moment. If someone texted for financing rate information, it stands to reason they may be closer to a purchase consideration than others. Ford also received information to be used for later marketing as an added benefit.

"If you took the first step and did not consent to be contacted by a car dealer, we would reach out to you in about a month and ask you are you still interested in the Focus," says Hasen. "That is important because through the system we track the phone number with the Focus automobile, so we're not giving them an offer for an F-150. So the more relevant you can be, the more opportunity you have to succeed. Ford told us they had never seen a lead conversion at that level, and obviously the program has been expanded and has multiple extensions with different cars."

GOING BACKSTAGE WITH SMS

When a mobile shopper is in store or on location, SMS can be used to influence quick interactions and engagement, the goal of many retailers. With many hundreds of stores, Macy's has been one of the more progressive marketers using mobile since its early days. The retailer wanted to target females over 25 years old for one nationwide campaign and it wanted to use mobile to gather related information to add to its customer database. The ultimate objective was to engage its audience interactively to drive traffic and increase sales through the campaign.

With Macy's Backstage Pass program, in-store displays are placed throughout various departments. Shoppers are prompted to text the advertised keywords to a unique short code or even scan a QR code on the sign. In return, fashion tips and exclusive designer videos were unlocked, giving shoppers an opportunity to learn about the latest fashion and keep them active for upcoming promotions.

"The Backstage Pass program was an opportunity for Macy's to make what used to be a passive activity, walking down the aisle in a retail store, into one that was interactive," says Hasen:

The consumer walks down the aisle and sees multiple calls to action that are mobile focused. If you want to learn about the fashion from Martha Stewart, or P. Diddy, or several others, all you need to do is take your phone out, which already is in your hand, and you respond to a call to action that is either in text prompt to go to the mobile Web and you get a URL for those few people who want to take a URL and go home.

This is what consumers want to do. They want to have the information at their fingertips and they want to access it without having to call over a salesperson, or they want to get as smart as possible in as quick a time as possible.

The most significant part of this is that Macy's is giving consumers choice and it's not dictating. For instance, Macy's isn't saying, "If you want to come to Macy's Tuesday you need to park in South lot and you need to drive a red sedan." That's ridiculous. They'll never be that exclusive. What they want to do is be inclusive.

SMS is the reach strategy in the Backstage Pass program. It allows every consumer to engage, but Macy's knows that not everybody wants a text. Some people want a richer experience, some people want a QR code, but other people don't have the scanner on their phone. So this is a great example of Macy's giving the consumer choice and also obviously tracking the activity. So what we're doing is monitoring and turn[ing] the knobs as the program is live, the whole concept of a postmortem is not playing when it comes to mobile because we can look at real-time interactions and make changes accordingly.

We've actually seen a lot of MMS and mobile Web because the beauty of this campaign is you're taken to richer assets. You're taken to video and you can see the behind-the-scenes look at how to accessorize. So SMS is the heavy lifter when it comes to Macy's for having people opt in for the Macy's loyalty club. There are hundreds of thousands of people who are in the club. In this particular case for the call to action we are seeing more folks who are getting driven to a mobile website or an MMS experience so they can get everything they can get from us.

We're seeing a fair amount of scans from QR codes and it also varies by location. The SMS part of this is the reach because if you don't have a mobile Web-enabled phone or a mobile scanner, they want to be able to give these shoppers an opportunity to engage. And it's not just in store. An extension to Macy's SMS is the program on NBC called *Fashion Star* where Macy's is the sponsor. Various fashion items are unveiled around the store or around the show. You're able to not only learn more about the fashion but we're also taking the passive activity of sitting on the sofa and making it a lean-forward activity by engaging with it.

RETAILER DATABASE VIA SMS

New York & Company is a nationwide specialty retailer of women's fashion and accessories with a target demographic of females over the age of 25 throughout the United States. The retailer wanted to leverage mobile to accumulate information to build its customer database. Retailers can effectively use in-store signage, prominently displaying offers suggesting that a shopper text a message, starting a potential discussion between customer and marketer. In the case of New York & Company, SMS offers in fashion magazines were also deployed.

After the first several months of the campaign, 37,000 mobile consumers had opted in to the New York & Company database. "Much like Macy's is driven by an offer in a variety of places, different key words, different media vehicles, in a fashion magazine ad we have one keyword," says Hasen. "What we are able to do is say, 'Okay, this particular buy is working and we should be doing more of that' or if we're not getting the activity we want out of something else, we can exit out of there.

"It is all about the CRM [customer relationship management] aspect to it and also the opportunity to gain the information from a consumer who is willing to give it to you. Macy's wants to know that I am interested in men's fashion and wants to give me offers that are entirely around that category as opposed to kids' clothes. I don't have kids. It's like the eyelash enhancements and the flying trapeze offers that are sent to me. Not only are they irrelevant but they are annoying. The more relevant you can be and the more you understand what the consumer is looking for, the richer list of interactions between a consumer and a retailer, the better you can be in terms in relevance. We see that with luxury retailers, but we see it primarily with retailers of all price points."

While on location, both cruisers and seekers can be walking the aisles of the store, passively walking by products. Deploying SMS on location can transform that passive experience into one that is interactive and more rewarding for the customer.

"You are on your own when you are out there shopping and you may or may not find the answer to the questions you have," says Hasen. "You may not even know the questions to ask. I am not suggesting that every customer experience should be in the store because, sadly, a lot of retailers don't provide these great customer experiences. There is an opportunity for retailers to combat showrooming by making the in-store experience that much better for the consumer. From a CRM perspective, this comes back to things like folks at Nordstrom's are doing. They are carrying a tablet and they know a lot about the consumer in front of them. They know their buying history and can get relevant very quickly and provide that better experience by knowing your name, knowing what you are interested in, and making it that much more special for you."

Using SMS on location leverages brick and mortar. A retailer has the advantage of regular store traffic, so it can easily display signage with text offers. Some other examples:

- **MillerCoors.** The company wanted its Blue Moon beer to become top of mind with consumers on the go. The objective was to target travelers, provide a way for the beer's fans to stay in touch with their favorite beer, and increase sales. The brand promoted opt-in offers at 28 U.S. airports so that when travelers arrived at the airport they received a message telling them which restaurants served Blue Moon beer.
- **Nestlé Waters.** The company wanted to grow affinity and drive sales of its Arrowhead water brand. Using in-store, SMS opt-in offers, consumers were offered a chance win a day at Universal Studios in Hollywood. Hipcricket found that 78 percent remembered participating in the program, 64 percent found it to be interesting, 38 percent had already purchased an Arrowhead product as a direct result of the program, 44 percent said they were more likely to buy Arrowhead products, and 24 percent were more favorable toward Arrowhead than to competing products.

PINPOINTING: RIGHT CUSTOMER, RIGHT TIME

In addition to reaching seekers and cruisers on location by SMS messaging, there are other types of highly targeted and relevant messaging platforms, triggered by a range of factors. These messages can be delivered to consumers' mobile devices based on customer segment, location, and mobile-app usage history. One facilitator of mobile influence that specializes in this approach is Xtify, a New York–based mobile start-up.

Located on the tenth floor of a building on Broadway in lower Manhattan, an area that numerous mobile start-ups call home, Xtify works on methods of continually tracking mobile consumers to provide messaging at the highest moment of relevancy. This form of momentary marketing is what I call *pinpointing,* the precise targeting both of consumer and message at just the right moment. The company started in 2009 with the intent of creating content and promotional offers delivered to consumers at the time and place in which they could immediately act on them, typically on location.

As a facilitator of mobile influence, Xtify creates and manages the pinpointing platform for brands such as Ritz-Carlton, PacSun, Jack-Threads, and InterContinental Hotels Group. The name Xtify came from a combination of "X marks the spot" and "identify." As is the case with many facilitators of mobile influence, consumers don't see Xtify, since it is the underlying mobile technology that empowers some on-location programs of many of the captains of mobile influence. The consumer sees messaging coming only from well-known brands, either through those companies' apps or mobile websites. The people most likely to use Xtify capabilities are those customers who downloaded a brand's app because they already are fans of a particular brand. "If you have an app, you likely are a brand loyalist," says Josh Rochlin, CEO of Xtify. "This is the next-generation CRM."

In the Mobile Shopping Life Cycle, messages are more effective when fine-tuned and well timed, especially during the on-location stage. With the Xtify system, a marketer can customize messages depending on when they are sent, based on time and location as well as frequency. For example, a person may be sent a mobile message when they come within a certain distance of a particular store. If the person opens the message, they may receive only one more message (a different one) within a four-week period. If they do not open the message, they may receive another the next time they are near that same store again. If the consumer does not open the app within 30 days, they may be sent a reminder message by email or SMS to open the app.

Xtify's technology can extract either the persistent location or "app-open" location of the smartphone, using technology built in to Apple and Android mobile devices that registers a user's location anonymously from their smartphone on a continuous basis. In addition to being depositories of information, smartphones also send information to the cloud. This allows marketers to send consumers useful messages when they enter a predefined geographic area, or geofence. Consumers don't have to open the brand's app to find if there is a special offer, since the offer is automatically triggered when the consumer in the vicinity to use it right away. "We took the push notification and built a cloud interface," says Rochlin. "We use dynamic segmentation for targeting and messaging."

With showrooming as a backdrop, the issue for Rochlin is how the retailer recaptures the initiative through mobile. "One way to go is putting out an app," he says. "With the Web, it's more of a pull when the consumer is on the site." While a cruiser is on location, the Xtify technology can be used to get targeted messages to them. They could be based on the particular time of day, current weather, and past messages opened. When mobile shoppers are viewing a brand's website, different messages can be sent based on whether the consumer is at home, in the store, or even in a competitor's store. In the platform, which supports 20 languages, the idea is that no message is sent to a person more than once and every recipient has to have opted in and agreed to receive the messages in advance.

The general idea of using geofencing on location is that if a person opens a page within a certain radius, they will receive value. It's up to the brand or marketer to determine how best to provide value to each individual and to influence intent. When a person does receive value in the form of a message, the system also allows the easy sharing of that message to other platforms like Facebook and Twitter. Here is how some companies use the Xtify approach to targeted mobile marketing on location:

- **PacSun.** Uses push notifications to engage mobile shoppers with imagery and coupons. The intent was to drive customers to the app or website.
- **JackThreads.** The men's lifestyle and fashion brand sends targeted push notifications to app users alerting them of sales that start each day at noon and pass quickly. These are quick reminders of the latest flash-sale deals.
- **InterContinental Hotels Group.** Sends messages to incent app users to join their loyalty program. Customer loyalty numbers are linked to the mobile app for better segmentation and user engagement.

- **Ritz-Carlton.** Created targeted welcome messages triggered by a person with a smartphone coming within a certain distance of the hotel entrance. Message suggests that the person open the Ritz-Carlton app for additional hotel information and to see special offers.

THE RULE OF SITUATIONAL RELEVANCE

The value of identifying someone on location is in providing products or services that are relevant based on the proximity of where the consumer is and what they are likely doing. Using this knowledge of location and likely behavior or state of mind at the moment provides what we call *situational relevance*. The services offered to the mobile shopper on location can be based on the situation rather than just the location by adding context and probability to the equation.

One company that leverages situational relevance is the 35-year-old 1-800-Flowers.com. With about $700 million in annual revenue, 1-800-Flowers.com was one of the first retailers to embrace what is known as So-Lo-Mo (Social-Local-Mobile), comprising social media, local stores, and mobile technologies.

The florist and gift shop company found that mobile had the potential to transform its business. "Mobile has fundamentally done two things to our business," says Amit Shah, vice president of online mobile and social at 1-800-Flowers.com.[19] "The first thing it has done is it has really opened up for us a very disruptive channel that is net accretive to our business and to the overall growth trajectory for the company. Number two . . . is that it has disrupted all our existing channels so thoroughly that it has changed in many ways how we think about our day-to-day business."

As other businesses also discovered, 1-800-Flowers.com found mobile behaviors were impacting how customers dealt with them not just within the mobile footprint but across the channels from retail storefront to on-line e-commerce. Says Shah:

Think of something as simple as ordering flowers for your wife the day before Valentine's Day. Traditionally, the shopper always thought about the perfect vendor experience at a storefront, so you could walk in and pick out those lovely red roses or you can get them online. So the demand in this case is based on a pre-conceived impetus and the affinity towards a particular brand.

But now, suddenly, we are doing something called situation-based targeting. You could be going to the mall to pick up a set of diamond earrings for your wife and maybe we're at 500 meters away from one of those jewelry shop locations. So now we are sending you an ad on your smartphone while you are near the jewelry shop telling you: "Hey, you are already in the vicinity of our flower shop, please come in and by the way, we'll give you a great deal on two dozen red roses for your wife that will perfectly complement your other gift of diamond earrings." The traditional way did not take the user's location or the situational context (picking up a gift for wife) into account; the more current mobile marketing efforts take location into account, but the real disruption occurs when you can also bring in this situational context in play. In our example, just using the location would be sub-optimal since the husband could be perhaps looking to just get his watch repaired at the jewelry shop and is not in the correct situation to be shown an ad for flowers that can be easily picked up in the same trip. So this has fundamentally changed our view of marketing to potential and current custom-ers not just within mobile but across all channels. Any retailer that underappreciates the enormous power of this context is not looking at their metrics. I challenge any retailer to just look at their traffic and ask their salespeople in the stores to ask the customers that they work with, "How many of you discovered or decided to come to this store because of mobile?" I think they would be very surprised at the number of customers pointing to mobile as an influencer, if not the deciding factor behind their visit—a "zero moment of truth," as Google calls it.

One very misunderstood thing about privacy in the mobile world is that customers do not want to share information and get upset when the information shared is used in other contexts without their authorization. Paradoxically though, we have discovered that customers are more than willing to give their information if you are the right steward of that information. If we used the information to make it more relevant for you to remember your wife's birthday, trust us, every guy on the planet is going to love you. It's about how you champion and use that context that is of relevance. And I absolutely think, not just from the retailer's perspective or of the consumer's perspective, but even from a regulatory perspective, we are moving toward very clear guidelines in the next couple of years on how context can be ingested by other parties. We absolutely think that the majority of the people will be more than happy to share the relevant situational information, the same way, people still put down their physical address on forms. You cannot get more contextual than that, right? People are going to keep on doing that because it provides clear value.

By creating marketing messaging based on a consumer's location, taking into account what else is in the vicinity, determining the current activity and likely mindset based on those factors, the savvy marketer can craft offers that play to situation relevance. When this occurs, both the marketer and the consumer benefit.

THE COOL VERSUS CREEPY SCALE

As location and technical capabilities advance, it will become easier for marketers to at least identify if not reach consumers via their mobile devices. Before computers, there was junk mail that came via daily delivery in printed forms. With the internet came spam, unwanted junk mail delivered electronically. Mobile marketers have been more careful, following opt-in and double opt-in rules to make sure the consumer agrees in advance to receive certain messages.

Location-based knowledge opens the door for marketers to have yet a new set of conversations, perhaps extremely relevant and helpful information closer to the product purchase decision. Many brands, marketers, and mobile industry companies will do it right. To help consider an on-location program, here is a simple guide we created to assist in deciding how the consumer might react. We call it the Cool versus Creepy Scale. Keep in mind that one person's cool could be another person's creepy.

Cool. Perfectly targeted information based on location and from a trusted brand. Clear value provided, such as interactive content or even live feedback. Could include instant gratification, such as discount or additional bonus offer.

Acceptable. Somewhat targeted information based on location, from a known source.

Off the Radar. Consumer has turned off location in their phone or company not using location technology. A missed opportunity in this case.

Iffy. Randomly targeted information to random consumers based on being near a location.

Creepy. Random or pushy information provided totally unexpectedly based on location and other factors the consumer did not anticipate. Could be using predictive modeling technology to provide suggestions that make the consumer wonder if they are being watched or monitored.

Some mobile consumers want their location to be off all the time so they do not feel they are being tracked, while others not only leave location on but actively check in at locations, continually broadcast their whereabouts, and opt in to multiple location-based offer opportunities. Before launching anything involving live, on-location mobile interaction, an easy early gauge is to ask a few different demographics of only smartphone users. Depending on the range of customers you expected to use the location-based service, describe the intended program to that demographic. Then ask those in a different demographic what they think. Once described, a location-based program can easily elicit a "That's cool" as well as a "That's creepy." That's using the Cool versus Creepy Scale.

By creating marketing messaging based on a consumer's location, taking into account what else is in the vicinity, and determining the current activity and likely mind-set based on those factors, the savvy marketer can craft offers that play to situational relevance. When this occurs, both the marketer and the consumer benefit. Physical retailers have a distinct advantage in the Mobile Shopping Life Cycle if it is properly leveraged. Whether by countering and taking advantage of showrooming, linking the digital and physical supply chains together like V&D, or using SMS in store, marketers can provide added value to mobile shoppers while they have them on location. There is additional opportunity as the mobile consumer shops the aisles, which we discuss next.

five

THE PLAY

selection process

THE ART OF NEARBUY MARKETING

Once the mobile shopper gets to the location where items can be bought, there is another mobile influence opportunity related to the products to be considered for purchase. As mobile customers roam the aisles, they are empowered to check and compare items, receive additional information, compare competing prices, and ultimately even purchase on the spot. During this phase of the Mobile Shopping Life Cycle, marketers have one of the last opportunities to exert mobile influence before the actual purchase phase.

Businesses face dramatic new opportunities to reach mobile customers based on their proximity to particular goods and services, which we call "NearBuy Marketing." They have a chance to influence individual purchase behaviors based on this proximity. And the increase in reaching mobile customers via Wi-Fi or NFC (near field communications) devices near products, known in the mobile industry as proximity marketing, will increasingly come into play.

There are multiple ways marketers can reach these shoppers based on their relationships to product locations. Mobile location capabilities are improving, so that customers can now be identified the closer they get to specific departments and ultimately products. In this process the customer approaches or reaches the intended product and may even pick it up to head to checkout or place in a basket, providing new opportunities for in-aisle mobile marketing, the art of reaching customers as they shop.

Appealing to these NearBuyers, who are highly involved in the actual physical selection of what to buy, scanning will go Main Street as more mobile shoppers will scan products using price-comparison barcode scanners such as ShopSavvy and Amazon's Price Check, putting pressures on retailers to price match. Best Buy, for example, decided to match prices from Amazon and other online sellers starting in March 2013.

Sales associates everywhere are struggling to keep up with mobile consumers. Customers armed with smartphones are checking items and tapping their phones to find more knowledge about everything from product information and customer reviews to ratings and recommendations from friends and peers. Some retailers are waking to this fact and arming their sales staffs with mobile devices. For example, Lowe's decided to give iPhones to its 44,000 sales associates, and retailers like Bloomingdale's, Macy's, and Sears deploy mobile devices in their stores. Starbucks employees learned how to scan codes from customers' smartphones at checkout, with transactions quickly reaching into the tens of millions.

MOBILE BARCODE SCANNING

Barcodes have been around since 1974, when a ten-pack of Wrigley's Juicy Fruit gum was passed through a handmade laser scanner at a Marsh's Supermarket in Troy, Ohio.[1] That 67-cent sale marked the beginning of the UPC (Universal Product Code) barcode era. Since then, these ubiquitous codes have helped track the sale of billions of items and speed shoppers through checkouts. UPC barcodes carry information and pricing related to a specific product.

The UPC barcodes are different from 2D barcodes. While the traditional UPC barcode is one dimensional, that is, read from left to right or right to left, the 2D codes are two dimensional, read left to right and top to bottom. You may have seen one of these 2D codes in a magazine or on a billboard. They typically are square, rather than rectangular like UPC codes, and some are even more sophisticated in appearance.

Over the years, cameras in smartphones have improved so that these codes can be quickly and easily read. The most common 2D barcode is the QR (quick response) code. Those codes can be rapidly read by mobile phones and instantly lead to any number of experiences, ranging from special websites to contests and videos. Many marketers initially used the 2D codes simply to route someone to a website, which was often an unrewarding consumer experience since the consumer could just as easily type in the website address and achieve the identical result. That evolved over time with sophisticated marketing programs, most notably from the two leading mobile code scanning companies, Scanbuy and SpyderLynk, which we discuss later in this chapter.

While 2D codes can present great innovation and consumer value, they have to be intentionally added to packaging with a distinct intent in mind. Meanwhile, UPC barcodes are on almost all packaging, primarily so that the products can be scanned at checkout. Both types of barcodes come into play in NearBuy Marketing.

Mobile scanning is only going to increase with the addition of more smartphones globally and the added incentives coming from a wide range of sources. There are numerous barcode scanning variations, but they all generally incent a consumer to scan. Here are just a few examples:

- **Price-Checking Apps.** These are mobile apps that allow a mobile shopper to use their smartphone to scan a UPC barcode on a product and receive information about where else the product is sold and for what price. The leading app of this kind is ShopSavvy (discussed in detail later in this chapter), but there are a number of apps that provide essentially the same function, including Amazon Price Check, RedLaser, and TheFind. Many major retailers also have scanning capability included within their apps, and some, like Nordstrom, provide additional information on the product scanned, since the codes they use are unique to them.
- **Loyalty Card Apps.** These are apps to store your reward and loyalty cards, so that you can stop carrying around plastic cards.

The two most prominent apps for this are Key Ring and CardStar, which is owned by Constant Contact. Key Ring, from Mobestream Media, allows you to add a card by scanning the barcode on the card or, if there's no barcode, to select the retailer or business from a large list and type in the card number. Offers associated with any of the cards are then sent through the app. CardStar provides a similar list to add a card, with similar deals associated with each of the cards.

- **QR-Enabled Scans.** Sainsbury's, one of the oldest retailers in the United Kingdom, introduced a program called Mobile Scan and Go in its Tadley stores in Hampshire, Clerkenwell Local, and Bethnal Green Local. Supermarket shoppers there can shop with their Android or iPhone and pay without unloading their carts or bags. They register for the program with their Nectar loyalty card, download the app, and then scan barcodes on products as they shop. The mobile shoppers check in and check out using a QR code and pay by credit card or cash.

- **Targeting In-Store Shoppers.** During a holiday season, Amazon targets shoppers in stores. The online retailer provides incentives for mobile shoppers to scan items in the store and provided a discount if they then purchased the item from Amazon. Target has also taken aim at in-store shoppers by adding QR codes to certain products so that a shopper can scan the code, buy the product, and have it shipped, all from their phone. The codes are placed on the store's most popular toys, and shipping to anywhere in the United States is free.

THE ONE-TAP BUY

Look around any shopping facility and you're likely to see someone using their mobile phone. While phone calls and texting are still occurring, there's increasingly more mobile activity directly related to the actual context of the shopper in the store. There are numerous research findings indicating that this is true, but the key to marketers, brands, and retailers is what mobile consumers will be doing with their phones in the future as they shop. Mobile scanning at retail during the selection process phase of the Mobile Shopping Life Cycle can quickly transport a consumer to the next phase, the point of purchase, all without the on-location shopper ever going to a cashier.

ShopSavvy is an app from a company named Big in Japan, although it is located in Dallas, Texas. The app has been downloaded more than 30 million times directly. It also licenses its scanning technology to companies such as Walmart, Macy's, and Consumer Reports and counts another 100 million downloads from applications that license the technology.

The company started as a simple utility to allow shoppers to scan barcodes to find the best deals. It then built connections with thousands of retailers to provide real-time inventory and pricing data to mobile shoppers. The app is also a two-way street, in that not only can shoppers find the best prices but also brands and merchants can advertise in the app to reach the consumers when they scan and shop. This is one way that marketers are reaching NearBuy shoppers. ShopSavvy created an advertising platform allowing retailers and brands to deliver targeted messages, offers, and deals to shoppers based on the store they're in at the moment and on the product they just scanned.

The company launched ShopSavvy Wallet, allowing one-tap purchasing after an item is scanned. Essentially, a mobile shopper scans a traditional barcode on an item in a store, views the pricing at other stores on the app, and selects the one with the best price. For example, you might scan the barcode on a product at Office Depot and instantly be provided an offer to buy that same product at Best Buy with free shipping through ShopSavvy Wallet. With one tap (the action is labeled "slide2pay," actually), the product is shipped to you. Like Amazon, with credit card and shipping information pre-entered in the ShopSavvy app, the mobile customer buys the item with one tap and the credit card is charged by the retailer, who directly ships the product based on information passed along by ShopSavvy.

At a MediaPost Mobile Insider Summit, Alex Muse, CEO of ShopSavvy, talked about the evolution of the well-known price-comparison app, boasting more than 30 million downloads.[2] As a further indication of the rise in on-the-spot buying, he says that 90 percent of the purchases made through the mobile wallet were by people located in retail stores.

Retailers will increasingly face the prospect of mobile shoppers looking, checking, and comparing details and product pricing via their mobile devices as they shop.

The challenge and opportunity for physical retailers is to transform the showrooming mobile shopper, who uses the retailers' brick-and-mortar assets to view products and then buy them elsewhere via mobile, into immediate buyers from them, as discussed in an earlier chapter. One way during the selection process phase is to reach customers as they scan in the store.

The checkout process used to be the final phase just before a customer left the store. With in-store scanning through apps such as ShopSavvy, many mobile shoppers may never make it to the traditional cash register checkout, having been intercepted during the product selection process itself. While some retailers may be looking at retail through the wrong lens, analyzing how point-of-sale systems and checkout might be modified to accommodate mobile shoppers, they could be missing a more significant dimension of mobile shopping happening at the product level in the aisles. Checkout and POS systems obviously are part of the equation, but they are far from the whole picture.

Shopping traditionally has been a linear function. A shopper goes to a store to find a particular item, selects it, and then heads to the cashier to pay on the way out the door. Mobile makes shopping an iterative function. The shopper is highly interactive, in real time, on location, as they move through a mall or store. They can get up-to-the-minute price information, be solicited by other online and offline retailers, and buy through one mobile tap. Marketers can reach them by *geotargeting*, a method of determining the physical location of a shopper and delivering location-based and relevant content. When the mobile shopper scans a product, they essentially geotarget themselves. And that's where barcode scanning comes in.

SCAN FOR NEARBUY MARKETING

Barcode scanning can help marketers identify shoppers' location and activities to improve their NearBuy Marketing efforts. When a customer scans a barcode in store, they can be provided with additional information to aid in a purchase decision. If codes related to certain mobile platforms are utilized, marketers and retailers can also receive instantaneous feedback triggered by the code scan. One facilitator of mobile influence that provides such a platform is Scanbuy, a New York–headquartered company that has been in the code business since its founding in 2001.

As is the case with many of the captains and the facilitators of mobile influence, Scanbuy has a global footprint, with more than 50 employees in New York and more than ten other offices worldwide, including in the United Kingdom, Spain, and Brazil. Its codes are on products sold and used around the world. "Half of our traffic is in the U.S., a quarter of it is from Western Europe, and a quarter from 145 other countries every day," says David Javitch, vice president of marketing at Scanbuy.[3] With such a range of customer locations, Scanbuy gets to identify differences and adapt to each market. "Japan is fully saturated and 90 percent of the people scan," says Javitch. "There they use smartphones as a PC. In Spain, Coca-Cola placed QR codes on every can and bottle."

The company has its own barcode-reader app called ScanLife, which can read other codes in addition to those created specifically to run on the ScanLife self-service platform that many companies use. To address barcode scanning by market, Scanbuy introduced language-detection technology into its scanning. The dynamic QR code action detects the language setting of the user's device to deliver content unique to that language. This allows a brand with products in multiple markets with different languages to create a campaign that can be read by each of the markets and automatically send the desired marketing message in the local language of each consumer.

Barcodes are being used on packaging of all kinds in hopes of attracting both seekers and cruisers as they pass by or near products, but no one can tell exactly when a code will catch the consumer's eye. "Unique QR codes have been used outside of Bloomingdale's, in catalogs, and outdoor media, driving people to scan again in the store," says Javitch. "Users of smartphones are more likely to buy in the store if they feel comfortable with the decision. It's about using mobile phones to become more informed shoppers. A lot of our customers are using QR codes all along the path to purchase to help them close a sale."

ScanLife was recording more than six million scans a month along with millions of thousands of downloads of its app in late 2012. Both 2D and traditional barcodes are being scanned, with more QR codes from platforms, in which companies can track detailed behavior and provide highly customized results after the scan. "We know what is scanned, by devices and location," says Javitch. "I know location, time of day, demographics, and scan frequency, making it more targeted and relevant for content."

Scanbuy looks at using its codes to supplement the mobile shopper's retail experience. "A retailer can't change the behavior of scanning in their stores," he says. "They need to deliver relevant information to that customer, making it as quick, easy, and relevant as possible. Using QR codes, they can say, 'Scan this code to get more product information.' The people who get mobile totally get it. On big-ticket items, you could set triggers so anything scanned over $300 would notify a salesperson to go to aisle five. It's the convenience of getting it right there, and that is great for all parties." Here are some other examples of marketers using the ScanLife approach:

- **Starbucks.** To promote a new line of signature coffees, the coffee chain wanted customers to learn more and engage with the coffee they loved the most. It also wanted a way to quickly and easily give customers information during the coffee purchase process. The company printed QR codes on millions of bags of coffee that linked to videos on the product and other demonstrations, such as how to brew coffee. Customers could scan, share, and vote, and 50,000 votes came from the mobile site alone.
- **Taco Bell.** Looking for an innovative way to promote its sponsorship of the MTV Video Music Awards and share exclusive content, the company put QR codes on millions of Taco Bell's Big Box Remixed packages and large cups around the United States. The codes linked to exclusive Video Music Award content that could be accessed only through the code. The content included video teasers, artist interviews, and performance footage. The content was updated weekly to provide return users with an incentive to scan again. The program generated more than 400,000 scans in a six-week period and found that 59 percent were male and 13 percent were repeat users.

Scanbuy provides a wide range of actions after the scan. For example, HP carries ScanLife codes on its printer line globally, providing customers with specific additional product information, such as details on accessories that make it easier to select products. For a contest at Staples, ScanLife codes were used on in-store signage and on circulars connecting shoppers to exclusive content and allowing them to enter the contest by scanning the code, causing thousands of scans within a four-week period. The real key for scanning, though, is what happens after the scan.

GETTING SOME LIFE AFTER THE SCAN

Using 2D barcodes only to send someone to a website is finally becoming a thing of the past. More interestingly, the follow-on actions after a scan are starting to provide more value with measurable results. Another way to look at this is that there are two distinct occurrences with scans: the action with the phone that activates, and then the activity following the activation. The early use of QR codes typically led to a website, which tended to give codes a bad rap, since the end experience was rather routine—just seeing a website on a mobile phone.

The current use of many of the newer QR codes is routing a consumer to an activity or experience. The activation is what the consumer is able to do using their phone. This could be the scanning of traditional barcodes, such as using ShopSavvy or Amazon Price Check to compare prices elsewhere while shopping. While the action of scanning a QR code is somewhat obvious, there are numerous activations involving mobile motion:

- Phone scanning of either traditional or 2D barcodes.
- Taking a picture of a code and texting it to a number.
- Bumping a phone, such as phone-to-phone action to exchange information.
- Waving or touching a phone to a receiver, such as to connect via NFC chips.
- Aiming a phone camera to identify a certain building or location, as in augmented reality.

All these activations are simply to trigger something, hopefully to bring a consumer to a valuable experience. Another facilitator of mobile influence is Denver-based SpyderLynk, which has created unique codes called SnapTags. Rather than the square-looking QR codes, SnapTags are round and can contain a brand's logo or other images inside the circle. Consumers with smartphones or even standard camera phones can activate the code by taking a picture of it and sending it via text or email. SpyderLynk also has a free app that can be downloaded and used for quickly reading the codes. The tags are commonly used in a number of places, such as on consumer goods packaging, in taxicabs, and in magazines.

For SpyderLynk, the focus is less on the scan than on what happens after. "It's about the action behind the scan, it's not about the scan," says Jane McPherson, chief marketing officer of SpyderLynk, who has been focused on after-the-scan for several years.[4] "The value of the activation is what the consumer is able to do, get, or achieve." Rather than simply linking to a website, SpyderLynk connects consumers to a range of marketing platforms creating multiple action routes, such as leading a consumer to "like" the brand being promoted, submit their email for an email coupon, submit info to be entered into contests, submit info for a free sample, or enter info for a VIP membership, all with the ability to share any of these with friends.

In one of the larger concentrated uses of codes, *Glamour* magazine inserted SpyderLynk's code on multiple pages in one issue, resulting in several types of actions and activities. The company registered more than 500,000 activations, including scanning the codes with the app and taking and sending a photo. McPherson says the actions also led to multiple activities:

- Sixty-seven percent "liked" the magazine or brand to access a deal.
- Eighteen percent shared the deals with friends.
- A secondary activity of entering sweepstakes with an 85 percent conversion rate.
- A secondary activity of getting exclusive content.
- A secondary action of receiving coupons or promotion codes.

The measurements of codes can then move from how many were scanned to what activities occurred, which gets one step closer to measuring what was actually bought after being scanned with the consumer having a valuable activity.

In another example, when EA Sports launched the latest version of its NCAA football game, it used SnapTags on the package. While in the store looking at the package, a consumer scans the code and the activation brings the box holder to a video with clips of the new game, highlighting new features. It also allowed consumers to instantly "like" the game on the EA Sports Facebook page. Success measurements included video views, Facebook "likes," and EA website visits.

"The real opportunity is to offer consumers something meaningful or of value," says McPherson, who noted that several major brands are pushing for post-scan actions. It's no longer about the scan or the activation; it's now about the activity after the scan. Here are some other examples of marketers using the SnapTag approach:

- **Foot Locker.** The retailer wanted to increase participation in its Foot Locker Family and Friends promotion. Tags were printed on Foot Locker advertising materials offering a 25 percent discount on purchases. After consumers activated the SnapTag, they received a text message containing a coupon code that could be shown at checkout to receive the discount.
- **Office Depot.** The office supply retailer wanted to drive in-store traffic for back-to-school shopping. The company used tags on in-store signs, advertising, and direct mail. The offer was for 100 consumers a day to win a $100 Office Depot gift card. After the consumer activated the tag, they replied with their birthday and state location and instantly learned whether they had won the gift card. Winners could show the code on their phone at checkout to cash in the offer. The store received a 30 percent increase in participation compared to the previous year without using codes.
- **Toyota.** With the intent of increasing consumer interaction and knowledge at dealerships across the United States, Toyota placed tags on vehicles. The idea was to engage consumers during the

decision-making process. By snapping the tag and texting it to the short code, Android and iPhone users were provided with the opportunity to download the Toyota Shopping Tool app while other Web-enabled phones could receive information via the Toyota website. This was another example of directly engaging with consumers to provide information and drive sales conversions.

In each of these cases, marketers were able to facilitate interaction with customers during the selection process phase of the new Mobile Shopping Life Cycle. These interactions can influence behavior and activities directly during the product selection process, as potential buyers are viewing, comparing, and evaluating all their choices. Whether about an expensive item like a car or back-to-school supplies, there is the opportunity to quickly initiate a conversation starting with a code scan, the art of NearBuy Marketing.

AUGMENTING REALITY

In addition to the scanning of codes, there is another mobile technology that can add a different dimension during the selection process. This technology is called *augmented reality* (AR), which shows additional information when aiming a phone camera at a place or object. For example, pointing a phone camera at a building could show the building as well as data that augments the reality of what you are seeing, such as the date the building was built, the number of tenants, and a list of companies housed there.

One of the AR pioneers and another facilitator of mobile influence is Layar, headquartered in Amsterdam with offices in New York. Layar was founded in 2009, leveraging the compass in Android phones. "It was this idea of actually plotting over the camera image the locations that are around you in the right position because we know where you are pointing the phone," says Dirk Groten, chief technology officer of Layar.[5] "That's how Layar started."

The initial business focused on real estate, targeting houses for sale in Holland. "You have signs on every house for sale but when you actually want to know more about how much it costs or how it looks from inside, you just take your phone, open Layar, point it to that building and you'll see a dot and you just open it," says Groten.

Those were the early days of AR. The next evolution used camera recognition, bringing Layar to its current focus on traditional media, augmenting the reality in print magazines.

"For us, media companies are more interesting to sit down with," says CEO Quintin Schevernels.[6] "They reach out to the agencies or the brands and advertisers to embed in the advertising."

"Print is maybe not a dying industry, but in very big trouble," says Groten. "For at least the next five years there will be a lot of innovation in how to connect users that are actually reading something to all kinds of content that's online."

A magazine using Layar's AR app typically notifies readers early in the publication of pages with a Layar call-to-action logo, such a button to make an instant purchase. Holding a phone over a page can quickly provide additional pieces of information relating to what's on the page.

Augmented reality can be used on any number of areas during the mobile shopping process, all the way from on a retail building itself to products on the shelves. "Magazines are where we are focused now because magazines are a very easy way to enter, but the next step is packaging," says Maarten Lens-FitzGerald, cofounder of Layar.[7] "There is a lot of stuff we can do there and one of the printers I'm talking to wants to do this with packaging. Of course this packaging is round and crinkly, that's hard to see by the computer. I want cartons and hard surfaces."

Millions of people have downloaded the Layar app, available for both Android and Apple mobile devices, enabling them to see additional information as they move about.

Both the front and back cover of this book contain Layars, so if you want to see how it works, download the Layar app, open it, and point your camera phone at the cover of this book. You then can see and interact with various examples of what Layars can do.

HOLD THE PHONE

As more mobile shoppers scan items in stores and find a lower price at another store, the number of phone screens shown to sales associates is certain to increase. Retailers and store owners will have to determine how they want to handle the actual transaction. Does the salesperson take possession of the customer's phone during the course of a transaction or require the customer to hold it showing them the price match on the screen?

With the increasing number of smartphone-enabled consumers, the issue is only going to become larger, since customers in general are ahead of marketers when it comes to mobile.

Some businesses are less affected than others, such as Starbucks, which set its mobile scanners at checkout to be easily reached by customers. With tens of millions of mobile transactions since it launched the program, Starbucks likely considered the dropped-phone scenario. The Starbucks employee handbook states: "Stores should place the scanners in a location that customers can easily access and hold their device to scan the barcode. Partners should never handle the customer's mobile device."[8] The policy for Starbucks was rather straightforward, since the code on the app could be easily scanned at checkout, which is not always the case at other businesses.

At your local supermarket checkout, a customer may open their Key Ring app, which can store rewards numbers and barcodes. If the supermarket scanner can't yet read mobile barcodes, the phone is often handed to the cashier to enter the barcode numbers.

So what if an employee does drop and damage a customer's phone? "If they take the phone they're on the hook," says attorney Edward Lake of Gacovino and Lake Attorneys in New York, though he questioned whether the value of a mobile phone would be worthy of a lawsuit outside of small-claims court.[9]

Some brands, like Starbucks, have hard-and-fast rules that employees not touch customers' phones, while others have less formal guidelines or no policy, for varying reasons.

After contacting more than a dozen major brands to find out their policies on mobile phone handling, we found that there is not yet exactly what could be considered an industry standard. In their spokespeople's words:

- Target: "We ask our team members to have the guests hold the phone while they scan the screen."[10]
- Macy's: "We do not have a policy but there is no reason for us to handle a customer's mobile device unless they ask for help."[11]
- Sears: "The customers are asked to hold the phone for the operator to scan the barcode."[12]
- Best Buy: "It is not our SOP or price match policy to handle customer devices for price checks. In the instance a customer pulls up a coupon or offer on their device and hands it to us for redemption, we would certainly allow that type of interaction with the customer's permission."[13]
- Walmart: "Our national policy at this time is to bring a printed copy of the ad to the store."[14]
- Staples: "While there is not a formal policy in place regarding the handling of customers' smartphones, we encourage our associates to get the information necessary without handling the phone, if possible."[15]

And once a policy is adopted, a company still needs to filter the word to all its employees, which can be more challenging than devising a policy.

"Our training covers what to look for when the customer presents their mobile device, so it would be more of an eyes-only policy," says BJ Emerson, vice president of technology at Tasti D-Lite and Planet Smoothie, an early pioneer in mobile rewards and checkout.[16] "There should be no need to take or handle someone's phone."

As in retail, major airlines also have varying degrees of mobile phone handling policies. They say:

- United: "While at security or boarding a flight, the customer scans their mobile device over the scanner. The CSR [customer service representative] does not touch the phone/mobile device."[17]

- American Airlines: "There is not a policy that states customers may not hand over their phone to agents. They can either pull up the coupon themselves or hand it to the agent."[18]
- Jet Blue: "We do not have a policy."[19]
- Delta: "Our scanners are configured so that customers can hold their phone and scan the boarding pass themselves if they desire, but an agent is always present to assist should they have difficulty with the scanning device."[20]

With more smartphone barcode scanning coming, sure-to-be glitches while paying via mobile, and more on-location usage, customers and businesses are going to have to determine their own rules on who holds the phone.

SUPERMARKET SCANNING

Ahold USA is a $25-billion holding company for businesses that together operate more than 750 supermarkets with more than 100,000 employees in the United States. Its brands include Stop & Shop, Giant Food, and Giant Food Stores. Ahold USA also owns online grocery pioneer Peapod and is one of the ten largest food retailers in the country. In the world of mobile scanning, Ahold is the leading grocery pioneer introducing and was experimenting with in-store supermarket scanning by shoppers years before it could even be done on smartphones.

All of the early scanning technologies, experiments, and in-store execution were developed by Modiv Media in Boston, Massachusetts, a company involved in mobile scanning for more than ten years. In 2012, the company was bought by Catalina, headquartered in St. Petersburg, Florida, and Modiv became Catalina Mobile.

"The company started with the idea of linking e-commerce with in-store commerce," says John Caron, vice president of marketing at Catalina.[21]

Not having sophisticated handheld technology with scanning capabilities available, Modiv decided to create a makeshift scanner to test shopping behavior to see if consumers would actually scan groceries as they shopped.

"It started with this really big idea," says Caron. "In 2001, it was a tablet attached to a shopping cart. The idea was that if you could connect the internet to the shopper, there are ways to let them build a shopping list, scan, and bag their groceries while they shopped. This expanded into giving shoppers offers based on where they are in the store. It worked but it was massively expensive to outfit a store with enough tablet devices and install a tracking system."

Modiv began using the tablet system with Ahold, and then evolved the program as additional scanning technologies came to market.

"In 2007, it really started to take off with a Motorola device," says Caron. "It combined the capabilities of previous technologies and provided features like quick scanning, ease of use, and a high-quality screen to present offers and coupons. This was all before the massive adoption of smartphones. Over the next few years, we focused on increasing the quality of the display and displaying content in multiple digital formats. This was a complex process since an offer for a shopper had to go through multiple channels, including the handheld device, a screen in the store, payment terminal, kiosk or website. What we were uncovering was the ability to influence a shopper's behavior by giving them the most relevant offers as they go through the store."

At the time, Ahold was the only company that bought the device, as other grocery retailers found them too costly. "It was quite expensive per store, but they (Ahold) love to drive innovation," says Caron. "In this space, they are considered an innovator. They've always been looking at ways to be different and have a different experience. Innovation, as they define it, is very different than how others might and they like the idea of this technology and they got behind it and kept pushing and pushing it."

Ahold was Modiv's only mobile shopping client at scale from 2001 until 2011, when it launched with true mobile device scanning. "Months after we launched mobile, we picked up our second client," says Caron. "Shortly thereafter, Modiv was acquired by Catalina, and it became clear that mobile commerce was going to be big."

Before introducing grocery scanning by smartphone, Stop & Shop had kiosks at the entranceway to stores where shoppers swiped their loyalty cards and grabbed a handheld scanner they could use while they shopped.

When they finished shopping, they simply returned the scanner to the kiosk on the way out of the store.

Once smartphone scanning capabilities matured, it was logical for Stop & Shop to capitalize on the consumers' devices, hoping to lessen the need for owning and managing hardware and kiosks while leveraging the power of a device that is always with the shopper. The handheld guns are in more than 350 Ahold locations and the mobile app is being enabled in an increasing number of the 750 total stores.

From the consumer's viewpoint, the value is not only in the cost savings by receiving on-the-spot coupons based on location in the store, but also in that the mobile scanning app makes the last stage of shopping painless. "Once you can pay by phone or you have expedited checkout, where you're out the door in seconds, we think that's going to be a game changer," says Caron. "At Stop & Shop, the scanning app is fully integrated with the grocer's rewards program and point of sale systems, making the shopping experience friction-free for the shopper.

"Imagine a scenario where you walk into your favorite retailer, open their app and it immediately presents personalized offers for you based on your purchase history, in-store location, current cart contents and brand preferences," says Caron. "This is in-store mobile commerce. Where we start to see real traction and lift in mobile is when the experience is more like a personal shopper that says, 'Hey, how'd you like a dollar off this?' or 'You should try this product too.' This is the promise of personalization—it allows the store, at a massive scale, to treat every shopper individually."

CHANGING CONSUMER BEHAVIOR

It turns out that convenience trumps savings for consumers using the mobile scanning app. It also remains to be seen how many new customers can be attracted to in-store scanning and how high the ultimate customer retention of those mobile shoppers will be. And since there is only one major grocery store chain scanning effort, there is not yet enough data to determine the main drivers of scanning while grocery shopping.

One of the advantages of Modiv's acquisition by Catalina is the access to the major trove of shopping data, behavioral targeting, and manufacturer content that Catalina brings. Stop & Shop is also monitoring the attrition rate or churn rate, which is the rate at which customers who have been scanning stop, for whatever reason. "Right now, the primary reward is speed," he says. "The secondary reward is savings. As we ramp it up and make savings even stronger, and then multiply the speed with express checkout or payment by phone, it goes to a whole new level. It's kind of like the toll booth. When E-ZPass first came out there was one lane and now they're about half the lanes. And, it's the norm. You know there's a more efficient way to pay your tolls that saves you time and money."

The question is when or whether supermarkets outside the Ahold properties adopt in-store scanning and whether it is pushed by the stores or demanded by consumers. As more mobile consumers become accustomed to scanning items in other types of stores, the demand or expectation to expand across all categories may become obvious. Coupled with the move to mobile payments, such as by using mobile wallets or NFC (near field communication) technologies, scanning to receive savings can become simply one more automated and integrated step.

Caron expects to see some form of mobile payment with integrated mobile coupons within the next few years. "You'll see some form of what we do, or ideally our solution, within the next few years in every major grocery chain. In the top 20, absolutely," he says. "You'll be perceived as a dinosaur if you don't go in this direction."

When it comes to Ahold and its scanning efforts at Stop & Shop, Caron says they welcome other retailers doing it as well. Since the Stop & Shop mobile launch, Walmart introduced mobile self-checkout for shoppers. "They don't want to be the only company doing this," says Caron. "They absolutely want to see other retailers doing this as broader awareness of mobile commerce drives adoption for everyone."

The early Modiv transformed itself from an in-store technology company to a mobile technology one, and ultimately, to a mobile commerce company, long before it was acquired. Caron looks at Catalina and the technology as enablers of smarter marketing.

"Catalina Mobile is looking at out-of-the-box thinking in how to influence customer shopping patterns. Catalina is one of the largest behavioral targeting companies in the world. So in some ways you could say we're the conduit for this big data to be applied to influence the shopper in the aisle."

· TARGETING AND ENGAGING

For NearBuy Marketing, the combination of the former Modiv with Catalina can increase the potential marketing mix to reach more grocery shoppers in the aisles with real-time offers. The combination increases Ahold's capabilities by providing deep capabilities for offers, analytics, and precise targeting. "Catalina has historically been known as a coupon company but its heritage truly lies in its personalization capabilities and behavioral analytics," says Caron. "Personalization will be a core requirement in mobile commerce and companies, like Catalina, are the ones who will drive this."

The combined Catalina and Modiv solution creates the ability to bring more brands through the grocery store channel, adding more value to the mobile app. Says Caron:

> It's about targeting and engaging shoppers in a way that boosts loyalty, value, and a better experience. And, there is the big difference between mobile ecommerce and in-store mobile commerce. Mobile commerce actually connects the physical store and the shopper using the mobile device and retailers can use that mobile device (in a similar way to websites) to personalize the experience as you're going through the store.
>
> That's where the big win is. How can retailers treat you differently? How can they treat you as an individual? How can they make their labor costs more efficient? How can you replace some or all of your checkouts? Imagine what you can do with that extra space if the front-end registers went away. Imagine the experience where associates are engaging shoppers throughout the store and not just at checkout. Companies like Nordstrom and JCPenny are already moving in this direction.
>
> In early 2011, when we were talking about what we were doing and we were in pilot at three Stop & Shop locations people said, "That's neat

but I don't know if it's actually going to fly—is it practical?" The biggest shift I've seen in the last twelve months is that we've gone from this feeling of "Oh yeah that's interesting" to "We need to do this now." And, Mobile is now a real strategic initiative, it's not a side project.

As these retailers start to look at showrooming, it's just accelerating. You think that people didn't do this before but it just took more time. If you look at it and embrace and say, "Yeah, okay, we're ten bucks more—so what?" Instead of price matching how about price awareness? So yes, it's $2,000 from us, and its $1950 from them. And in that same day you could say, "Right there, here is why to buy it from us. We'll install it," or whatever it is.

We will see the start of rapid growth in mobile in-store commerce. Retailers are going to start to look at it as a way to integrate the shopping experience. These retailers are realizing there is no path of purchase anymore and mobile provides a way to stay always-engaged with their shoppers.

Within three years all grocers will have some integrated mobile savings, coupon, payment, and mobile commerce capability. I think it actually needs to happen faster. But if you look at the top 25, they'll all have it in the next three years. The best ones will have it within the next 12–24 months. This is the optimal engagement tool for retailers.

CUSTOMIZED OFFERS

The future for Catalina Mobile and Ahold, and likely other supermarkets, will be to add the depth of Catalina's offers and ad inventory with loyalty programs, all tied to location, with the art of NearBuy Marketing. Part of the driver will be consumers standing in a supermarket checkout line watching mobile shoppers walk out the door, their groceries already bagged and paid without having to pass through a cashier. Combined with mobile check-in services, highly targeted offers provide a powerful mobile influence tool.

As the paths of coupons, scanning, and payment begin to intersect, marketers will be able to provide more relevant offers to NearBuy shoppers based not only on location but also on past behavior initiated by the explicit or implicit distance from a particular product.

A GROCERY STORE SCANNING EXPERIENCE

To observe firsthand in-store supermarket scanning, I went grocery shopping with an executive of Catalina Mobile, the company that has been working on in-store scanning with Ahold and Stop & Shop for the past decade and the one that developed the mobile app.[22]

We entered a Stop & Shop in Danvers, Massachusetts, and charted our course around the store.

Before even starting our mobile shopping, I watched a woman with two small children in her shopping cart (one with a car and steering wheel in front) pick up and scan items, put them in a bag in her cart, and move on to the next aisle. She did this throughout the store looking as if she had been doing it all her life. No big deal.

At checkout, the shopper uses the scanner to quickly check out and pay, with the groceries not having to be removed from the bags (there are various security profiling measures built into the system).

The iPhone and Android apps were launched in 2012, and we used the iPhone version for our shopping. Products of various categories were read easily with the app and as we scanned certain items, we received instant coupon offers. When we scanned items in the dairy section, we received coupon offers for items in the same section. The selection was based not only on location, but on past purchase patterns and other criteria, which was true of all products scanned.

In the produce department, there are scales where shoppers typically weigh produce, except these now have instant printers that spit out a barcode to be read by the app, thereby automatically entering the item into the shopping cart.

As shoppers with full shopping carts waited in line for their turn at the Stop & Shop checkout registers, the woman with the two small children was on her way to her car, groceries scanned, packed, and paid.

THE NEARBUY FLY-BUY

Mobile consumers will shop for and buy just about anything via their mobile device. Some are scanning groceries as at Stop & Shop, some are snapping 2D codes of Scanbuy and SpyderLynk, and others are purchasing travel. While proximity to an item is one factor for NearBuyers, time is the other. A consumer may be near a physical item in a store, making them a mobile influence candidate. A shopper also could be nearing a certain time that a purchase decision has to be made, so the closeness to that time is the major factor. An example of this is airline travel, in which the mobile influence can be providing either ease of booking or offers around a required date of travel, such as a necessary business trip. Another influence can be impulse offers, such as attractive travel deals that provide high value, maybe due to heavy discounting.

JetBlue, headquartered in New York, has been observing its customers' mobile behaviors and has found that some are the same as traditional online behaviors and others are different. It has also found patterns based on whether the person is using a mobile phone or a tablet.

"We see very high tablet usage by our customers," says Michael Stromer, vice president of customer connections marketing at JetBlue.[23] "JetBlue customers in general overindex on Apple devices—to our knowledge, more so than our competition. It might just be the nature of our customer base, our heavy New York and Boston presence, so it could be a function of geography. I also think it's the nature of our demographic, which skews to a more technology savvy customer. And so with that we see very high usage of customers using the iPad when visiting jetblue.com. We also see very high iPhone usage when accessing our mobile website. That said, we have seen a continual increase in the penetration of Android usage across our customer base, which was a main driver for our recent Android application launch."

In addition to different devices being used to access JetBlue, customers are using different features based on various types of travel. Says Stromer:

> From a purchase behavior standpoint, we're not seeing, for example, the time in which people are starting the purchase process change significantly with mobile. I believe the tradition of when customers begin thinking about their vacation to the time in which they buy, hasn't really changed that dramatically. We have seen the timeline shrink a bit but not significantly. Business travelers still tend to book last minute and leisure travelers tend to book several weeks out.

Where mobile has provided us a more significant opportunity is around travel that they didn't plan. We're able to put messages in front of customers that traditionally may have sat in their email box for a day or two or may never have been opened at all. Whether it be through push notifications in the device, text messages, or more targeted content in our mobile products, we are able to use customer preferences and behaviors to put more compelling offers in front of them. This has allowed us to improve the quality and timeliness around our communications and to create more urgency around buying.

With social tools such as Twitter we have been able to create purchasing opportunities through a feed we've called "cheeps," which is a separate feed from our regular Twitter following. And we use it just to post distressed inventory and other great deals. And we find buying behavior there is obviously much different than with a planned trip.

Essentially, what people really want is a "one-click" buying experience, or at least as few clicks as possible. I don't think there are many companies that have gotten there yet. However, mobile buying experiences are getting better and companies are spending more time in optimizing the experience. Tighter integration with payment services is key. I believe this has been a big part of PayPal's success in this space.

Consumers also use mobile for research. When I'm sitting on the train for an hour on the way to work each day, I'm using it to do things I don't have time to do during the workday. We're all struggling to find time in our day. It could be as simple as researching my trip on my iPhone on my way to work but ultimately closing the booking on my tablet or desktop later in the day or on the weekend. That behavior is not really a new behavior, I think people have used mobile for research for a while now, but I believe as the mobile experiences improve, and the technology gets better, people are a lot more willing to close a purchase via mobile. We are seeing this with an increase in our mobile conversion rates.

When someone is buying a vacation package from us, a five-day, all inclusive hotel, car included and everything else, there are a lot of steps to that process. So, there's a much lower chance someone is going to close that deal over a mobile device. But they might click to call and speak to a customer service representative and to close the purchase or begin their research via mobile and close the purchase later or vice versa. So I don't think it's about the price; it's more about how considered is the purchase and how complicated is it to buy via that channel? And you're probably doing a lot of research on buying that television or that vacation package before you make that purchase, but you have no problem buying it on a mobile device versus a desktop as long as the process is simple.

When we re-launched jetblue.com this past February, the idea was to build a site that would be optimized for tablet devices. If you look at even the format of our site we went with a much more vertically oriented site than we have traditionally. When designing for the Web, most companies are focused on delivering content above the fold but with tablets, the traditional fold has changed. Optimizing our website for tablet hasn't ruled out building tablet specific applications. In fact, we recently launched a promotion called ThinkUp, which is a Facebook application seeking customer feedback on what they would like to see in our tablet experience. Customers vote on their favorite ideas, which we then bring to market. The voice of the customer is extremely important for our product development process.

With mobile and tablet development it is important to remember the unique benefits of the device. Location services, touch screen, the ability to turn the content sideways, and voice commands, are just a few examples of those benefits and so building out our products to fully leverage those benefits will be crucial for a fully optimized experience. Those are the types of things that we are actively designing to. Our initial efforts were getting solid mobile applications into the market and now we are driving in with deeper innovations. Mobile is here to stay, so for JetBlue, it means ensuring we have the right talent in place who can keep us at the very forefront of innovation.

The size and price of the purchase clearly can be factors in how a marketer looks to exert mobile influence. For groceries, the influence can simply be coupons with new deals or incentives to try a new product. For big-box retailers, it may mean matching the price of the nearest competitor on a big-ticket item. And for airlines, it may mean providing tools to contribute to a long-term travel decision or offers providing great deals on otherwise empty plane seats.

The art of NearBuy Marketing is about interacting and engaging with customers as they see, feel, and touch the products. In some cases, they may be persuaded to purchase elsewhere, after a quick mobile price comparison. In other cases, they will be provided with the ability to receive additional information and on-the-spot mobile influence after scanning a barcode. They may be incented with coupons offered after the scan or a particular item or series of items. In the Mobile Shopping Life Cycle, the selection process is that last stage when the marketer has one more chance to influence both seekers and cruisers. Then they move to the actual transaction, the point of purchase, which we address in the next chapter.

PEOPLE SYSTEMS VERSUS TECHNOLOGY SYSTEMS

As more customers scan and check product prices during the selection process in the Mobile Shopping Life Cycle, sales associates will need to be trained to interact with ever-more-savvy shoppers. Technology can play a role, but in many cases the ultimate transaction will be between the shopper and the person at checkout. Mobile technology still can ultimately lead to people dealing with people.

One example involving mobile technology and people may help illustrate the point. Staples, the well-known office products retailer, has gotten quite efficient at mobile price matching, with checkout personnel actually knowing what they're supposed to look for on the customer's screen, as we detail in a later chapter. However, at any store, when multiple elements are mixed in with in-store scanning and price matching, not to mention customer service, the results can prove tricky.

For example, in one of its campaigns HP ran a promotion with Staples for customers to receive a free comparable ink cartridge for every two purchased, labeled in an email campaign as "buy two, get one free." Staples also promoted an additional coupon to save $20 on a purchase of $100 or more on ink cartridges of any brand. To complicate matters further, as a Staples Rewards member, I also had coupons within my app from past purchases.

I selected two sets of different ink cartridges, one set of two at $39 each and the other at $28, to pass the $100 threshold. So far, no problem. Just before checkout, I used the ShopSavvy app to scan the cartridges and found them each to be several dollars cheaper at another store. It was an online site, though a store with a physical presence. Major retailers in general will match the prices of brick-and-mortar competitors, and mobile scanning makes the price finding instantaneous.

The next stage is where the many retailers face the challenges of integrating the various reward, processing, and product-tracking systems. A point-of-sale system may have preprogrammed rules, which may not account for all the external factors mobile brings to the table. At Staples, the checkout technology would allow either the discount of the price match or the three-for-the-price-of-two deal, but not both.

However, the fine print on the ad says "not valid with any other offer," so we made the point that a price match was not another offer, just a different price. After about 20 minutes of the store manager and sales associate battling the POS system, they figured how to provide the two discounts. But when entering my rewards number, the entire transaction went back to original pricing and they had to start all over again.

The helpful duo at Staples persevered and ultimately did figure how to provide all the discounts, including the price match and the HP deal. The people system made it work, to the advantage of the customer.

As more customers turn to real-time mobile information, such as in-store price comparisons, and combine that information with traditional marketing offers like coupons and online deals, retailers will be faced with more, not fewer, integration challenges. "Staples is always looking for ways to make things easier for our customers, and that includes providing the best cross-channel shopping experience," says Prat Vemana, director of mobile and e-commerce acceleration at Staples.[24] "We know that more and more customers are turning to their mobile devices to do research as well as to make sure they're using their Staples Rewards."

It is this cross-channel challenge that both the people and technology systems at many companies face. The short-term approach is likely the workaround, as executed by the checkout team at Staples. The longer-term solution is to create more integration of programs into the mobile mix, factoring in the issue of on-location price matching. But rather than hardening the technology to decrease customer-facing workarounds, IT leaders now have the opportunity to view and measure how the people systems are actually making things work on location.

Retailers worried about showrooming, discussed in a previous chapter, might take a lesson from the people system. Brick-and-mortar retailers that follow their traditional, rigid rules of deals and don't leverage in-store, mobile price-matching customers have the unenviable opportunity to become their geography's showrooming headquarters.

Interestingly, I called Staples's national order number and after many minutes of discussion I was transferred to the supervisor of the call center who said they could either price match or provide the HP deal, but in no case could they do both. Those are the rules. They were basing their response on the technology system, while the store employees on location based their response on the customer in the store. Through lowering the price of a few select products matched by mobile app, the store also sold an additional bag full of office supplies, including Staples brand products that could not be price matched.

six

THE WRAP

point of purchase

THE NEW LAWS OF MOMENTARY MARKETING

Mobile changes the finality of the point of purchase or point of sale. The convergence of mobile wallet technology, on-scene scanning, product information, and rewards programs allows the creation of a more fluid moment of the point of purchase. With mobile customers self-checking products and ultimately self-checking out via smartphone, the role of the retailer will forever change. The ability to influence purchase behavior now extends to the actual moment of the purchase.

In some stores, mobile shoppers already can scan a product, instantly check if the product is in inventory, select the product, pay for it with rewards points, and receive the item at a pickup window. No salespeople, cash, or credit cards are involved.

During this stage of the Mobile Shopping Life Cycle, companies can attempt to influence behavior by incentives through real-time scanning programs already in use by retailers such as Macy's, Target, and Best Buy. With such apps, consumers are automatically checked in when they enter one of the participating retailers and are then incented with points to scan certain products, for which they receive credits that can be cashed in at any of the stores.

The marketing opportunity is to work to influence and change the minds of mobile shoppers during the checkout process. Real-time bidding for and by customers for products will grow as the m-powered consumer becomes the premier customer with access to all products from inventory-aware organizations, so that tapping-in-place shoppers receive the highest value.

With the new value of brick and mortar (as discussed in an earlier chapter), mobile provides retailers opportunities facing customers who are accessing real-time information about products as they shop the aisles. Large and small brands have been awaiting this development, and they will now have the option to conduct what I call *momentary marketing*, interacting with a customer for even just a few seconds, but at the time and location most relevant and valuable to the customer. This allows companies to market to a customer at exactly the time and location that is of most value to the company and the retailer, the actual moment of the purchase transaction. These moments will come and go quickly as shoppers move from one item to the next, providing many opportunities to exert mobile influence.

THE MONEY BEHIND MOBILE PAYMENTS

People in the mobile industry have been talking about mobile payments for years. Generally, the discussions focus on the actual paying of something on location using a mobile phone. Highlighting those discussions are typically mobile wallets and NFC (near field communication), where a consumer taps or waves a phone at or near a terminal to execute a payment, sometimes referred to as "contactless payments." In effect, it all comes down to buying something and paying using your phone rather than, say, cash or a credit card.

The move to mobile payments is a global phenomenon, with some countries ahead of others. For example, more than half (52 percent) of mobile users in China use mobile wallets, while only 12 percent use them in Spain, Germany, Argentina, and the United States combined.[1] There is mobile payment activity in all markets around the world, since transferring currency for products and services has no borders. Numerous companies of varying types and categories are aligning with partners, forming new partnerships, and launching payment trials.

Telefónica, one of the largest telecommunications companies in the world with a strong presence in 25 countries, and most notably in Europe and Latin America, formed a number of mobile payment initiatives. The company, with 300 million customers globally, formed strategic partnerships with Visa to drive new business opportunities within mobile commerce. It also created a joint venture with MasterCard to expand mobile financial business in Latin America by creating a new corporate brand called Wanda. The intent was to provide mobile payment services linked to mobile wallets or prepaid accounts to allow mobile money transfers, bill payments, and retail purchases. "I am convinced that Wanda is headed toward becoming the leading force behind mobile payments in the region, driving economic growth and promoting financial inclusion," says Richard Hartzell, president of MasterCard in Latin America and the Caribbean region.[2] MasterCard also hosted leaders of major banks from throughout Latin America at a summit in Colombia, where both Hartzell and MasterCard Worldwide president and CEO Ajay Banga discussed the significance of the role of mobile in the future of payments with the bankers.[3]

The obvious opportunity mobile payments provide is the elimination of the need for consumers to carry cash or credit cards to buy things. Along with that comes the associated challenge of when or whether consumers will trust paying by phone. Some experts are split on the issue, with 65 percent saying consumers will come to fully trust and embrace smart devices and mobile wallet services to buy things in stores.[4] The study from the Pew Research Center's Internet and American Life Project also found that a third (33 percent) believe mobile payments will not succeed because of security and privacy issues.

Mobile payments will grow as more NFC-enabled phones spread throughout the marketplace. There is little doubt that NFC is coming, with 35 percent of handsets sold in 2016 to be NFC-enabled.[5] It will take some time for NFC-enabled phones to totally saturate the marketplace as older phones are gradually retired, however. In addition, there are competing methods of mobile payments, and NFC has not been embraced by all phone makers, most notably Apple. With many established brands as well as new mobile start-ups competing to be the mobile payment method of choice, it likely will be some time before a dominant method emerges.

MAKING MONEY MOBILE

Announcements about new mobile wallets and mobile payments have been occurring over a relatively long period of time. There are small devices you can plug into an Android or Apple mobile device that allow personal swiping of credit cards, which generally works easily, as well as payment methods by swiping or tapping a smartphone to a terminal at checkout, much like the credit card terminals at which consumers have become conditioned to self-swipe to pay.

At the popular SXSW Interactive, the annual conference in Austin, Texas, a panel on mobile payments tackled the why and the when of mobile payments. The panelists were specialists on Isis, the joint venture with Verizon Wireless, AT&T, and T-Mobile aiming to provide a mobile commerce network for merchants, banks, and other carriers.[6] Isis launched consumer trials in Austin and Salt Lake City in late 2012. To use the service, consumers with an NFC-enabled smartphone receive a new SIM card from local retailers and download the free app. Those consumers could then pay for merchandise by tapping their phones at terminals of participating merchants.

The panelists agreed that a considerable amount of mobile banking already was taking place outside Isis and that the adoption of any mobile payment options, including Isis, is going to take a considerable amount of time for mass acceptance, a common mobile industry perception.

Part of the initial consumer interest in contactless payments is the novelty factor. The idea of tapping a phone to a terminal to pay intrigues many who have not yet done it, especially in the United States, where it is not yet commonplace. "It's just a shift in experience," says Ryan Hughes, chief marketing officer of Isis.[7] "The technology [NFC] is nothing new," he says. "VeriFone says 100 percent of their terminals are NFC." For example, Hughes and his team brought an Isis-enabled vending machine as a demo for SXSW attendees. At the booth, on the main floor of the Austin Convention Center, large crowds of people continually waited in line to see the machine in action. One of the many Isis marketers would tap an NFC-enabled phone to the front of the machine where you'd normally insert coins and the phone would be charged the 50 cents for a promo booklet to drop out of the front slot of the machine.

Privacy concerns are also commonly woven into any discussion of mobile payments, with concerns about unauthorized use of the mobile wallet, such as because of a stolen phone, for instance. Generally, all the mobile payment services and platforms have security at the top of the list, especially banks and credit card companies, both of which are highly regulated and protective of their brands. Hughes cites security as the number-one concern of customers, and Isis has security built into the system itself. In addition, "a single call to your carrier can shut your wallet down," says Hughes.

While Isis is focused on serving retailers, other mobile payment approaches allow consumers to send money to each other and individuals to accept credit card payments via their mobile device. No matter the approach, all of them involve behavioral change, and are transforming how consumers will expect to pay when ready. Competing for the mobile payment space are a range methods of payment from a range of companies, both start-ups and well-established brands. Here is a sampling of some of the mobile payment operations.

- **Boku.** The mobile payment processing company enables online merchants to receive payments made through their mobile phones without a credit card or bank account. The charges go directly to the consumer's wireless phone bill. The mobile payment option can be embedded within mobile apps. The payment platform is available in more than 60 countries over more than 250 mobile networks. A merchant's loyalty programs can be integrated into the service. Boku also has a strategic partnership with Telefónica and its mobile wallet services.
- **Dwolla.** By charging a flat fee of 25 cents per transaction, this mobile payment network, started in Des Moines, Iowa, raised an

initial investment of $5 million from various investors, including a fund of actor Ashton Kutcher. The peer-to-peer (p2p) transfer of money can be done quickly from a mobile phone with funds being transferred from bank to bank, and for transfers under $10 there is no fee.

- **PayPal.** One of the most well-established of digital payment services, this eBay company has more than 100 million active accounts in about 200 markets around the world. The company, founded in 1998, is headquartered in San Jose, California, with its international home base in Singapore. PayPal handles about $10 billion in mobile payment transactions a year, with a large portion coming from outside the United States. It also provides a large percentage of eBay's overall annual revenue. With more than 50 million U.S. consumers, PayPal has its own card to be used at retail and offers a free PayPal Here device that is connected to an Android or Apple mobile device, allowing credit card swiping and payments. The company conducted mobile wallet trials across a range of retail brands, including Home Depot, American Eagle Outfitters, Foot Locker, Office Depot, and Toys "R" Us.

- **Square.** Plugging the small Square device into an Android or Apple mobile device transforms that device into a virtual cash register. The mobile user takes payments by swiping a credit card through the device. The device caught on due to its simplicity of use, so that small business owners, restaurants, taxi drivers, and individuals could easily take mobile payments. The company was founded in 2009, is headquartered in San Francisco, and processes more than $8 billion in payments annually. The mobile payment company has raised several hundred millions of dollars from various investors, including Visa and Chase. Square also received $25 million from Starbucks, with the associated benefit of having the Square Wallet enabled for use in the 7,000 Starbucks stores in the United States. Consumers can link a credit card to the Pay by Square account, open a tab at a restaurant, and pay without leaving their seat, since the establishment can detect the phone's location in the store and automatically transfer payment. This could also be accomplished by telling the cashier your name or showing them your photo on a Square account. Square expanded its service into Canada in late 2012.

Numerous companies have introduced credit card readers that easily attach to smartphones, instantly transforming them into currency-processing computers. For example, even though eBay owns PayPal, it also introduced a direct Square competitor named Here, with its own dongle.

No matter the approach or the platform, the value is not so much about the actual payment using a mobile phone as it is the value a consumer could potentially receive because of the mobile payment capability. The idea is that with on-the-spot information about customer location and payment history, retailers could provide coupons and other deals with higher relevance to enrich the shopping experience. This is a dramatic improvement on the age-old supermarket coupon arrangement that at checkout, based on what you bought, you receive coupons for competing products, in an attempt to sway you at the next supermarket visit. Just as that process has become highly sophisticated over the years, mobile takes it to a totally different level.

At mobile checkout, more real-time information is available. This can include precise location, whether in a store aisle or at checkout, time of day, past mobile behaviors, past purchase behaviors, immediate preceding behavior, and current weather outside. Additional innovations in payment options like Square and Dwolla will likely continue while credit card companies and banks look to secure their positions in the mobile world.

ENHANCING THE MOBILE PAYMENT EXPERIENCE

Financial institutions, some with many millions of customers, are learning to deal with a world gone mobile. In some parts of Latin America, for example, bankers are looking to acquire new customers who never had access to banking before mobile phone capabilities, as discussed later in this chapter. One bank also sees a significant opportunity to make the customer experience better at the point of purchase.

By any measure, Bank of America is big when it comes to mobile. Here are some of the well-known bank's mobile stats as of late 2012:

- Of the 30 million online banking users, 11 million use mobile.
- The bank has about 100 million mobile sessions a month.
- Mobile usage is growing by 40,000 customers a week.
- The bank sees a 74 percent year-over-year increase in mobile as primary usage.

Even with numbers like these, rather than taking a mass mobile marketing approach, it is spending its time and resources looking to enhance personal interactions. "We're living in a more connected, digital world," says Marc Warshawsky, senior vice president and mobile solutions executive at Bank of America.[8] "Each transaction represents an opportunity to be more deliberately human to build ever more personal and human connections. Our focus is finding ways to bring a better customer experience to the market."

As is the case with other major brands, Bank of America sees an opportunity in working with others rather than trying to solve all the mobile purchasing issues by itself. "In this space, it's difficult for a single player to do everything on their own," says Warshawsky. "Partnerships will help bring these capabilities to life because everybody has a different piece of the puzzle [and] has potential to create a better customer experience. For example, we're partnering with merchants to make targeted cash-back offers through our BankAmeriDeals program when they use their Bank of America credit or debit card for a purchase."

Bank of America spent much of 2012 exploring and experimenting with various mobile payment approaches, ranging from NFC to using QR codes for payments. But rather than putting all its chips in one bucket, such as betting that NFC will be the ultimate payment solution, the bank focuses more on the one-to-one customer level in all aspects of their interactions with the bank, not just payments. "Customers want choice and simplicity in how they interact," says Warshawsky. "Each interaction is uniquely important to that customer."

This idea of simplicity brings to mind the initial launch of Quicken by Intuit. At its introduction, all the software did was print onto a check the information you'd normally write on it and automatically balance your checkbook. But it turned out that was the simple thing that customers wanted—to find a replacement for balancing their checkbook. Intuit captured a massive customer base and then expanded from there into a myriad of financial services products. This does not mean starting small, but rather doing small things—simple interactions that make a person's life easier. The small things done by Bank of America are being done at a very large scale, for millions of people. For example, banks including Bank of America allow customers to use their smartphones to take a picture of a check and deposit it via mobile to be deposited, thereby avoiding a trip to the bank or to an ATM machine. While not the biggest innovation in mobile history, the process was made available at scale to millions of people and made their lives easier.

The point is to provide functionality that customers value, even if those things are seemingly small. Bank of America has found that mobile customers are more engaged than online-only customers, which means the bank wants to ensure that interactions are simple and intuitive so that customers choose their phones to transact and interact. Simple things in mobile can go a long way, and you can build from there. At the moment of the actual transaction there is a great potential to exert mobile influence. Warshawsky continues:

> As I think about the point of purchase and some of the changes that will continue to evolve at the point of sale, it is really an opportunity to add value to the purchase experience—to leverage technology to help customers inform their purchase, save on their purchase, and make the purchase more convenient. We believe that as these technologies mature, and it doesn't matter what specific technology, mobile can assist customers with a variety of purchasing tools.
>
> We are looking at ways to make the payment experience more valuable and more convenient. We're trialing and testing and evaluating a variety of solutions that can help enrich the purchase

experience. There is a lot of runway in this space to help make that experience better.

We are also focused on helping customers manage their finances on a day-to-day basis. It goes beyond can I save money on that purchase, to how does that fit into my budget, and do I have enough money in my account to pay for this purchase? We're trying to bring together all of those into a cohesive, seamless experience that really helps customers manage their daily finances more effectively.

Consumer behavior can be influenced at the point of purchase by providing additional information at the transactions stage as well as making the product selection process more interactive with smartphones along the way. "From a product comparison standpoint, that is the beauty of mobile devices," says Warshawsky. "They are anytime, anywhere, and a wealth of information is available at your fingertips. If you walk into a store and are looking at a particular product, you can scan that barcode, look at reviews, look at what other people have purchased, look at detailed product info, and so on. Down the road it's conceivable that we'll see tighter integration of those experiences. What we may see is product research, product reviews, product comparisons, offers, payments, all being presented to the customer in a very seamless fashion. Certainly all of those on their own add value to the customer, but that value gets amplified as we see a trend towards packaging those into an integrated experience."

Even though the mobile transaction experience can become richer, it still does not mean that credit cards will go away, especially since mass usage of mobile payments on a global basis is a ways off. "The truth is, plastic works and it works very well today," says Warshawsky. "There is value in making that transaction through a mobile device, but there are some things that have to occur to make that a reality. Any of the mobile payment technologies that are out there would have to be more prevalent. Merchants and customers have to see value in adopting this technology to drive acceptance at scale. It must be secure, as reliable, and more convenient than what they do today."

While small, mobile start-ups can quickly launch products and services, they can start small and then grow over time. In many ways, large companies with well-known brands have a higher bar, since they have customer expectations that their new products or services will live up to their current—and often well-liked—offerings. Brands also often have to build for massive scale, as in the cases of MasterCard and Bank of America, which are global entities. The advantage of the brands is that they are well known and have a large customer base at the start. They also typically have a corporate culture of creating, launching, and maintaining bulletproof products and services. Says Warshawsky:

> Customer experience is the most important thing. Those that have established brands that people trust and people know start out with an advantage. When Bank of America looks at a new technology or new solution, we have to make sure that it is secure, reliable, and scalable. We are solving for millions of customers and millions of transactions every day. That makes that solution inherently more difficult.
>
> We're not focused on being first to market, we're focused on being right to market. To us, right to market means the right customer experience, the right security, the right reliability, the right timing, with the necessary scale to bring that experience to millions of customers every day.
>
> As we look at new technologies we have to ensure that they are bank grade from a variety of perspectives. A lot of the payment innovators are not held to these same standards as banks. So they can create a technology and put it out to market very quickly because they don't have some of the considerations that regulated financial institutions do.

BANKERS CHASE MOBILE IN LATIN AMERICA

Banking leaders in the United States are not alone in looking at the impact of mobile on their business and how retail banking in the future will be done. Mobile is also taking center stage in financial services in Latin America. After I addressed hundreds of IT and banking executives from throughout Latin America gathered for their annual meeting in Panama, several of the executives brought up the issue of who will dominate mobile payments in the future. While numerous mobile payment schemes are under way in the U.S. market, the executives at the CLAB Banking IT Conference in Panama, sponsored by the Latin American Federation of Banks, are examining the role of carriers there.

Unlike some markets around the world, parts of mobile in Latin America are developing somewhat differently. Mobile penetration in Latin America is relatively high, exceeding 107 percent of the population, though markets differ, with Panama mobile penetration at 204 percent, as one example. Some other examples, according to the International Telecommunications Union (ITU):

- Brazil: 251 million mobile phones, 203 million people
- Colombia: 45 million mobile phones, 43 million people
- Argentina: 57 million mobile phones, 42 million people
- Chile: 22 million mobile phones, 17 million people
- Venezuela: 29 million mobile phones, 28 million people

Twenty countries in Latin America had more mobile subscriptions than total inhabitants, and 20 countries accounted for 98 percent of all mobile subscriptions. But the key statistic in relation to mobile is that Latin America households with internet access number only 29 percent, according to ITU. This means a significant number of people will have internet access through mobile devices rather than computers, with huge implications for the bankers in the region. Many express a fear that mobile carriers will get involved in mobile payments, to which the carriers say they will not. Their main argument is that they are too busy running and growing their own businesses to want to wade into the bankers' space.

Many financial services firms are focusing on the developing markets in what they refer to in Spanish as "Bancarización," getting more people to choose banking services rather than non-banking services. This is why mobile payments are of such significance in the region, since whoever dominates the payments space can potentially become the first financial services (or banking) experience for millions of people. The bankers are working to make sure they fulfill the coming market capabilities.

There also are facilitators of mobile influence in Latin America, such as Arango Software International, known as Grupo ASI, in Panama. The company develops software for microfinancial and other banking institutions. It was founded by Julio Arango, a specialist in financial software applications, in 1985 in Panama and later expanded to other markets, including Mexico and Costa Rica.

The company created what it calls a channel manager to extract information related to banking over data communications and reroute it to different mobile channels with a high degree of security. "ABanks Mobile gives the clients the ability to do any transaction that they usually do in a branch, or through the internet, through a mobile phone," says Julio Alejandro Arango, representative of Arango Software.[9] "It works pretty much with any mobile phone. All it requires is that the phone has a browser that supports HTML5."

The system manages all the security, following different regulations of the different countries. "We have it here in Panama, Colombia, and in Venezuela for some of our customers," says Arango. "In Latin America, pretty much any country uses mobile apps. Much depends on in the country which phone is most popular. For example, in Ecuador, most popular is BlackBerry, so they use the BlackBerry app. Here in Panama we have pretty much an Android family, but in Colombia and Mexico they are more into iPhone and iOS devices, so that depends. We have the application that can be set up in any Android phone or tablet as an app in Google Play and any iOS devices, either and iPod, iPad, or an iPhone in the App Store. The other ones can access it through a URL, or a Web browser. Most use it in smartphones."

For customers without smartphones or who do not have data plan contracts with their mobile carriers, Arango sets up a different channel. "You then can make a phone call and do transactions through the phone just by pressing keys," says Arango. "We have that in Venezuela. The idea is especially to bring new people into banking. It's the possibility to do transactions through the phone by following instructions."

There are some mobile differences in the U.S. and Latin American markets. For example, BlackBerry still commands a significant presence in some of the countries, for various reasons. There also are several noticeable similarities in mobile usage in Panama. At the Panama Canal, most visitors, from various geographies, use their phones to take photos and videos of massive ships making their way through the canal. When I handed both my iPhone and my Samsung Galaxy Nexus to total strangers to take a photo at the canal, no one needed any verbal directions in any language to know what to do. Some functions of mobile are instinctive, for anyone anywhere in the world, no matter the business market situation.

In Europe, Latin America, and South Africa overall, less than a quarter of the mobile population uses mobile payment services, and almost half (46 percent) have used their mobile device for some type of banking transaction.[10] More than a third (39 percent) are interested in or plan to use mobile payments.

CREDIT CARDS IN A MOBILE WORLD

Major brands involved in any stage of the move to mobile payments are highly involved in ensuring a role for themselves in payments of the future. In many cases, their core business is payments or payment processing, so adapting to the mobile future is an imperative. The companies involved have to balance the needs and capabilities of multiple stakeholders, including consumers, merchants, and banks, all of which are involved in giving or receiving money. All those constituents have certain expectations, such as reasonable fees, high security, and ease of use.

One of the most common methods of cashless payments is the credit card, commonly used around the world. Following the creation of the first common credit card, the Diners Club card in 1950, several other companies entered the business with varying business models. Some cards are free, some charge interest rates, some charge merchants varying rates, and some come with multi-tier services. No matter the type, the global marketplace is well established to accept the cards as payment.

Rather than the credit card vanishing because of mobile payments, the more likely scenario is that the number of transactions will be increased by the sheer number of people with mobile phones who may have never had a credit card. "I don't think the piece of plastic will ever disappear," says Mung Ki Woo, group executive of mobile at MasterCard Worldwide.[11]

"The overall volume increases. I'm convinced there will be incremental transactions."

MasterCard, whose stated vision is "a world beyond cash," processes more than 23 billion transactions a year. As a payments processor, the company has wired the world for commerce through the MasterCard Worldwide Network that connects financial institutions, merchants, and cardholders with payment-processing services.

"We're going through a digital transition," says Woo. "There's always a degree of looking at the past to predict the future." Woo is part of Master-Card's emerging payments team whose focus is on making payments work on new technology platforms around the world. "Payments is our core business," says Woo. The transition to mobile at the point of purchase does not mean a total replacement of the past or a total replacement for the credit card but rather the potential added value that can come through the mobile device.

As in other transitions to new technologies and platforms, companies figure ways to add value, and consumers seek that new value. This does not mean the previous platform was not functional, but rather that new value can be added in the next wave. For example, books being downloaded onto mobile devices and e-book readers did not eliminate printed books. "Books were not broken," says Woo. "E-books are another service and they provide instant gratification. Old media doesn't go away."

MasterCard has a stated strategy of partnerships and is involved in a range of areas, such as being one of the early credit cards as part of Google Wallet and linking its rewards program into the mobile check-in app, shopkick. Like many of the large companies moving to mobile, Master-Card has to think big. "If you want scale, you need planning," says Woo. "Digital feels the same as plastic, but it's not. We have 35 million merchants and 450,000 PayPass terminals. Mobile is the only medium where you can reach the individual, and a small level of additional convenience is enough to change consumer behavior." MasterCard sees the potential for an increase in processing due to mobile payments. "Overall, it's going to have an increase in transaction volume," says Woo. "It's about the overall packaging of the service. You can communicate over the air and cause an action in the physical world."

MOBILE PAYMENTS VERSUS PAYMENTS WHILE MOBILE

Aside from mobile wallets, NFC, and other forms of on-site mobile paying, there is another side of mobile payments with a far larger scope. Mobile payments generally refer to using a mobile phone to pay for things where you are. The much bigger and more significant market involves using a mobile phone to pay for things where you are not. This is the issue of mobile payments versus payments while mobile, and payments while mobile are substantially more significant.

For example, by 2015, payments while mobile are projected to reach $1 trillion, according to a global study conducted by KPMG. That's close to 100 percent a year over the next two years, fueled by the increase in the number of smartphones and tablets. By the second half of 2012, a third (33 percent) of U.S. consumers had already made payments while mobile, almost twice the number from the previous year.[12]

Consumers buy a wide range of products and services while mobile, such as music via iTunes, electronics via Amazon Payments, and clothes via PayPal Mobile. While many digital goods, such as music and games, are bought while mobile, the majority of mobile shoppers are buying physical goods.[13]

It is this end—payments while mobile—where the real money and potential reside. As more people become comfortable buying from their phones, more purchasing will occur.

As another data point, 23 billion tickets (for concerts, etc.) are expected to be delivered to mobile phones worldwide by 2016, according to Juniper Research in the United Kingdom.[14] The benefits to facility operators include savings by selling and delivering tickets directly through mobile without the need for extra staff or real estate. This also extends the mobile influence beyond traditional marketing avenues, since many of the mobile ticket buyers will also be researching event or travel information via mobile in advance of the purchase. This means the marketing messages have to be in the mobile arena and on the customer's mobile platform. The key for marketers is to realize that focusing all their efforts at the end offering of the transaction through any number of point-of-sale strategies and tactics is shortsighted.

Payments while mobile will affect all products. The decisions in shopping—and buying—are being made all the time in many places, most of which the product or service seller has little or no control over, and the change in buying (and shopping) is fundamentally behavioral.

Using mobile devices to shop for, find, and buy pretty much anything is becoming a totally iterative process that can be done anytime, anywhere. Payments while mobile is about the behavior of the consumer more than the technological intricacies of mobile payments.

RELOCATING THE POINT OF PURCHASE

In the traditional shopping and buying process, a consumer goes to the store, shops the aisles, selects the products, and goes to the checkout to pay and leave. In some larger stores like Walmart, this could be a process of varying lengths of time, depending on how crowded the particular store is at the moment and how many people are simultaneously trying to pay and leave. Over time, many retailers passed along some elements of the check-out task from the cashier to the customers, such as by installing carousels for items at checkout that can spin, allowing the consumer to take the filled bags and put them in their cart themselves. No instructions were needed for the customer; the task at hand became obvious.

To make this process faster over the years, businesses introduced self-checkout systems. Shoppers then could scan each of their items themselves and pay without dealing with a cashier. This type of system proliferated at many locations, such as supermarkets, big-box retailers, and airports. While these systems passed along some of the point-of-sale actions to the consumer, they still required that the person go to a physical checkout location. The behavior of shopping and then paying as the last step before leaving a store has been ingrained in consumers as being a serial process. While this habitual process has worked both for consumers and retailers for decades, the move to mobile totally redefines it.

When you think about it, why do shopping the aisles and paying have to be separate tasks, one fully completed before being followed by the other? The consumer walks around a store aggregating goods by putting them into their shopping cart. When all the goods have been selected and aggregated in the cart, they then are hauled by the customer to the check-out location. At that station, all the goods then are disaggregated as the detail of each item—generally in the form of a UPC barcode—is yet again checked and registered by a cashier and a computer system. The goods then are reaggregated for the customer to take home. When broken down, the in-store shopping process can look quite convoluted:

- Customer walks around store checking items.
- Certain items checked are then selected and put in shopping cart, one at a time.
- Customer wheels cart to checkout station.
- Customer waits in line.
- Customer takes out items one at a time and puts on conveyor belt.
- Cashier again checks each item, one at a time.
- Items passed along to another person, who reaggregates items into bags.
- Bags are placed into shopping cart again.
- Customer wheels cart out of store.

Major retailer such as Lowe's, Home Depot, and Staples are making mobile devices available to sales associates to aid in the in-aisle shopping process. There are various mobile technologies that can leverage the potential to interact with customers at the closest possible time to the actual transaction. For example, the Boston-based start-up AisleBuyer created a virtual shopping assistant that allowed in-store customers to bypass checkout lines, paying directly through their mobile phones. The system allowed shoppers to bypass self-checkout locations as well with their credit cards associated with the mobile app. The company ultimately was acquired by Intuit, where it joined that company's mobile payments team. The technology would then be used to transition Intuit's point-of-sale solution as well as its Square competitor, GoPayment.

Another mobile app called aisle411 allows brands to reach consumers as they select products in a store's aisles to influence which products are selected. The technology can be included in a store's own branded app, and a two-way connection can be live, allowing a brand to make real-time product selections depending on the customer's precise location and what products they are considering. An added benefit is the data marketers can receive from actual shopper behavior in the aisle. Walgreens uses the app, so if you go into any Walgreens store, the aisle and content are displayed on the phone. If you looking for powder, for example, type that word and all locations of all powders appear at the shelves on which they are located.

Mobile shoppers can use the app to preplan a trip, add shopping lists, search, and navigate to the section of an aisle with indoor maps of the stores. The app allows brands to target customers based on unique purchase-intent metrics and contextual location tracking, keyword search triggers, and user-generated information.

As more technological innovation is introduced at the point of sale, more of the transaction capability can be moved to the location of the shopper rather than waiting for the shopper to go to a fixed location to pay. The customer already is mobile with enough processing power in their hand to be able to execute a payment transaction. Here is a shopping scenario with more use of mobile technology:

- Customer walks around store checking items.
- Certain items checked, scanned, selected, and put into shopping bags in cart.
- Customer wheels cart out of store.

Product tracking has gotten very sophisticated over time, with RFID (radio frequency identification) chips and readers and other inventory-tracking systems. Combined with mobile tracking technologies, the logical next step is to link the product locations and products with mobile shoppers and their behaviors and current needs. The goal would be to make the trips through the aisles faster and the exit from the transaction points more efficient and friction-free for the consumer.

LONDON AIRPORT GROCERY SHOPPING

Sometimes relocating the point of purchase can take the form of a re-thinking of where something has traditionally been purchased. Aside from online purchases, for example, clothes are typically purchased in a clothing store, electronics are typically purchased in an electronics store, and groceries are typically purchased in a grocery store. Mobile can change all that and influence purchase behavior by disconnecting the products sold from their logical location.

Consumers in the United Kingdom are well acquainted with Tesco, which has a footprint of more than 3,000 stores and more than 300,000 employees. The retailer's Finest and Everyday Value are the two largest food brands in the United Kingdom, bigger than Coca-Cola, each with more than $1.5 billion in annual sales. Outside the United Kingdom, Tesco has stores in 14 markets across Europe, Asia, and North America. In the United States, the company has about 200 stores and more than 5,000 employees in its Fresh and Easy Neighborhood Market stores in Southern California, Arizona, and Nevada.

In the second half of 2012, Tesco decided to try allowing its customers to tap into its mobile capabilities to shop for groceries in a different way and a different place. On the idea that airline travelers have extra downtime at the airport after checking in and clearing security, Tesco introduced airport grocery shopping at London's Gatwick Airport. Unlike at its typical stores, Tesco created a virtual grocery store at the airport. The company installed interactive billboards that smartphone travelers could use before their flights.

The billboard displays what look like shelves stocked with products, each with their own barcode. Using the Tesco app, consumers scan the codes on products they want and then select a deliver date and time so they can receive groceries after their trip. A vacation traveler leaving for a two-week holiday could then feel comfortable they would be supplied with necessary groceries upon their return, skipping that post-holiday trip to the food store. While a consumer could also order groceries online from their phone, the electronic billboard at the airport is a highly visible reminder at just the right time and place. In addition, entering items onto a list is fast and easy for a consumer. The electronic shelves are brightly lit and mimic what a person would see in the physical store. The refrigerator section, for example, looks like a refrigerator, with various milk selections on the shelves.

Tesco's virtual grocery store at Gatwick follows a successful trial of the concept in South Korea, where the company's Tesco Homeplus has virtual stores in subway and bus stops. Customers there can use their smartphones to scan QR codes to purchase products that are then delivered to their homes. The South Korean operation also has more than 270 physical stores, comprising both large hypermarkets and small express stores, and is the top only grocery retailer there.

Both the U.K. and South Korea virtual stores are examples of how a company can move the point of purchase of items in its traditional stores to locations and venues far from those stores. This allows mobile influence at the point of sale to be relocated and, in many cases, increased.

CLOSING THE MOBILE SHOPPER GAP

Marketers have been talking about organizing around the customer for many years. During the heyday of the early Net, IBM organized into Industry Solution Units (ISUs, in IBM-speak), each of which focused on a particular industry, such as banking, retail, or entertainment. For a big company selling big hardware and storage to big companies, it made a lot of sense. It was practical at the time to at least organize around markets, the thinking being that expertise in any given market could be aggregated for a company to provide greater and more relevant solutions for each set of customers in that market. In many ways, that was the ultimate B2B play.

But for Business2Consumer (B2C), the existence of mobile creates the time and opportunity to come closer to organizing around individuals, as many agencies and leading brands have preached for years. The mobile industry has the words, such as "microtargeting," "location-based," and "hyperlocal," though they are more easily said than done. Organizing around and serving customers has some great potential with mobile, though it likely won't be technology hurdles that get in the way of ultimate success. Often, it will be internal company structure or culture that delays or even prevents what would otherwise be a successful mobile influence approach.

While a technology solution may be introduced at one end of a company, the customer may be at the other end, which becomes even more pronounced with mobile. For example, when the rewards-rich shopkick app was introduced some time ago, the idea was that a shopper would walk into a store such as Macy's or Best Buy, a signal would be silently sent to the person's phone as they entered the store, and they would receive rewards (called *kicks*) just for being there. They would also get bonus points for scanning the barcodes of particular products.

In the beginning, the process was rocky. But it was not so much about the technology as about the trickle-down knowledge at the employee level. In the early days, we were looking for certain products to scan, as specified by the app. I'd ask the nearest Best Buy employee about where the products for shopkick scanning were and would get such responses as "What's shopkick?" But over time, these types of comments from Best Buy employees evolved. They went from "Let me get you the person who knows shopkick" to "Yes, I'm familiar with shopkick, what are you trying to do?" This is a somewhat typical, normal evolution of the introduction of a new mobile approach on a massive scale.

The next phase was the checkout process. Best Buy has its own rewards program, and shopkick has its own "kicks" rewards programs. Again, an evolution at checkout: At my first attempt to use shopkick to receive points at checkout, it took two employees and the manager on duty to figure how to find it in Best Buy's POS system. The next time, an employee and one manager found it. The third time, the checkout cashier found it on her own, as well as the Best Buy rewards program, applying credit to both.

The lesson here is that the shopkick technology worked; it was all the people-involved processes along the way that needed to be modified. And therein lies one of the key challenges in moving to organizing around the customer. The best mobile technology may be at one end of the organization and the totally willing customer is at the other end. The problem is everything in between.

These issues can range from effectively introducing new ways of doing things with mobile customers, such as with shopkick, to convincing specific profit centers or franchisees that they should adopt and deploy what corporate is introducing. The retailers that win will figure out how to streamline the evolution of everything in the middle. "The most scared will succeed and those not will fail," says Jeff Sellinger, cofounder and chief product officer of shopkick.[15]

In the case of shopkick, with more than four million users, mobile consumers also were pushing back into Best Buy store associates, forcing them to learn about the features of the app. In many cases of mobile influence, the mobile shopper is the catalyst. Shopkick is an example of an influence right at the moment of purchase. They know you're in the store, they know what you have scanned, they likely know your purchase behavior if your rewards card is linked to your shopkick account, and they can present real-time suggestions based on all that knowledge.

Another typical roadblock to being customer-centric within an organization is the silo effect, with division or group A focused on its mission and success metrics working next to group B, with its own set of the same. If group A and B are aligned, then there is sure to be a group C or D.

These also add to the obstacle course between the mobile innovators and the customers, both of whom get it. During the point-of-purchase phase of the Mobile Shopping Life Cycle, the gap between the mobile innovators and the customers has to be closed. Otherwise, the company risks losing at the transaction stage, a critical point that many marketers work toward all the way through the other stages of the Mobile Shopping Life Cycle.

There is little doubt that mobile will eventually transform the way people buy things. Mobile shoppers will come to expect different types of activities and offers at the point of purchase, just as they will come to expect the availability of additional information on products delivered to their phones as they shop the aisles. Even after the transaction, the Mobile Shopping Life Cycle continues into the post-purchase phase, which we address in the next chapter.

seven

THE TAKEAWAY

post-purchase

SECURING THE MOBILE CUSTOMER CONNECTION

In the Mobile Shopping Life Cycle, the sales process does not end at the actual moment of transaction when the customer makes a purchase. The new mobile buyers tap into their social networks to share information about their new item as well as their purchase experience, both the good and the bad. This can range from a quick text just after a sale to a photo of the product shot with a mobile phone and posted to Facebook. This is the equivalent of every sales experience having the potential to be on the nightly news, in real time on a global scale.

Businesses, especially those selling big-ticket items, need to remain connected with the buyers to ensure that the product experience lives up to expectations created in earlier stages of the shopping cycle. There are multiple ways to stay connected after the transaction. One way to think about it is that the actual transaction is part of a continuous shopping process in the Mobile Shopping Life Cycle. Ensuring that a post-purchase customer is satisfied obviously increases the likelihood of an additional future purchase down the road. This is another reason marketers need to be involved in multiple stages of the shopping cycle.

The other potential benefit in the post-purchase phase is new customer acquisition. A satisfied customer can easily share their viewpoints with others in their circles. They are likely to text, send photos and mobile videos, and share through social media. Many captains of mobile influence empower these activities in multiple ways. They include sharing capabilities within apps and mobile websites and often offer incentives such as future discounts if they share with others. As discussed in an earlier chapter, using SMS can be effective for sharing. Likewise, MMS can add rich images and video to the equation.

MMS IN THE MOBILE SHOPPING LIFE CYCLE

Mobile video is big and getting bigger. Better and more powerful smartphones and tablets are fueling the growth, and much of the increase in data usage will be driven by mobile video. By 2016, mobile video traffic will account for 71 percent of all mobile data, according to the Cisco Visual Networking Index Global Mobile Data Traffic Forecast.[1] That would be the equivalent of 33 billion DVDs, 4.3 quadrillion MP3 files, or 813 trillion text messages. The growth in these numbers is being driven by more powerful mobile devices using faster networks accessing much more video. There are numerous studies showing that consumers watch video on their mobile devices. You may have watched a movie trailer or a video sent from a friend on your mobile phone. If you watched a video message from one of your favorite brands you opted in for, chances are high it was sent via technology you may never heard of called Mogreet.

Mogreet is another facilitator of mobile influence and is the leading pioneer in MMS marketing. Founded in 2006 in Venice, California, by James Citron, the company focused almost exclusively on enabling brands to deliver mobile videos to their customers' mobile phones via MMS. Mogreet boasts that it was the first company that could enable MMS video delivery to consumers' phones regardless of which wireless carrier the customer used. Several years later, Mogreet has become the largest MMS platform in the industry.

Like many of the other facilitators of mobile influence, Mogreet did not become a household name because it became instead the silent platform that brands use under their own names. These include a large list of well-known brands such as Walmart, Kohl's, Nike, Turner, Bloomingdale's, Fox, and ABC, among many others.

Unlike SMS text messages, which we discussed earlier, MMS (multi-media messaging service) can include pictures, sounds, and videos with nearly unlimited text characters, and the messages can be viewed on a very wide range of phones, including feature phones and smartphones. MMS has a place throughout the Mobile Shopping Life Cycle, and using it in multiple stages on the way to post-purchase can successfully solidify a customer's brand engagement.

One company that uses the Mogreet MMS platform is Charlotte Russe, a mall-based specialty retailer. The company wanted to increase personal interactions with their customers and become top of mind for females 16 to 26 years old. Its research indicated that particular demographic interacts with their favorite retailers via social media and mobile. Since the retailer already had more than 500,000 Facebook followers, they decided to delve into mobile.

As is the case with many retailers during the early stage of the pre-buy, the first step for Charlotte Russe was to capture initial customer information. "Nearly all of our retail customers do a great job of capturing their customers' mobile numbers when their customers are on their Web properties," says James Citron, the founder and chief executive officer of Mogreet.[2] "For example, Charlotte Russe does this by prominently featuring an incentive to join their mobile club and in return receive an immediate 10 percent coupon. By providing a compelling incentive, their customers are more inclined to provide their mobile numbers and consequently these retailers can now start pushing out targeted content to them."

Charlotte Russe launched a "mystery date" contest utilizing a mobile Web video MMS campaign over a three-day weekend. Shoppers participated by texting a particular keyword (MATCH) to a short code and selected their mystery date from among three provided choices. For those who opted in, they received a prize delivered by MMS video. Mobile coupons were used as an incentive for shoppers to enter the contest, which were delivered by MMS video from their winning mystery date. To promote the campaign and involve shoppers, Charlotte Russe promoted the program, including putting up signs in windows and at checkout terminals at all 500 of its stores around the United States. Employees also encouraged shoppers to participate, a key component in many cases of mobile influence. The company also leveraged its social media presence by encouraging its Facebook fans to take a chance to meet their mystery date in store. In the case of the Charlotte Russe mystery date campaign, the company saw a 33 percent growth in its mobile database in one weekend and a 300 percent higher participation rate than its past SMS programs.

"In-store-only offers can be simple to execute and they can leverage the significant store footprint that many retailers have," says Citron. A simple call to action at various parts of a store can enable a retailer to capture their shoppers' information and/or deliver relevant content (i.e., an incentive like a coupon, a video about why this product is a hot new item, etc.) to increase the likelihood of the consumer to purchase at that time.

"Charlotte Russe utilizes a wide range of promotions, as well. One of their popular promotions is an instant win promotion available in-store, which says 'if you go in a store and buy something, everyone gets one of three prizes.' And the prizes are amazing, jewelry, a cool pair of socks, a new shirt. And consumers love it. They view the offers as being valuable and highly engaging. Everyone wants something for free and if you can only redeem it in-store, then customers have a better chance to engage with the merchandise, leading to higher average sales."

Vans Shoes is another retailer that does a great job of encouraging its customers to subscribe, or opt-in to their mobile database. Promoting on the homepage of their website, they ask additional qualifying questions about their shoppers' interest in different sports (i.e., surfing, skating, BMX, etc.) and create a mobile profile of their customer, so they can start delivering highly relevant and engaging content to their shopper and, in turn, drive awareness and sales of specific products. MMS is a unique vehicle for interacting with mobile shoppers since they can watch a quick video message on the fly, during or after their in-store experience. "You can use video to tell a story and increase the customer's consideration of purchase," says Citron. "Our central premise is that while 140 characters is effective in delivering a message, video provides a better customer experience and is three to five times more effective in communicating an experience, deepening loyalty and driving a sale. The overarching differentiator in our business is that we help brands use video to move customers through the purchase cycle." The company says it has grown 400 percent in a year with hundreds of millions of MMS messages delivered to consumers through its system. Mogreet projects ultimately hitting a billion messages delivered in a year.

INCREASING TRAFFIC

Like SMS, discussed in an earlier chapter, MMS helps drive traffic and action. For example, Charlotte Russe found that using MMS compared to sending email drives more store traffic. "That is very specially a clear benefit of mobile messaging," says Citron. "When you send a consumer an email and say, 'This new shirt is available today $10 off only today or online,' the marketer hopes the consumer will click and buy it online. However, multiple studies show that brand emails tend to land in the spam filter and suffer from a lag time open rate of anywhere from ten-minute or so lag time. When a consumer receives that same information by text, they can easily tap into one of the key benefits of mobile, which is location. They can then say, 'Okay, here is the closest Charlotte Russe store, I'm going to go in and buy.' And because mobile truly is all about location, it is really activating consumers to go in store, the top goal for most retail marketers."

MMS can also be used to interact with the customer while in the store. "The simplest way to engage with a consumer in-store is to understand the customer's position within the aisle. In-aisle, customers face a wide range of products that may be indistinguishable to the consumer," says Citron. "Smart marketers provide them with the information they need to make the right decision. While a sales incentive like an incentive coupons can drive immediate action, consumers cite that videos showcasing product features and competitive differences are frequently used to aid in the purchase process. If a consumer is shopping, the best thing to do is give them a quick video highlighting the differences. Home Depot does a really good job of this with their store QR codes. Home Depot products feature a code customers can scan to receive a video with important information aimed at demonstrating why you should buy a particular product. For stores with multiple competitive products in-aisle like Best Buy's wide range of flat screen TVs, savvy brands and manufacturers are including a shortcode and keyword on their packaging enabling consumers to text in and receive a video back on their device with the information that explains why the consumer should buy their product." Another interesting Mogreet campaign is by the toy company Melissa & Doug. "They have a hot product, The Trunki, for young kids," says Citron. "It's a piece of luggage for kids, which is very popular with young kids because it enables them to pack their travel items, while also riding on it when they go traveling with their parents. Showing a product like this in action is also another great way to drive interest in the product. Mogreet customer Melissa & Doug prominently featured the call to action 'Text this code or scan this QR code to find out why your kid needs to buy a Trunki' on all of their product tags. As soon as users texted it, they received a great lifestyle video showing kids happily riding around on their Trunkies where the product sold nationwide.

"Bloomingdale's is another brand utilizing this marketing tactic. You might be in Bloomingdale's where you will see an interesting product, like Tommy Hilfiger's new line of clothing. Right there, you will find a text code prominently displayed. You walk into the store and Bloomingdale's store associates are actively encouraging shoppers to text in or scan a QR code to find out more about a particular product. Bloomingdale's does this with their wedding registry catalog as well. When you get the catalog in the mail it has QR and MMS codes for you to get more information on any featured product. It brings to life gift registry items and turns print ads into direct sales tools. In these cases, depending on the audience, these types of MMS marketing programs receive two to five times higher engagement from a text code versus a QR code. A younger audience, high school and college aged audiences rarely, if ever, scan QR codes. The mid-20s to early 30s are the QR code user sweet spot, and the over–30-year-old audience never use QR codes, particularly females in that age range. They are all texting. The mom today uses her smartphone and texting as her primary way of communicating with her family. That's it."

PHONE NUMBERS MATTER

Capturing mobile phone numbers is an obvious and critical component of MMS marketing, especially as it relates to the shopping cycle. Just as numbers can be captured when customers come into a location and while they roam the aisles, they also can be captured during the checkout process before the customer leaves the store.

"Point of purchase is the primary place for our retail customers to capture the customer's mobile number," says Citron. "That is the number-one place where consumers are most likely to take out their phones and join a database and to get more information or receive an instant one-time offer. Steve Madden does this and Charlotte Russe promotes their mobile campaign, whether it's their database, or sweepstakes, or contest at point of purchase. It is typically a little sign at the register. While you are waiting in line, why not join the mobile club and receive a 10 percent discount if you are a customer? Customer data is currency, so it is key for brands to offer something valuable to users. Another offering that drives database subscription offers users a free prize at purchase for joining in the club. It works because the offering is valuable to the customer."

Another opportunity to capture mobile numbers is at certain payment terminals at checkout. When a customer is signing and selecting your credit card, there can be a call to action on the pin pad for consumers to enter their mobile phone number and click to opt in. It should be noted that marketers and brands need to follow guidelines for opting in to messaging, whether MMS or SMS. For example, if a customer is waiting in a checkout line and a cashier asks if they want to join the mobile club, the customer agrees, and gives their mobile phone number, that is not sufficient. The customer should be asked to text in, as with the in-store signage previously described, and then sent a message back asking if they are sure they want to opt in for messages from that particular company. Every message should also provide an easy way to opt out, to stop all future messages.

AFTER-THE-SALE SHARING

Immediately after a transaction, the moment when a product is finally bought, marketers have another great mobile influence opportunity. You likely have a happy customer and a short window to turn that customer into a brand advocate. It is the moment that you can decide to let the customer be, having made the sale, and focus more on the next customer acquisition opportunity. However, the Mobile Shopping Life Cycle continues after the point of purchase, providing both a chance to keep that customer satisfied and to recruit that customer to help spread the good word about your product or service.

After the transactions, marketers can drive goodwill to the brand or immediate reaction from their friends. "We always try to give them incentive like 10 percent off on their current purchase, by sharing the offer with one's Facebook or Twitter friends," says Citron, who recommends that his customers take a picture of a product and post it. For example, in one Mogreet campaign with Converse, buyers could text in a picture of their favorite Converse moment and it would show up on the Converse website hosted by Kohl's. Everyone who texted in built goodwill for the brand and it was promoted on every Kohl's store nationwide.

"The progressive marketers realize they are not in the transaction business, they are in the relationship business," says Citron. "These brands have to build a relationship with their customer increasing sales in the short run and building loyalty and relationships to drive long-term sales. An important challenge for many marketers is how to deliver something of such great value that it turns customers into advocates, sharing the great experiences with their friends and driving sales form their current customers' friends and repeat sales from the existing customer."

Mogreet also has a feature called social poster, by which every message that gets sent to every MMS video through its platform (as long as the customer wants it, which Citron says almost everyone does) includes the ability to share that product instantly and directly to Facebook, Twitter, and Google Plus if they so desire. "If the customer is happy with the MMS or if they get something of value worth sharing, like a coupon, viral video, etc., people will share the message. On average, 3 to 10 percent of people will share the content or offer with their social media friends and followers. When consumers do share it, our customers have seen the amplification of their offers reach audiences 10 to 100 times larger than their initial mobile audience. For example, let's say I just bought some surfing gear from Vans, and as a part of buying them, I opted in to receive video messages from Kelly Slater (one of the most popular surfers in the world). If I receive a video from Kelly Slater and it says 'share this with your friends to get 10 percent off your next purchase from Vans,' I would be very inclined to share it and get the coupon back on my phone. By sharing the coupon with my friends on Facebook, I've received my coupon and Vans has grown their mobile audience and reached hundreds of my Facebook friends."

In the case of the Charlotte Russe mystery date campaign, the company saw a 33 percent growth in its mobile database in one weekend and a 300 percent higher participation rate than its past SMS programs. MMS can be used in all areas of the Mobile Shopping Life Cycle and, especially at the end, can be used to bring in more potential customers by sending them messaging that may even move them into the pre-buy stage of the cycle. While apps and sophisticated mobile websites may be a focus of many companies, MMS can be a critical component of mobile influence all the way through the Mobile Shopping Life Cycle.

FOURSQUARE'S POST-PURCHASE KNOWLEDGE MARKETING

In addition to providing an opportunity to leverage the viewpoints of satisfied customers, the post-purchase stage of the Mobile Shopping Life Cycle also provides a chance to aggregate and use data from the consumer's previous activities. By capturing and analyzing a large amount of behavioral activities of mobile consumers, a company can use that data to create offerings that add value to that consumer in the future, in many ways taking the Mobile Shopping Life Cycle full circle. One company based in New York does just that.

When I first profiled Foursquare in my earlier book *The Third Screen*, the popular location-based service was on the fifth floor of a building in Cooper Square in lower Manhattan. In early 2010, the company had leased space from another start-up company and was sharing space with them in the same office. As Foursquare grew, it leased additional space on the third floor, so its employees were scattered between two floors. Then the company raised $20 million from venture capitalists, renovated the entire top floor of the building, and relocated to the new space. The company has now grown to more than 150 employees and has yet again relocated, this time to Broadway in New York. Just as the location and company size of Foursquare evolved over time, so has its business model.

Foursquare started as a check-in service where millions of users would receive credit in one form or another for checking in to locations. Through location tracking in smartphones, the names of nearby locations are presented, the mobile consumer selects where they are, and, with one tap, they check in. Any of the person's selected friends then could see and even be notified by email where they were and vice versa. Within its first 16 months, there were 100 million check-ins on Foursquare, and two months later there were 200 million, highlighting the rapid growth of the location-based service.

Consumers could link their Foursquare accounts to their other social media accounts and share information across platforms. A check-in could be shared over Twitter, for example. One of the drivers of the check-ins was competition, since badges are issued for a number of check-ins and friends can be notified about who is checking in to places more than someone else. The person who checks in at one location more than anyone else is bestowed the title of "mayor," and anyone else checking in to that place can see who is the mayor.

The idea at the time was that local businesses would want to be able to incent potential customers nearby to come to their establishments. They could advertise a special offer, such as a 15 percent discount shown to a Foursquare user when they checked in at a location a short distance away. There were initially several mobile check-in services along with Foursquare, though now it is essentially the last man standing in that arena.

Foursquare learned a lot along the way and captured a substantial number of insights about customer behavior. Over the years since its launch, Foursquare registered more than three billion check-ins. Along with many of those check-ins are recommendations and various comments about the place, left like breadcrumbs along the way for others to see when they check in later.

Foursquare grew to be used by more than 25 million people around the world, with more than a million businesses using its merchant platform to incent mobile users to visit their locations. Foursquare is in the category of company known as pure-play mobile, which means it was created specifically for the mobile world and was not an extension of an on-line or traditional brick-and-mortar business. As one of the captains of mobile influence, Foursquare launched, grew, and closely monitored the behaviors and changing needs of its customers. Over that period, it found innovative ways to use location information to provide new value for its customers. It took a unique approach to the post-purchase stage of the Mobile Shopping Life Cycle by leveraging post-purchase or post-visit information to create future value.

"There has been evolution of the product," says Eric Friedman, director of sales and revenue operations at Foursquare.[3] "You can now use Foursquare to find out the best places and the best things that are going on around you. If you go to Foursquare.com, you are met with an intelligent-looking map and search box and you can just dig right in to all of the data. We look at the evolution of all the check-ins that we are collecting and are still happening, which are what power as the world's best recommendations for places and we have over three billion check-ins. If you think of that as a data set, we can actively use that. You can leverage and draft off of the effort of all the people who came there before you and type in 'coffee,' or 'pizza,' or 'cheeseburger,' and all of that data is what powers those results. So if you think of the idea of local search, previously, when you opened a map and two people could get the same results when you search something. Foursquare now powers a unique set of results tailored to you."

SOCIAL JUSTIFICATION

Foursquare can also be used without checking in. Location-based services such as the Yelp and Poynt apps provide information and reviews of nearby locations you may be considering, such as a restaurant for dinner. Those apps carry reviews from past visitors along with overall ratings based on user votes. The Foursquare approach is to provide more personalized information, such as which of your friends have frequented the establishment along with their comments after their visit, with the system learning as it goes.

"From the very first check-in, we get smarter at what we recommend," says Friedman. "If you check in to a series of places, we will make a better guess at what you are looking for. If you love small coffee shops and you go to a new city and type in 'coffee shop,' guess what we are going to recommend? A small, independent coffee shop. If you are a guy that loves a big coffee house and you go to a different city or country and type in 'coffee,' we are going to give you recommendations based on your history. If we were friends on Foursquare and I was in downtown Boston and I saw Chuck had been to a cheeseburger place five times, that is a great signal for me to go to the same place for lunch because I know Chuck and he knows good cheeseburger places and I like Chuck.

"You can use it without any previous information. The more you use it, the better recommendations we can give and the more friends you have on the system the better the experience as well. We call it *social justification*, because if someone has been somewhere 15 times, and they are a buddy, and you know their taste, that is a great reason why you should go somewhere. We use tips that a person can leave at a place and another person can find a week later or a year later and it is still relevant. A tip is like a 'go here and do this.' It could be at a monument, a restaurant, or a park. It is like a buried treasure you left two years ago. For example, 'Sit at the back corner, the music sounds best from there.' It is something that lives on forever and we use it to make recommendations."

Even though check-ins are no longer its primary focus, Foursquare still records more than five million check-ins a day and has grown around the world. The platform has become big in Russia, Brazil, and elsewhere in South America, is in 12 languages, and exists on every major mobile platform. When a Foursquare user travels to a new place for the first time, they can get trusted recommendations.

In a major redesign in 2012, Foursquare introduce a feature called Explore that highlighted locations based on the user's current location, including nearby specials and places they may not have previously considered. As more people discovered the Explore feature, its usage skyrocketed, enabling the company to build the next steps of communication tools for merchants. Foursquare is a conduit for merchants to reach customers and potential customers, coming up with new ways for offers and deals and their versions of a deal.

"The product we rolled out is called Update," says Friedman. "This is something we got a lot of feedback about from merchants who were interested in talking to their customers. Update is Foursquare's version of a chalkboard that sits outside of a restaurant. We built a digital representation of that and gave business owners the opportunity to advertise on them, write on their digital chalkboard. Something like 'Take a look at these cupcakes that just came out of the oven' or 'Take a look at this juicy T-bone steak that is back on the menu,' or 'Chef Johnson is working this week.' Those types of very timely, very relevant, interesting facts have nothing to do with an offer. Those are things we want people to post. It is just an update. You can imagine walking down the street and seeing a chalkboard. Foursquare allows you to deliver this message without people having to walk by it. It is a digital chalkboard that allows customers to see what is going on in your business when they are far away based on their interests, if they had been there or 'liked' it.

"The people who see this are the people you have checked in multiple times or have 'liked' it. We have so many people using Foursquare, over 25 million, so when you come for the first time you are drafting off of those people. We know places that have closed, places that are busy, and we know places that are great. We introduced rating so that based on 'likes' and check-ins, and a bunch of other features, every place now has a score, and that is a big driver for whether we recommend a place or not. That is a big asset to small businesses. If a place just opens, chances are a Foursquare user will add it. It has become a real asset to small local businesses and big businesses."

As in many mobile businesses, Foursquare has grown primarily by word of mouth. With people continually using the service, the volume of post-purchase data continues to grow. One of the key points of mobile influence in the post-purchase phase of the shopping cycle is to leverage not only the customer, such as by incenting or following social media interactions, but also personal activity and aggregate consumer behavior data. Foursquare has more than 40 million points of interest or locations worldwide and more than a million merchants. Outside its New York base of operations, it also has a London office. In Turkey, one of the largest carriers has Foursquare preloaded into their phones to give its customers the service automatically when they get a phone.

FOOT TRAFFIC ROI

Foursquare is still a city guide, though with the Explore feature it has become more interactive, allowing a consumer to discover a place for the first time without knowing anyone in that city and to take advantage of actions of others that left digital breadcrumbs for followers on Foursquare. As one of the early members of the Foursquare team, Friedman's role at the company evolved along with the company's business model and approach. He recalls:

For the first two years I was at the company, we were building two sides of the marketplace, the consumer side, and the other, the merchant side, which is what I've been focusing on. We went from zero to over a million verified merchants. These are merchants who have access to their dashboard, see all the check-ins, and use the Update feature.

For the first time, we have started Promoted Updates, which is the first Foursquare revenue. Update will show up first in the Explore tab as the first result. It is promoted and they pay for it. We started with a pilot program with a handful of retail partners currently in the U.S. It is three-quarters national companies and major brands and one-quarter small, local companies. Some are Gap, JCPenney, Hilton, and Whole Foods. What they are doing, such as Whole Foods, is using promoted updates and they can have a photo and text that they promote. Unlike a banner ad, these are from an actual place. Let's say Whole Foods is doing a promoted update. You only see it if you are in the Whole Foods area. We think that the check-in is actually a stronger signal than geofencing because you tell us exactly where you are in what location, instead of just being "I'm in New York." It is a very different thing than just saying, "I'm in the neighborhood." We were able to target people based on past behavior, so the things that go into whether a person sees an ad we think is very smart. Has this person been there before, have their friends been there, what time of day is it, is it lunch time or a great time to go shopping?

Foursquare sets up all the targeting, we take out all of the work, so all the advertiser needs to do is give us a photo and text, such as an offer, an event, a new line, or a deal for back to school. An Update does not have to be a discount.

Old Navy can update that it has a new line, they upload a photo and text, and Foursquare decides who sees it, by who has been there or is near one, based on their past check-ins and likes. We charge when someone clicks on the ad, not for who sees it. The impression is free, but when someone clicks on the ad that is an action and we charge the merchant. It is search advertising for the real world. You aren't at your desk or at work or at home, you are out and about on the street with a phone in your hand and someone shows you an ad for something that you like and is near you. If someone searches bicycles, we can show them a shop close to them.

Companies are finding amazing results; they can actually track and prove ROI through a channel that didn't previously have strong ROI. Better than social media. You can push people to a site or social media, but I don't think there is another service that can prove foot traffic coming through the door. When check-in goes up, there is a direct correlation to your advertising versus building a following on social media or building an audience. It is very hard to quantify that audience.

Where we are headed is using some of the deals we already have in place, such as American Express, where if you spend a certain amount you get a certain amount back. An example is Best Buy, who is a pilot partner. They obviously want you to come in and make a purchase, so they made a spend X, get Y promotion. They can push up the average basket size by giving purchase incentive. Whole Foods ran a promotion like this. Dunkin' Donuts ran a spend $10, get $2 promotion. Gets you to spend more and is an important milestone for marketers because they have never been able to track if they put more money into a channel will they get it back. It's how we differentiate ourselves from television, print, coupons, FSI [free-standing inserts], et cetera. Foursquare is about showing actual foot traffic and in some cases sales with credit card purchases.

On the local side, American Express has become a customer so they can promote their offer. American Express can get people to use their card by offering cash back. Come spend $20 and get $5 back. The waiter, the managers, et cetera, they don't have to do anything, people just use their card. No one wants to print something out, unfold it, and hand it to a waiter at dinner, or have someone scan it. You don't have to go through the awkward exchange. It is important as people want lines to move faster and people want things to be more automated. They don't want to print and hand in a coupon. Because this relationship exists with American Express, Foursquare can recognize what stores accept American Express. If a restaurant participates in Restaurant Week, American Express gave users cash back. We can do promotions around the world to restaurants that participate in certain events. Foursquare is a great way to deliver value to both the merchant and customer.

We made a bet that explicit actions are more powerful than implicit, and I think a lot of other companies had location tracking for everywhere when you walk down the street. That's not as interesting as "Hey, I'm around the corner at this restaurant," or "Hey, I'm about to see this movie." So the next time you see me you could ask how I liked the movie, versus this is a loop you went around the park in. We made a software bet on explicit activity and a lot of companies made a hardware bet. You need two pieces of the puzzle or you need to turn it on and have everyone know where you are constantly, and I think that is something that worked out very well with Foursquare.

Implicit is a passive location tracker. If I was using loop you could literally see me walking down the street taking a left-hand turn. I'm in SoHo right now and on my block alone there are probably 15 places, but you have no idea where I actually am. But, if I check into Forever 21 that is a really strong signal versus checking into the Juice Bar, which is right next door. Those are two completely different places.

Friedman's 12-person team works on revenue-driving partnerships by meeting with merchants, a far cry from the early days of Foursquare. "At the beginning we had no idea, and we listened and had merchants come in and did case studies," says Friedman. "We listened and we watched and saw what happen with other companies, like Groupon. We heard that we need to communicate with all customers. The big guys wanted a platform that they could put up against other advertising channels. That is really what we started to do with this pilot program. What we want to do is figure out the best part and put more resources behind it. Listen to the feedback from the partners and then eventually roll this out to a larger set of hosts.

"We now have a full-service team and self-service tools for merchants. Chances are they are already on Foursquare. We now have a fully automated way to claim your business to make sure that the person is the real manager. You can do this on the phone for $1. You can start using Updates within a minute with no cost. We let businesses syndicate Updates to Facebook or Twitter. We are finding that businesses have a bigger audience on Foursquare than data networks. If you have a business and claim it, we have three years' worth of data, so your business could already have thousands of check-ins. You don't start with zero like on Facebook or Twitter. When Best Buy first came in and claimed their business, they already had a built-in audience. We solved the cold start problem. We know that people want to hear from you because they have liked you and checked in."

The specials that merchants can offer to nearby mobile Foursquare users are free and generally offer some kind of incentive to sway a consumer to their location. "The big revenue for Foursquare is on the promoted side," says Friedman. "If you think of search in the real world, that is the perfect analogy. Businesses will pay to reach customers at the highest point of relevance."

By aggregating data from billions of check-ins by many millions of mobile consumers, Foursquare capitalized on the post-purchase phase of the Mobile Shopping Life Cycle and ultimately crafted a new business approach for itself and its growing customer base. While the check-in can be classified as being within the on-location stage of the cycle, Foursquare took the aggregate data and treated it as being in the post-purchase phase.

AFTER-THE-FACT COUPONING

While mobile influence can be exerted well before, up to, and during an actual purchase, it also can be extended to activity after the sale. Coupons traditionally have been clipped in advance of a store visit, or with mobile loaded through an app or mobile website. But in all those cases, the activity occurs before going to the store. With in-store mobile coupons, as with the case of Stop & Shop discussed in an earlier chapter, the activity happens as the consumer moves through the aisle while shopping.

Established offers have included numerous check-in and reward programs, all with various tasks assigned to the customer. Some of the tasks are intuitive, and others require explanations and even help from sales associates at retail.

- Consumers entering stores that use shopkick earn points that can be redeemed at any of the participating stores, like Old Navy, Best Buy, and Macy's. The check-in is somewhat automatic, if the consumer's phone receives the signal sent from the shopkick device at the store. The app provides the following directions: "Open shopkick on your phone, walk into the location and stand inside the entrance and wait for the shopkick signal to find you."
- We Reward allows businesses to set themselves up on its platform and provides cash back to customers who show they visited the store and bought the product. Rewards are issued after a customer proves they were there by taking a photo of themselves enjoying the product and sending it in for verification, done by the business owner.
- ShopSavvy allows consumers to real-time price compare by scanning traditional barcodes on products in stores.

All these approaches have their pluses, with some requiring more consumer effort than others. However, mobile innovators continue to find new ways to cause influence within the Mobile Shopping Life Cycle, even by moving something traditionally done at the pre-buy and point-of-purchase phases into the post-purchase phase of the cycle.

Coupons and offers in the world of mobile continue to find their way looking for the paths of least consumer resistance. In reality, not all shoppers will use their phones to scan products to receive a coupon while they shop. Some may feel too self-conscious about walking around a store pointing their phones at barcodes, while others may either not learn about it or decide that it's not worth their effort. One company devised a novel approach to product identification, product manufacturer offers, and shopper purchase data insights that bypasses both the one-off product scanning and the retailer's POS integration. The system and platform is from Endorse, a well-funded start-up in San Mateo, California, and it is challenging the age-old concept of coupons.

A consumer downloads the free Android or iOS mobile app and receives ten instant offers, ranging from 10 percent to 100 percent cash back for recognizable brands from top CPG companies, including Kraft, Mondelez, General Mills, and PepsiCo. For example, if there is an offer for a particular frozen pizza and you buy it, there is no need to scan the actual product, print anything, or associate a coupon with it. Rather than scanning the products, when you get home you take a picture of the receipt, which is then uploaded to the Endorse system. That's all the system needs. After an hour or so, the reward is posted in the app. The rewards are in cash, which can be sent by check or via PayPal.

From the consumer standpoint, there is no product scanning and no coupon tracking. "The more receipts someone has in their account, the more personalized and targeted the offers become," says Steven Carpenter, Endorse's founder and CEO.[4] "We already personalize offers, meaning that if you and I download the app on the same day, we each will see different offers, and they refresh regularly." There are many variables used to determine which users receive which offers. "Our ad server is flexible so we can segment by whatever our brand partners wish, by geography, demographic information, retailers, basket size, products purchased, category spend, purchase frequency, brand loyalty, light brand buyer, coupon user, just to name a few," says Carpenter.

BYPASSING RETAILERS

As a consumer shops and uploads more receipts, the Endorse system *learns* what offers should be sent to which consumers, which could benefit both the consumer and the brand, since more relevant offers are sent. "Brand marketers need a more efficient, higher ROI channel than what exists today," says Carpenter. "Blindly blanketing coupons to 70 million households and praying for a specific redemption rate is arcane thinking. With this approach, brands can set a specific offer budget and we manage to that, rather than the other way around."

Endorse's technology platform recognizes the individual products based on the sales receipt. For example, if a consumer has an offer for, say, Cheerios on their phone and they purchase Cheerios and scan the receipt, the system automatically detects they bought Cheerios and that it was one of the offers on the user's phone. If a person uses a traditional coupon at checkout, they still only have to take a photo of the sales receipt.

By working directly with brands, most notably consumer packaged goods, Endorse essentially bypasses the retailer as well as the point-of-sale system. From the consumer standpoint, the entire process can occur post-purchase, and they have several days after the purchase to scan the receipt. "We're the next-generation offers platform for brands in the online world," says Carpenter. "We provide the direct connection between consumer brands and the people that buy their products. And we do it in any store. That is really the key. We have decoupled the traditional promotional offers from the point of sales infrastructure. And when you do that, all kinds of new offer types are suddenly available and the data insights become incredibly rich and actionable. Our brands are enthusiastic about it, and we can work with certain retailers. Our offers don't require any type of integration with the current and traditional coupon or loyalty card systems or anything involving retailer coordination."

Shopkick, discussed earlier, also has somewhat of a post-purchase component in that points gathered while in a store are accumulated for later use. "The difference between shopkick and our approach is that shopkick made location and checking in at a retailer their monetizable unit, their partner is the retailer" says Carpenter. "We have gone directly to the brand manufacturers to help them be successful in this new mobile environment and haven't spent a lot of time thinking about the specific interests of what retailers are trying to do."

The Endorse platform also has a post-purchase social media component. For example, when you install the app and connect with Facebook you see various product offers that can be increased by sharing a deal you got on Facebook, some up to 100 percent cash back. By sharing the post, you receive a half-price rebate on the product, what the company calls a "social offer." Endorse partnered with PayPal, so you can sit on your couch and transfer your Endorse balance to your PayPal account. In one promotion, Mountain Dew posted an Endorse offer to its Facebook page, with nearly eight million "likes," and ran an offer for 50 percent off on two-liter bottles through Endorse. When someone "claimed" the offer on Facebook, it automatically was added to the user's Endorse app. In one week, Mountain Dew reached almost two million people, saw 35 thousand new actions and, for the first time, was in a position to being to make some connection between people that followed the brand and whether they buy the product in stores.

Endorse developed technology to analyze store receipts, to decipher what a person bought, and to provide analysis in as real-time as possible. "We are able to make sense of all the receipts and everything that is on there," says Carpenter. "We are able to extract all the relevant pieces of information and then analyze and crunch it. We've built a national loyalty card infrastructure coupled with old-school post-purchase analysis that looks across retailers. We are able to do that on an actionable, consistent basis so that you are not just looking at individual snapshots of somebody's purchase behavior, you can have an ongoing relationship over time so that you can learn which offers are best for the right customers, which segmentation is best, the replenishment cycle with certain customers over others, and what it means to trial certain products based on consumption. You can do all those things in a very actionable way."

The objective in the new post-purchase approach is to influence behavior. "We want to be able to drive purchase behavior," says Carpenter. "Most importantly, we want to drive that connection. What is cool about mobile is that it is the best thing that has ever happened to brands. They now have a direct way to connect with the people who want to buy their products. Brands do not need to be held hostage by the retailers anymore. What we have done is taken every step along the current offers and promotions value chain and we've made each of them better for shoppers and brands alike. In terms of offer creation, we can do that in a day because you don't have to do any upfront planning and/or printing and distribution. We don't care about redemption rates because the brand can just give us a budget and we manage towards the budget. So we don't have to worry about overages or even fraud because you can't take our offer and duplicate it and send it out to millions of people and fraud the system. And because there is nothing to present at retail, we have all the data on the redemption loop and we're all able to provide all of the traditional analytics to our brand partners who meet offer spend thresholds for free. It is part of them being in the system."

The company focuses on everyday items such as grocery, coffee, fast food, gas, and clothing but can easily expand to other categories as well as to international markets. The system also can be used to drive consumers to specific retailers by providing special brand offers at their locations. The app works with Android and iPhone and the receipt uploads go directly to Endorse rather than being stored in the phone's photo library. Endorse says once people start using the system, they typically upload multiple receipts a week.

This post-purchase approach challenges businesses built on the traditional, existing infrastructure. "They either have to figure out how to get on mobile very quickly or figure out a way how to get off the reliance on the point-of-sales purchase," says Carpenter. The other key piece of information Endorse can ultimately provide brands is knowing, for example, that people who shop at Target also go to Walmart and to five other stores. "We get a complete share of wallet and a complete picture to create better incentives for shoppers," says Carpenter.

The uniqueness in the approach is that the process itself occurs pre- and post-POS with only one step involved, taking a photo of the sales receipt, which can be done once the shopper gets back home. Ironically, this new couponing brings the process full circle back to the home where the consumer used to clip coupons before going to the store. Now they can just take a picture of a receipt and the coupons clip themselves and are retroactively and automatically applied to what was already bought.

EVERYWHERE MARKETING

Part of the challenge for an automaker in the Mobile Shopping Life Cycle is being front of mind at the right time, when someone meanders into the market to buy a new car. Typically not an impulse purchase, car buying is affected by mobile in various stages of the cycle, all the way from the pre-buy through in-transit, on-location at car dealers, during the selection process, at the point of purchase at the car dealership, and most notably after the sale and delivery of a vehicle. Toyota, for example, recognizes the role of mobile throughout the process.

"What part of the shopping process isn't being impacted by mobile?" says Kimberley Gardiner, national digital marketing and social media manager, Toyota Motor Sales USA.[5] "We see it throughout when people have the initial inspiration around a vehicle, when they're refining their decision and looking at what's the right car for me."

Shopping for a car can be complex. Mobile consumers tend to access information all the time and while in motion, and looking at a car purchase is no exception. "The dynamics of where people are seeking information and how they shop are changing and it will be in the next few years that things can happen at any given moment," says Gardiner. Toyota anticipates the role of mobile in the car selection and ownership process and looks to it to help extend the brand relationship post-purchase.

Toyota plans its marketing and advertising strategy to be in front of the potential customer at all the influence points. "You never know where influence will happen," says Gardiner. "You want to be there whenever that is. They're one moment away from 'How does that work? How can I get one? How much can I afford?' The exciting part for us is that we have to be in a thousand different places. The hard part is that we have to be in a thousand different places. But mobile is a great tool to help people get from one stage to the next."

THE CAR, POST-PURCHASE

Buyers of expensive products, such as cars or major appliances, tend to spend more time in various stages of the Mobile Shopping Life Cycle. They may linger in the pre-buy phase as they continue to research and price compare. They likely will be on location more than once and spend time at the selection process phase. Until the purchase, there are many potential influence points for marketers to reach the potential buyer. However, after the purchase, the buyer can play a significant role in influencing others in a positive or negative way.

Buyers in the post-purchase phase of the Mobile Shopping Life Cycle become a main source of those in the pre-buy phase, taking the Mobile Shopping Life Cycle full circle. Markets that disconnect from customers after the point of purchase not only risk a negative impact on those at the pre-buy phase, they also miss a significant opportunity to tap into all the goodwill built up during all the other phases of the cycle. Toyota recognizes the importance of mobile in the life of the car buyer and knows it needs to be involved in all phases of the shopping cycle. Says Gardiner:

> One of the things we're looking at with an owner focused application is, how can we lay out the entire life cycle of somebody owning a vehicle? From the moment that they buy the vehicle, they drive it home, they want to understand how the different features and functions on their car work, they want things like how-to guides and helpful tips to make the most of their ownership experience.
>
> We want to be there for them whenever that moment comes up. So we're looking at places in the application where people can look something up, they can take a picture of a dashboard icon and find out what feature or function it relates to. In the past you'd have to look it up in the owner's manual in the glove box.
>
> I think that's ultimately what owners want. Map it all out for me, make it really easy. Finding information about your Toyota should just be really easy and intuitive. Much like Apple has done with their products. You don't need to have an owner's manual like you had in the past. They make it so easy you open up a few pages, you're done. And it's so intuitive that you don't have to go back and reference something. Ownership of a car should be that easy.
>
> It's all about keeping up with technology, keeping up with consumer insights, and ultimately finding some inspiration from a place that is radically different. Otherwise you won't stay two or three steps ahead and create ground-breaking digital experiences for your customers.

Whether using MMS to stay in touch with customers after the sale or to fa-cilitate the sharing of happy experience or using after-the-fact couponing, marketers need to stay in touch with the customer at the post-purchase phase of the Mobile Shopping Life Cycle. While it looks like the last step in the cycle, it can actually become the first step again for that customer as well as the first stage for a potential customer who received shared, post-purchase insights from a friend. Companies that succeed in the mobile revolution at retail will participate in many, if not all, phases of the Mobile Shopping Life Cycle, as we discuss next.

eight

MARKETING THROUGHOUT THE MOBILE SHOPPING LIFE CYCLE

PROVIDING CUSTOMER VALUE ALL ALONG THE WAY

The impact of mobile on retailing extends well beyond the in-store experience, as you have seen throughout this book. Mobile takes shopping past the boundaries of the brick-and-mortar location, and businesses that focus too much on the in-store mobile actions may be too late, both in time and location. Conversely, companies that focus too much on the earlier stages of the Mobile Shopping Life Cycle can see all that effort wasted if they allow competitors to exert mobile influence on that customer at later stages of the cycle. Success depends on activity at multiple influence points. The mobile shopper traverses in and out of all the phases during the new mobile path to purchase, and the opportunity for influence and decision change exists at each stage of the cycle.

Both seekers and cruisers can be reached at multiple stages and multiple times throughout the Mobile Shopping Life Cycle. Precise targeting to mobile consumers whether at home, in transit, or on location is getting more sophisticated. More relevant messages can be crafted and sent to mobile shoppers based on numerous factors such as location, time of day, and past behavior. Companies will be more tightly linking their rewards programs to mobile activities in the marketplace. Mobile customers will expect to receive value when they want it based on what they are doing at the time. This may mean helpful information, assistance with a purchase, or special offers.

Once consumers start using smartphones and tablets during more stages of the Mobile Shopping Life Cycle, they do not go back. They become continuous shoppers. On the other side of the equation, this transforms retailers into continuous sellers. This means that both buyers and sellers will be continually active and interactive in all stages of the shopping process. Mobile consumers will come to expect more from the people from whom they buy. One major retailer has been focused on ways to use mobile and tablet functionality to bring more value to its shoppers, both in and out of store.

STAPLES MOBILE ON MAKING SHOPPING EASIER

Part of the challenge many companies adapting to the Mobile Shopping Life Cycle find is not why to start but rather where to start and how to start, as well as defining which areas of the value chain can and will be most impacted, how to integrate with various channels, how to tie to online, and what to test. Perhaps the most important consideration, though, is determining the most effective way to provide customers value through mobile and what it is their customers will want and likely expect or demand in the future.

Staples is the world's largest office products company, with annual sales of $25 billion. With 88,000 employees, the retailer has operations in 26 countries throughout North and South America, Europe, Asia, and Australia. Staples was founded in 1986 and ranks second in the world in e-commerce sales. For Staples, whether or not to incorporate mobile was not an option, it was an obvious imperative. Staples is another captain of mobile influence company.

"Initially, when we first started exploring the mobile space we found some very simple assets to market very inexpensively and very quickly," says Brian Tilzer, senior vice president of global e-commerce at Staples.[1] "We created a very simple mobile website and a very simple app. We got to the market quickly, which is probably more important than inexpensively, just so we could start understanding what this thing meant. At that time, we did not know who downloaded the app and what it would be used for versus the site. That's how we started, and that step gave us some real foundational insight. Insight number one was that yes, small businesspeople do use mobile devices. It isn't only a consumer thing. We saw consistent growth in usage among our core customer segment."

Getting to market with mobile quickly enables a company to see what works and what doesn't. Companies of all sizes should take a *test-and-learn* approach, since smartphone and tablet usage patterns are still evolving and growing, especially as more consumers utilize more of the devices' capabilities. Mobile shoppers will try new things. It is after a company launches mobile initiatives that it starts to learn more about mobile shopping behaviors, which are difficult to predict without real market situations. Staples found it could learn more by being early and active in mobile.

"Another insight was that this was an opportunity that is not about purchasing online," says Tilzer, who has worked at Staples since 2007. "What it is about is enabling customers to make easier, more informed, powered decisions before purchasing in store, in some cases before they get to the store, and in other cases when they are standing in the store. Everything we have done has really been about that on-the-go and in-the-store usage as opposed to just buying stuff online. Our ambition with mobile is to be a leader for our customer, and we're always looking for better ways to do this. We're big believers in testing, learning, and being really nimble. The future hasn't really happened and the story hasn't played out.

"In a space like this, very dynamic, we don't know how it's going to play out, so what do you do? Do we write a three-year strategic plan or do we actually dip our toe in the water and get some customer feedback? We took a real onwards experimentation approach, especially initially. A lot of it was written out, but we didn't really know what mobile was going to mean to our customers. At the time, there was a portion of our group that thought we serve small businesses and mobile is just for consumers, it's like kids on cell phones, and that was years ago."

Staples found early on that mobile was going to provide additional ways for its customers to shop by using many different features of mobile.

It also had a substantial amount of knowledge from its years of online selling. "There was an overwhelming usage of find a store, look up a deal, and usage of rating and reviews were off the chart," says Tilzer. "I view myself in the website responsibilities as responding to corporate assets. We've long believed that customers go online to buy, but sometimes they are researching to go in store. I think we were the first retailer that invested in integrating the in-store kiosk to the POS system, because we realized there was that linkage."

Once customers began using the Staples app and mobile website, the company could easily determine usage patterns, which helped them better target what features to add and modify. They also learned what types of customers gravitated toward mobile. Says Tilzer:

> It was more about the decisions we made and the functionality we oriented around. If you look at everything we have done with our mobile website and our app, it has all been about eliminating pain points in shopping. Everything we have done falls under that category very, very simply.
>
> This multichannel, on-the-go, and solving the major pain points was the second insight. I think the third insight was specifically around the app. What we saw was, the customers that actually downloaded the app and used it are our brand loyalist. Some people thought you could acquire new customers with some cool app, you can attract the younger crowd or whatnot. And that's not what we saw. What we saw was the person that was most apt to go and download the app and use it were brand loyalists who love Staples and were looking to engage us in a different method.
>
> We think of it as our loyal small business customer. That is who we really designed this around. If you look at the app, this really informed the design of the app where we can really harness this, the app is all powered by our loyalty data. It's powered by what we know about the customers and all that information. It is making being a best customer easier. So if you think about things like how we used to mail you a check and say, "Here are your rewards dollars." And you know what game we were playing, we were hoping you forgot it, our

accounts loved it. It's called breakage. Woohoo, we saved 36 cents! But did we get more customer loyalty out of it? No, probably not.

Using that history to solve things like you're standing in the store and you need a toner cartridge for your printer but you can't remember what your printer is. Customers have been saying this for years. They don't know what their toner cartridge is. They had to drive back to their office and get it and then they wasted an hour of their day. Well, using your loyalty information, because we know our best customers who downloaded, we have all that information at your disposal. A couple clicks away, you can pull that up easily and it is in your hands. Initially, that is where we started.

We got these basic insights around our smartphone assets, which then informed us of two things. One is how we approach making those better. We designed our mobile site and app around solving these pain points for small business customers on the go or on the road, really making the app about loyalists.

MOVING MOBILE FASTER

Headquartered in Framingham, Massachusetts, about 20 miles west of Boston, Staples wanted to increase its process of digital innovation, so in mid-2012 it opened an e-commerce innovation center called the Staples Velocity Lab in Cambridge, Massachusetts. The company then added IT, product management, usability, and creativity positions at the center to further its work on multichannel customer experiences across mobile devices. The intent was to leverage the location in Cambridge as a magnet to attract talent from the world-class universities and technology companies in the general area. The goal of the center is to rapidly bring breakthrough new ideas to market in emerging online technologies of mobile commerce and social media.

Located in a large office complex in Kendall Square, the center has open spaces with a long row of side-by-side work areas so that employees from Framingham could drop in for a remote workday or two to link the innovations being created at the center with the everyday work of running the global retailing business in Framingham. The innovation center is headed by Prat Vemana, director of Velocity Lab and mobile strategy at Staples.

"Our mission for the center is to deliver growth through multichannel ecommerce innovation," says Vemana.[2] "That's what this center is about." Vemana has responsibility to develop mobile experiences for Staples worldwide that includes smartphone and tablets via mobile Web and apps. "What we are trying to do is take, in some respects, the more you can get that is in the app into the mobile site the better, because you don't have the barrier of customers having to download the app," he says. "There is a natural linkage between the two, and then we have the additional challenge of scaling these assets globally and across our different geographies. We are still learning in that space. We do see more people access mobile Web, and people who access the app use are more and more repeated uses. So there are different patterns on how much cross-pollination is still a learning."

In addition to its mobile operations, Staples has had a substantial online business for many years. However, the behaviors via mobile are not the same as online behaviors. Says Tilzer:

People think Staples is the huge store on the corner. We're actually more of an online company. We are 60 percent delivery products versus 40 percent retail globally. We're in 26 countries and we're the second-largest retailer in North America, and then we're in another 24 countries.

The piece of Staples you are probably most familiar with is B2C business, so Staples.com and the retail stores. We think of it really as B2B, small businesses. Then we also have our B-to-big-B-business area that we call "Staples Advantage." Like in extreme cases if Bank of America wants our office supplies, we have a website where admins can order it.

The 60 percent delivered is approaching all online. There are still a few percentages that are still in the call centers. In that portion [of the 60 percent] is mobile.

From a phone, the story is more about doing research before going into the store, although we have some purchases online. The other interesting thing that is coming on this journey is tablet sites as another component to mobile. Tablet is another real order device. At one extreme, desktop is where you are doing proportionally more buying than just researching before you go in the store. Mobile device is the flip of that. Tablets are somewhere in between. We are in the journey of learning. Part of our learning is from our initial assets as we went off and decided to put major bets on our smartphone website and our app. At the same time this initial learning gave us confidence to continue the R&D journey.

Two R&D bets that we made were around the tablet site. That is a different user experience optimized around that. The other bet we made is around putting that device in the hands of our associates. So we have that in five of our stores and we're testing it. That's one example, but this is literally empowering our associates by giving them an app built just for associates that are on tablets.

They can access customer information to help them answer a question like with the toner cartridge. Another big application is that we have much larger assortment breadth online, so it is a tool. These are scrappy test and learn and we're trying to figure out how to make these really relevant to our business.

Proportionally, tablets are doing more transacting than smartphones, significantly so. Tablets are a smaller channel in terms of traffic, since there are a lot less of them. But proportionally it's a bigger buying story, although there is still an element of research that is stronger in that media. If you start thinking about smaller tablet devices that are more portable the story has not played out yet. I think we are pretty clear that purchasing on the device is going to be more important than on the smartphone. What we can say is this device's experience is really about enabling customers to have a great in-store experience.

TABLET TRANSACTIONS

Over time, Staples found that sales on tablets were two times more than those on smartphones. The number of tablet visits to Staples grew ten times and sales from the device grew five times. The retailer also discovered there were ten times more sales in store with the app coupon than with just the app alone. Vemana sees higher expectations of mobile shoppers:

> If you look at the store experience when you walk in as a customer the fact tag with five bullets is no longer enough for me. You need that social profiling. "My cousin has the same chair" doesn't cut it anymore. Customer behavior has molded so much that they are expecting the store to be digitally lit up. As you probably saw in Staples, we now also sell more complete tech solutions. You can buy a cloud software and backup solution when you are buying the laptop, so our store associates create the right package options for our customers. Tablet is a better vehicle to bring content and tools that are much more sharable without overriding personal space and actually provide more choices and information to the customer at that moment so they can make the right decisions. Going with the philosophy of test and learn, we are in a few stores with proof of concepts.
>
> We are learning what is working both from an associate's perspective and a customer perspective. Are the customers bettering from the information in their hands at the moment in the store? And also, what information is more powerful? For example, the tablet application that is actually deployed in some of our stores allows you to quickly provide all the categories of products that you look at. Maybe you can find the products and compare side by side and make the right decision, build the right solution, and see that the baskets that you really want, several tools, memory finder, ink, and toner finder. The thing about ink is you want to remember the printer that you bought so you can easily pick up the cartridge right there. If you are our Staples rewards customer and you don't have the printer details with you at the moment, we can actually go look up and see what your rewards history is and find the printer or cartridge from the history. By putting this power in the store in the associate's hand, now we are putting that same power that we enable the customers with, with the associates.
>
> The different angles we are trying to measure from are which areas of the product content are more useful? Where they are spending

more time and how they are learning. How is it influencing the decision? From that perspective it's not just the metrics, there is also store walkthroughs. We are big believers in usability and user testing.

Our folks are actually walking through the stores and observing the engagement. What does the dialogue look like? Are we being helpful or are we distracting? In the sales process, how engaged in the conversation with the customer, if I stumble around and lose more than two seconds, the customer will lose the confidence. The information content both from [the] customer perspective, product perspective shares the same platform. So it's basically the same information as we have on the desktop site. What is different is the experience of how you actually provide the information. For example, this one is built in a way that you don't have to take your eyes off for more than a few seconds. So the associate can quickly navigate and help you right there. But the information content is laid out from the same source.

INCREASING CUSTOMER INTERACTIONS

The captains of influence companies generally work with some of the facilitators of mobile influence, depending on the particular need. And like many other companies that experienced explosive growth during the early internet years, much of the knowledge and experience from those times carried forward to mobile. Says Tilzer:

One of the things that our company really rallies around is the notion that more engaged associates will mean better customer experience. So another area of aspiration is to say is associates go through the natural learning curve that happens with any tool. In the end, we have more confident, more engaged associates who can deliver a more engaged/better experience to our customer. We also have integrated other applications within the website.

I would say one of the secret sauces we're finding around mobile is really having the right expertise around user experience. If you think about how we have staffed our teams and what we are choosing to outsource versus insource, and having the best usability and expertise.

We have a usability team in house that is part of reports in my organization and we have members of the team now down here (in the innovation center). So that's a core piece of that. To keep that team sharp we also invest strategically in bringing out outside expertise where they are learning and participating. Having the asset in house, yes, but we do use outside as well.

That is what we are accomplishing in this facility. Back in Framingham we had people sitting in different areas. Here we are going to have it embedded in one team. Technical, creative, usability, and business people.

Staples has been through this journey a little bit before. Back in the go-go years of the Internet, Staples as a company set up a tracking stock and had visions of spitting out the dot-com business separately. At the time, the dot-com business was like the chosen one and got extra stock grants and free food, but they were in the same building as people who were not getting free food, so you had people like stealing the free food. When we set the vision for this it was not just innovation with what we deliver but innovation with how we work. Prat's mandate is to take those innovations and leave one person on the team who works on this explicitly, takes innovations and codifies them and brings them back to the mother ship.

We've sent out the official, internal communications about the people moving down here and one of the things I was very clear to say in that is our mission is the whole team, not just the people down here, is bolder and more aggressive in innovation. This is just one of the assets we have along those dimensions.

MOBILE ACROSS CHANNELS

No one really knows for sure how smartphone usage will evolve at retail and whether it will depend on the type or category of business, including Staples. "I actually have a theory, but I don't have any proof, it is just a theory," says Tilzer. "At some point there will be a tipping point where this actually becomes a buying device again. Particularly for a lot of stuff that we sell, which are replenishable goods. The more that we can leverage information we have about the customer, the more we can present it in a way that we're reading their mind of what they need, the more potential I think we'll have. At some point they'll say, 'Why can't I order on this thing?' 'Why do I have to go into the store or travel over to my desktop?' I think we will be able to get that much more precise in what we present to make it more frictionless. In just three years of using these devices I think it will become a natural. That's a theory I have. Right now it is a researching tool."

Retailers with both physical and online stores face the problem of how to integrate all their customers' evolving behaviors as they become mobile and move throughout the Mobile Shopping Life Cycle. For a host of reasons, it took years for many retailers to integrate online and in-store so that a consumer could simply buy online and pick up the item at the store. Staples considers the implications across its various channels. Says Tilzer:

> We have seen this natural drumbeat over the years of people becoming more and more cross channel. More and more retail customers purchasing something online. That doesn't mean retail business goes away, but proportionally moving that way. I don't know why that would happen. I guess the question is whether or not there will be segmentation by shopping occasion.
>
> If you think about Staples, our business is fundamentally three types of purchases. One is consumable, repeat purchases like stocking up on office supplies. And that has very simplified research needs you could imagine purchasing on this device over time. We have another group of products that are a more considered group of products, like a computer, as an example. You want to see it, you want to touch it, you want to feel it. I think the role of this device in enabling better decision making, but probably still in a lot of cases part of the physical product category is going to continue. The third one I'm not sure of how it is going to play, and broadly speaking, I think it is in the services category. We're selling more copy and print services every day. It's actually a great business for Staples, generally. We're seeing both

channels grow. But we are seeing it growing proportionally faster online. I don't know how that research process evolves into what extent. I would say there is more segmentation around what people are shopping for. The same person can go into different modes based upon that list.

We have a single view of the customers across channels for years. Staples has a key asset. We have two mechanisms. We have what customers have done and what they tell us they have done. We do regular research around what they tell us they have done. In terms of what we know they are doing, it's all from our assets. We track price matching. I don't know if we have actually chosen to track price matching with a mobile device versus price matching with a printout online.

We just don't know the link that is "Oh, it's because they scanned." I still think there is a lot of value people get from the instant gratification. We've gotten the question that is how much do we worry about that kind of behavior? We worry about a lot of things. What this puts emphasis on to me is that we need to continue to improve our mouse trap every day. Fundamentally, we can offer the easiest office supply buying wherever and every day someone makes the other price-driven stuff easier. The good news is that small business customers are very busy people, so if we can continue to find ways to save them time I think we have a good weapon against other stores.

We have had our kiosk in the store for a generation now. That business has been growing fairly consistently. Traffic on the mobile website is many multiples larger than our app. By definition, I think a lot is going to happen there, but we're not sure. I think there is something to be said for mobile website because people are smart enough to get that a smartphone is just like a different type of computer. I think the basic behavior of going onto a browser and entering Staples.com is very natural and very transferable for people. We know a large percentage of our emails are opened on a mobile device and that takes them to a mobile website.

That was the other learning I think as we went off those basic assets, was how important from a core marketing perspective being currently vulnerable. If you think of how much time we spend as a retailer manicuring those emails and getting the message perfect and the creative purpose, with this device you can blow that out of the water in a fraction of a second.

Our orientation towards SMBs [small and medium businesses] and towards solving pain points in ways that are really valuable to them was our big focus. Pushing coupons to them is more about what we want to do as opposed to what our customers want from us. Research from SMBs and SMS is like private space, not that there isn't a segment we could try and go after. We haven't gone there yet.

Staples observed that customer smartphone visits grew by four times, with a third of all emails being opened on a mobile device. It has no doubts about the direction its customers are heading, and through initiatives like its Velocity Lab and its focus on the future, Staples plans to move along with them.

MOBILE AND CORPORATE CULTURE

In addition to adopting and adapting to new technologies like mobile, many businesses also have to deal with new ways of doing things and integrate them with the particular company culture. This is part of the reason some companies are aggressive and become captains of mobile influence and others tread so cautiously that they risk the explosive mobile shopping market passing them by.

"Staples as a company has been very good at saying if you focus on doing the right thing for the customer good things will happen to you financially," says Tilzer. "I think we try to do that as much as we can with our online assets and online business. I think that has really been the orientation of this. Staples is a company that responds to facts and thoughtful reasoning. Once we see that wind up and it's really getting the right people like any company behind it, then you can get behind things."

Already familiar with the tremendous impact the internet had on its business, Staples could easily see which way the wind was blowing with mobile. "There is this chart that we made early on in the journey which shows the adoption rate of mobile devices relative to original Internet technology," says Tilzer. "In Staples language, where 60 percent of our business is online, we understand how transformational the internet was for our business. I think to make the jump to a new technology that is being adopted faster than that thing that really transformed our business, you know what we better figure this out.

"I was just talking with our CEO about are we doing enough with mobile, what else should we do, and how can we be bolder with the R&D and the learning agenda idea. If you asked our CEO what he'd love to see coming out of this center is a lot of things, but mobile and innovation is the thing on the top of the list. I presented the mobile strategy work we were doing to the board and that was my joke initially. I said I bet you are on other boards that say you have to have an app, and my perspective is you have to have an app, but mobile is bigger than that and there is this thing called a mobile website that might actually be more important."

Captains of mobile influence like Staples understand the integration of mobile with their online and brick-and-mortar actions. They also tend to be involved in most if not all phases of the Mobile Shopping Life Cycle. And like Staples, many are closely monitoring mobile shopping behavior with an eye toward both the short and the long term. Much of the focus on whatever is done with mobile at retail is the satisfaction level of mobile shoppers with the shopping process.

ON MOBILE SHOPPING SATISFACTION

As customers move through the Mobile Shopping Life Cycle, the goal should be not so much selling as satisfying the needs of the mobile shopper, in which there are many opportunities. Consumer expectations are evolving as they move from online buying to buying while mobile, giving rise to obvious comparisons among the different buying experiences. ForeSee, a customer experience analytics firm, created a scientific benchmark of the user experience on the mobile platform. In its Mobile Satisfaction Index, Retail Edition, ForeSee conducted an in-depth study of how customers rate their mobile experiences.[3]

With mobile, it is very easy for an unsatisfied customer to switch. It might be caused by a negative experience with the mobile website of a brand that did not invest enough resources to ensure an optimal mobile Web experience. It could be a poorly designed mobile app or even a lack of product insight on the mobile site. In its analysis, ForeSee examined 20 major retailers through the lens of customer satisfaction.

Overall satisfaction with the mobile experiences of the measured retailers was high, though the retailers measured are some of the most widely used retail mobile sites and apps. In its process, a score of 80 is the benchmark for excellence in customer satisfaction, which almost half (45 percent) of the measure mobile experiences scored at or above (see Table 8.1).

The study points out that just because the lowest score is a 76 does not mean companies that score below 80 are necessarily doing a bad job. "It's quite the contrary; 76 is a very good score for a mobile experience but there's always room for improvement," the report states.[4] The study also found that first-time users of a company's mobile website or app tend to be less satisfied with their mobile experiences because they are

table 8.1

MOBILE SATISFACTION INDEX*

Amazon	84
Avon	83
Apple	82
Victoria's Secret	81
Barnes & Noble	80
eBay	80
Netflix	80
Staples	80
Walgreens	80
Best Buy	79
Groupon	79
JCPenney	79
Dell	78
Home Depot	78
Living Social	78
Macy's	78
Walmart	78
Sears	77
Target	77
Toys "R" Us	76

*Based on "ForeSee Mobile Satisfaction Index: Retail Edition," based on 4,500 customer surveys.

less familiar with the layout, navigation, and functionality of an application or site. About a third (35 percent) of first-time visitors were less satisfied with their mobile experience than the 65 percent who were repeat visitors.

The more brands engage customers within the Mobile Shopping Life Cycle, the more likely they are to have success through the entire buying and selling process. The ForeSee study also found that visitors who were influenced to engage in a company's mobile experience due to a prior experience with the company ended up more satisfied than others. Familiarity with a brand goes a long way in the mobile world. Almost 40 percent of those engaged in a mobile experience because they already were familiar with the brand, company, or site. ForeSee also found:

- Customers already familiar with the brand who received promo emails or mobile text alerts from the company were highly satisfied with their mobile experience.
- People driven to the company's mobile site or app via search engines or shopping comparison sites were less satisfied.
- Word-of-mouth referrals resulted in well-matched users with high satisfaction.

Somewhat like when they use the Web, when consumers visit mobile sites and apps they have a wide variety of tasks they perform. In the study focused on retail, the most popular activities found were looking up product details (28 percent), looking up price information (19 percent), and finding whether a product was in stock (17 percent). Visitors whose main purpose was to purchase were the most satisfied, and those looking for price, delivery, or shipping information were less satisfied. Of those who purchase using a mobile device, their mobile satisfaction score was 86, well above the benchmark for excellence.

With the stages of the Mobile Shopping Life Cycle, brands and retailers need to be in all places all the time. This means mobile apps for the larger brands, most of which already have them (some with a larger number of apps than others). It also means creating and maintaining robust and well-thought-out mobile websites, since not all smartphone shoppers download apps from all companies. Many who move to smartphones tend to use them in much the same way they use computers: to find things near them and to search the Web. Among mobile Web users in the ForeSee study, 68 percent use the retailer's website from their mobile device, while about a third (32 percent) most recently used the retailer's app. The app users were very slightly more satisfied than those who used the mobile websites. The highest app usage in the retailer study was for Netflix (59 percent), eBay (53 percent), Groupon (52 percent), and Walgreens (48 percent).

Savvy marketers and advertising agencies monitor where their shoppers come from digitally, whether from the traditional website, smartphones, or tablets. They also need to watch for where the shoppers are physically, since in the Mobile Shopping Life Cycle they can be anywhere. They may be a seeker, conducting research or even planning to buy from a tablet in their living room, or they could be a cruiser, on the go and traveling near the retailer's location. Three out of five (59 percent) of all users in the study most recently accessed the measured retailers' mobile sites and apps from home. More than two-thirds (68 percent) of Apple and Barnes & Noble visitors accessed their mobile sites or apps most recently from home. Meanwhile, visitors to Walgreens (27 percent), Target (25 percent), and Sears (24 percent) were more likely than others to access the retailers' sites or apps from anywhere in preparation to go to a store location. Sixteen percent of all users said they were planning to go to a store from anywhere during their most recent mobile visit or use.

REMOTE SHOWROOMING

Many retailers that focus on dealing with showrooming, discussed in an earlier chapter, tend to view it as an in-store-only phenomenon. A key finding in the ForeSee study is that a large percentage of the mobile usage related to retail is being done at home while preparing to visit a store. This is precisely the pre-buy phase of mobile influence. This means that the actual showrooming may not be as significant in scope at the physical store, since the activity of shopping via mobile is not location-dependent. It can be done anywhere. "Showrooming is happening, but it's not happening at breakneck speed," says Larry Freed, president and CEO of ForeSee.[5]

"Retailers need to be aware of it but realize it's just another method of competiveness," he said.

At the start of the Mobile Shopping Life Cycle, well-known brands have an advantage. Any earned loyalty may transfer to the mobile environment, at least at the start. The study found that the top influence for someone to visit the mobile site or use the app is familiarity with the brand, with the least influence being a search engine. So at least if the mobile shopper knows you from the non-mobile world, you have an edge going in. The challenge and opportunity for marketers is to create mobile influence by satisfying the customers as they move to mobile.

MULTIPLE CUSTOMER TOUCH POINTS

Many of the captains of mobile influence participate in many if not all stages of the Mobile Shopping Life Cycle, as you likely noticed throughout this book. Some companies, like Rue La La, have the opportunity to move a consumer from one stage, the pre-buy, directly to the transaction, the point of purchase. Other companies, like Guess, look to link all their channels together so the mobile shopper has a seamless experience. Depending on their category and industry, different businesses can find they have stronger opportunities within some parts of the cycle than others. Some businesses have recurring and ongoing opportunities within the cycle, such as in the case of an expensive purchase that takes a consumer a longer time to decide. Different businesses can adapt to the cycle depending on what they are trying to sell to whom, even in the case of everyday food and groceries.

Giant Eagle is one of the largest food retailers and distributors in the United States, with annual sales of more than $9 billion. Founded in 1931, the company is privately held and has grown over the years to 175 corporate and 54 independently owned supermarkets and 169 fuel and convenience stores. Its stores are located throughout western Pennsylvania, Ohio, West Virginia, and Maryland.

Giant Eagle looks to interact with its customers at multiple stages of the Mobile Shopping Life Cycle. "The way we look at that we illustrate that with an infinity loop," says Donna Pahel, senior manager of interactive and online marketing at Giant Eagle, Inc.[6] "It has multiple loops that reside within it. We agree that the sales funnel is dead and throughout the shopping life cycle customers can be intercepted at different points in time and we have different ways to engage them."

The retailer views its customers holistically and looks at ways to interact beyond when the mobile shopper is in the store. "The way we are looking at that is at each touch point how do we leverage paid, owned, and earned assets to be able to do that really effectively with customers," says Pahel. "We also have added a social customer loop. We're thinking about how social is evolving and how the customer thinks about the shopping process. That is the way we have been looking at that, which we totally changed."

The mobile shopper tends to look at shopping not as a one-time event but rather as an ongoing one, since they are always connected and can shop from wherever they are whenever they want. Giant Eagle views the process of grocery shopping and buying as a continuous cycle and strives to actively participate and interact with their customers throughout that process. "We're saying basically it is that infinite loop," says Pahel. "We can engage the customer when they are in initial consideration, when they are actually honing in that search on a particular product. Obviously for us, because we are predominantly brick and mortar still, I mean we do some online commerce but we're trying, from a digital standpoint, one, to get the customer to choose Giant Eagle, get them into the store, and then assist them while they are in the store. And then on the back end of that, keep them engaged during the post-shop so that we can retain that loyalty on the next trip."

Some of the opportunity for traditional retailers is to integrate their traditional marketing efforts they may have developed over a number of years and merging their learnings from that into the mobile mix. During the pre-buy, Giant Eagle figured some ways to do just that. "Obviously, our traditional team is working on all of those traditional media assets where they are trying to create awareness," says Pahel. "What we are doing from a pre-shop experience is, we are launching an entirely new GiantEagle. com and mobile suite to match up with that. The predominant things are advanced placement, and a reconfiguration of our circular and e-offers and a product catalog which we have never had before because we're not really e-com, but we think it is really important to put the customer in that mind-set because they are showing high intent to shop at Giant Eagle. What we have done typically, a lot of websites put the marketing material up front and then they try to pull you through that to the more hard-core things that the customer is looking for, like the weekly circular and digital coupons. We have actually pushed all of that to the front. Nobody else is doing that right now.

"We put our circular directly on the homepage of the website. From a mobile perspective, if you look at our current mobile app we are slightly behind where everyone is moving to but everyone still makes you drill through to the different things. We are actually pushing some of the circular content and some of the coupons to the front and then we're adopting a Facebook-like menu to help them drill down into it. It is basically flipping that over from what everyone is currently doing. I mean you come on and people talk to you about their marketing messages and all the programs and customers will be able to get at that, but what is center and focused is the circular and e-offers and digital coupons."

THE ONE-TAP APPROACH

Moving the display of the circular applies to both smartphones and tablets. Giant Eagle also believes in customizing the consumer experience based on various factors, including the device being used at the time. "When you come onto the website, you can see a whole list of products that are in the circular and, obviously, we can't take that whole big list and put it on mobile," says Pahel. "So what we do is we pull items based on who we know, what store you are with, and in the next consideration we are going to personalize that. So all of the products based on your shopping history. And then we're also going to sort products by your interest data on social. Obviously we can't show with as much content as we can on the website so what we've done is create a highlight area giving the customer a one-tap direct access to those things. I would tell you it's advanced placement and it's a reorganization of, we've actually bundled up all of the things customers want instant access to. There's no drill-down that occurs." Giant Eagle is active throughout the Mobile Shopping Life Cycle in multiple ways. Says Pahel:

Let's go one step back in that initial consideration set in the pre-buy. We are utilizing social and mobile advertising to corner a customer's attention from that very initial consideration set. We're using the hottest deals that we have and the new programs that we have and trying to get into that consideration set, and then the next step is when they would actually engage one of our venues during the pre-shop. And then, all of that pre-shop stuff on the website and mobile are tied to planning tools. So a shopping list, a menu planner, and so forth so we can continue to get the customer to commit on a deeper and deeper level as they move towards actually going into brick and mortar.

Everything's integrated. All of the functions you can do on the website are integrated with what you see on the mobile app. So a customer can literally do these things anywhere with their mobile device. They can go through the specials, create a shopping list, clip offers on the way to the store or clip offers in the store. And those are loading, so all they have to do is scan their Giant advantage card and purchase a qualifying product and those discounts are coming off. Everything is tied to the rewards program.

On location the customer can access their shopping list, they can clip e-offers in the store, and have those come off by the time they reach point of sale.

We're making it a lot easier for them to do that because the app now is like a whole plethora of functions as soon as you come in the gate and we have prioritized those things because we know from the data that we have captured over the past year and a half that those are the things that customers are utilizing most. We don't want to have to make them work for it.

Currently what will be available for customers is they will have access to the inventory of digital coupons that we have available and they are able to clip them in line at the store and have those load to card and check out with them.

We did an integration with shopkick, and we had "kicks" in their app. We just concluded that pilot with them. That is more before the customer gets in the store than when the customer is in the store. Customers did scan in store, but we actually went a step further with them and had what they called "kick buys." They were digital coupons that a customer could load and we had them integrated. So they were actually loading to card as well.

The customer didn't actually get cents off, they got "kicks" for those. I would tell you the folks that actually did it and loaded them, the redemption rate was super, super high, but there were not enough people using. I don't know if they weren't using our app in our footprint or they weren't using their app with Giant Eagle. They didn't show up in our app, they were integrated with our offer load. So what would happen was if a customer said, "I want to use this kick buy" that loaded onto their Giant advantage card.

At point of purchase, Giant Eagle is evaluating self-checkout. And if we do it we are going to have it be through our app rather than a third-party device. And the other things that we're looking at are item location, and that would likely, if we do, be a partnership with aisle411.

The only thing is you can utilize the Giant advantage card from within the app, you don't have to use the physical card. We have a scannable barcode on there. The only issue is we can't accept it at 100 percent of the locations yet because the scanner can't scan it.

At post-purchase, what we have been looking at is how we engage the customer during that post-purchase cycle. It would be great to get to an electronic receipt. We're still far away from that. But then could we take some of the offers that we are currently doing through the Catalina printer and some of the things we are sending out via direct mail and sent that out to the customer through mobile and through email. And when we get to the point when we're doing the personalizing on social we will be able to push them through the social channels as well.

If we have an app out there that we already have you logged in there and we're personalizing it, we could actually push the offers there as well and have you click to load the card. So we are really advocating the click to load the card in all of this because we want the customer to show intent to purchase. We don't just give it to them and not have them create an action that shows this intent to buy.

We would do that after the purchase or if we had a data set that told us—we might use it as a retargeting method. You looked at us but you didn't purchase anything in a specific point in time, so we might push you an offer.

In using social media after the purchase, we will be looking to expound upon the ways the customers can share. We're doing that heavily from a website perspective, and we'll start to do that. We're creating social sign-ons for all the venues so that we can already have the customer connected and start collecting that data. Everything that we're doing, all the campaigns, we are trying to put that *share* component in there. We are actually looking at, and this is longer term, but rewarding the customer and creating a social currency that is tied to our loyalty program for those online behaviors. Being able to reward customers for those online behaviors. Let's say you clipped an e-offer and then you shared it with so many friends, we might offer you points that would then be tied directly into our Giant Eagle rewards program.

LESSONS LEARNED

As have many captains of mobile influence, Giant Eagle learned many lessons along the way by trying various mobile approaches and closely monitoring customer behavior. "The biggest thing that we learned is we have had a gap by not utilizing our traditional media to talk about digital," says Pahel. "We have invested a lot in a digital perspective to create the awareness, but we are just now starting to utilize some of the traditional vehicles to make customers aware. I would say it is an awareness issue more than anything else for us. And that is because we need to leverage our traditional media vehicles."

This can be a common occurrence when a company delves heavily into mobile. Businesses can leverage all their traditional and, in many cases, proven methods of spreading the word of their products or services and link that to their expanding mobile efforts, which is the Giant Eagle approach. "We actually spend a lot of time and put a lot of resources to engaging our influencer network," says Pahel. "So predominant bloggers in our geographical footprint, we are constantly educating them, holding events with them, and creating things where they can engage and incent their audiences and getting them to educate on our behalf and advocate on our behalf. We have found that those earned impressions are invaluable. When we do these events and we get those guys talking about us it is like friends and family talking about it. It's not Giant Eagle telling you their own stuff is great."

The grocery chain is looking down the road at self-checkout, as are many retailers. "If we could get customers to adopt to scan as they are carting and then have them go ahead and run through checkout, that is absolutely something we would desire to do," says Pahel. "The thought for us is we could then take those front-end resources and move them into the store to better engage the customer. They would use their mobile device to scan their products as they were putting them in cart or they could scan the product to find out more information. It is something we are considering, but we haven't committed to that yet."

Pahel says the scanning likely would be executed through Catalina Marketing, the company working with Stop & Shop on its current in-store scanning systems, as discussed earlier.

Many leading mobile influence companies execute their mobile shopping initiatives by using a combination of both in-house resources and companies that are facilitators of mobile influence. Pahel considers integrating with the apps of others. "One has product data that is really customer friendly and creates a different level of engagement with substitutions based on your wellness desires," she says. "Wellness is a big focus for us across the store. We have been expanding the healthy beauty wellness department across many of our stores. We even have in-store dietitians and aestheticians in some locations. Wellness is predominantly going to play a larger and larger role in the content layers that we have both from a mobile and social perspective.

"For us we have been doing a lot of development ourselves, and unfortunately that has made us a little slower to market than we should be, so we're looking at some really strong, third-party partnership to really help us leapfrog over the next year." Giant Eagle also is focused on long-term behaviors as they relate to the future of grocery shopping. Says Pahel:

I think customers are not going to need much prodding to adopt the tools, I think they are going to expect it. And I think the biggest thing from a grocery standpoint is keeping pace with the customer's expectations because I think part of our infinity loop shows the social customer and that is infiltrating all of your purchasing cycles. How you consider and think about everything, being able to have instantaneous information at your fingertips, being able to do comparisons and being able to tap into your network of friends and family, I think that grocery is going to have to keep pace with all of that to really continue to own the customer's business. Also, there are some really near-term opportunities for us to leverage digital and online shopping during the traditional shopping trip. For example, Target is doing the QR codes in store where you can order some of the top 60 toys that are going to be really hot over Christmas and while you are in line doing your traditional shop you can scan this code and order and have that ordered online and delivered to your house. I think there is some opportunity with groceries down that path and other retailers as well.

If you think of some of the things that are really hard to get at from a traditional brick and mortar, because you either have your club or your grocery and you don't typically see those things melded really quickly. Customers usually have to choose one or the other or they're shopping for both. And I really think some of that stuff can be put in line to be really convenient for the customer to do online ordering from their mobile device while they are in the store that you can really expand upon your selection set and what you are able to offer the customer. It is kind of like what they did in the subway with the online ordering but actually doing that in the brick and mortar.

We're testing curbside express in a couple of our stores. The customer orders online but then they still have to go pick it up curbside. It is convenient for them not to have to come into the store and find things and purchase it. So we are doing part of it for them, but they still have to go online and pick all of the products and still pick it up at the store.

The other thing from a mobile perspective with our gecko format, that is our fuel and convenience format. We will be leveraging mobile, social, and everything digital to first of all keep us in that pre-shop consideration set and making sure that we are top of mind when you are ready to fuel up or you are hungry. And then engaging the customer when they are at the pump to drive them into the store. We are going to use location-based services and different check-in functions to create compelling offers for the customer while they are at the pump. When customers are redeeming fuel purchases they have to scan their Giant advantage card, and when they do that we know who they are and if we have them opted in to receive a mobile message from us. We could message them at that time with an offer to compel them to walk into our store.

Giant Eagle mobile customers predominantly use the iPhone and Android app, downloaded 100,000 times, and they also use the mobile website that can be used from other mobile devices. As other companies have found, the number of customers accessing their assets from a mobile compared to a traditional device is growing exponentially year over year.

Captains of mobile influence such as Giant Eagle, Staples, and Rue La La figure what works best for each of their different customer sets. Whether mobile consumers are shopping in supermarkets, office supply stores, or through flash sales, they all are in stages of the Mobile Shopping Life Cycle.

CONCLUSION

Mobile influence is about providing value to customers as they make their way through the new path to purchase. Mobile shoppers come in all forms of mobile knowledge, ranging from novice to power user, and the influence points in the Mobile Shopping Life Cycle illuminate how marketers can interact all along the way. The consumer is now mobile empowered, and there is no turning back. Shopping has been forever changed.

As you have seen through examples in this book, the captains of mobile influence and the facilitators of mobile influence are leading the charge and collectively getting ahead. Those that take mobile seriously will make some stumbles along the way, but will ultimately succeed since they are moving with their customers. Those companies that dabble in mobile while awaiting some mysterious moment to decide if they should devote major resources to it will find themselves playing catch up, and some will not survive. Those who do nothing in mobile will get nothing out of it.

The question to ask is what percentage of your customers use mobile devices in the shopping process. The answer ultimately will be all of them. A telling statistic is that while most if not all of a company's customers are using mobile devices, less than 1 percent of a typical advertising budget is allocated to mobile, as discussed earlier.

As you have seen throughout this book, a wide range of products and service already are being bought via mobile devices. These range from cars to loans to gas to clothes to groceries. If it can be bought, it will be bought via mobile.

What do you do now that you have this information about the transformation in shopping behavior because of mobile? Here are some suggestions about how to move forward:

Check the Steps. How many of the six phases of the Mobile Shopping Life Cycle does your company participate in? Add those where you now know you should be.

Leverage Brick and Mortar. If you have a physical store, you already have the mobile shopper on location. Serve them while they are there. Add Wi-Fi so your customers can use their phones in-store.

Mobilize Sales Staff. Make sure your sales associates know and understand mobile and what mobile shoppers are doing with their devices while in the store. Arm them with mobile knowhow.

Think Global. Mobile shopping is a global phenomenon, no matter where you are located. Take advantage of potential mobile customers outside your geography.

Capture Phone Numbers. Without your customers' mobile phone numbers, you won't likely execute the most comprehensive mobile marketing with them. There are multiple examples of how do to this in various parts of this book.

Use Multiple Means. There are many mobile tools that can be used to interact with mobile shoppers. These include SMS, MMS, QR codes, apps, and mobile websites. Use the tools. Optimize your mobile website.

Price Check. Use price-comparison apps on your products regularly to see what competitors are charging. That is what your mobile shoppers are going to do.

Use Location. Location is one of the most powerful assets of mobile, providing the capability to provide highly relevant influence close to the transaction. Don't forget the Cool versus Creepy Scale.

Do Something. Waiting is not an option. Test and learn has been rule one in the mobile world since the emergence of the smartphone. Expect to make a mistake or two, then refine and continue.

The intent of this book was to provide some insight into the new shopping behaviors and the magnitude of the impact mobile is about to have. We hope it has given you some helpful ideas on how you can succeed in this continuing mobile revolution and how you can exert your own mobile influence.

appendix

MOBILE PENETRATION
EXCEEDS POPULATION

Country	Mobile Penetration	Mobile Subscribers	Population
Macao, China	236%	1,353,194	573,003
United Arab Emirates	228%	11,727,401	5,148,664
Panama	210%	7,281,074	3,460,462
Hong Kong, China	210%	14,930,948	7,122,508
Saudi Arabia	206%	53,705,808	26,131,703
Antigua & Barbuda	185%	162,773	87,884
Cayman Islands	185%	95,120	51,384
Russia	180%	256,116,581	142,525,588
Montenegro	177%	1,170,000	661,807
Libya	173%	10,000,000	5,767,159
Anguilla	172%	26,019	15,094
Suriname	171%	947,000	553,159
Finland	170%	8,940,000	5,259,250
Kuwait	170%	4,400,000	2,595,628
St. Kitts and Nevis	159%	80,000	50,314
Oman	159%	4,809,248	3,027,959
Austria	158%	13,022,578	8,217,280
British Virgin Islands	154%	46,825	30,391
Dominica	152%	111,000	72,969
Luxembourg	152%	764,973	503,302
Italy	151%	92,300,000	61,016,804
Guatemala	150%	20,715,677	13,824,463
Trinidad and Tobago	149%	1,825,200	1,227,505
Singapore	148%	7,755,200	5,246,787

(continues)

Country	Mobile Penetration	Mobile Subscribers	Population
Bulgaria	148%	10,475,083	7,093,635
Estonia	145%	1,863,120	1,282,963
Uruguay	144%	4,757,425	3,308,535
Seychelles	142%	126,594	89,188
Lithuania	142%	5,004,150	3,535,547
Viet Nam	141%	127,318,045	90,549,390
Botswana	140%	2,900,263	2,065,398
Bahrain	139%	1,693,650	1,214,705
Serbia	139%	10,182,023	7,310,555
Maldives	134%	530,449	394,999
St. Lucia	134%	216,530	161,557
Kazakhstan	134%	23,102,700	17,304,513
Germany	133%	108,700,000	81,471,834
Chile	132%	22,399,969	16,915,020
Argentina	132%	55,000,000	41,769,726
South Africa	131%	64,000,000	49,004,031
United Kingdom	130%	81,612,000	62,698,362
El Salvador	129%	7,837,000	6,071,774
Bermuda	128%	88,200	68,679
Poland	128%	49,200,000	38,441,588
Malta	128%	521,748	408,333
Malaysia	128%	36,661,261	28,728,607
Switzerland	128%	10,017,000	7,850,100
Denmark	127%	7,047,000	5,529,888
St. Vincent and the Grenadines	127%	131,809	103,869
Czech Republic	126%	12,810,000	10,190,213
Taiwan, Province of China	125%	28,861,762	23,174,265
Qatar	124%	2,302,290	1,849,257
Aruba	124%	131,800	106,113
Sweden	123%	11,194,000	9,088,728
Ukraine	123%	55,566,881	45,134,707
Israel	123%	9,200,000	7,473,052
Brazil	123%	242,231,503	197,595,498
Norway	123%	5,750,000	4,691,849
Barbados	121%	347,917	286,705
Faroe Islands	121%	59,446	49,267
Belgium	120%	12,540,603	10,431,477
Netherlands	119%	19,835,000	16,653,734
Thailand	118%	78,667,910	66,720,153
Hungary	117%	11,689,937	9,976,062
Tunisia	117%	12,387,656	10,629,186
Jordan	115%	7,482,561	6,508,271
Morocco	114%	36,553,943	31,968,361
Portugal	114%	12,284,594	10,760,305
Gabon	114%	1,800,000	1,576,665
Croatia	114%	5,115,140	4,483,804

(continues)

Country	Mobile Penetration	Mobile Subscribers	Population
Vanuatu	114%	285,300	250,716
Namibia	114%	2,439,281	2,147,585
Spain	114%	53,066,828	46,754,784
Greece	113%	12,127,985	10,760,136
Australia	113%	24,490,000	21,766,711
Grenada	112%	121,946	108,419
New Zealand	112%	4,820,000	4,290,347
Gibraltar	112%	32,500	28,956
San Marino	111%	35,465	31,817
Peru	111%	32,461,415	29,248,943
Belarus	111%	10,694,900	9,661,508
Iceland	111%	344,085	311,058
Brunei Darussalam	110%	443,161	401,890
Slovak Republic	109%	5,983,059	5,477,038
TFYR Macedonia	109%	2,257,118	2,077,328
Slovenia	108%	2,168,548	2,000,092
Armenia	108%	3,210,802	2,967,975
Korea (Rep.)	108%	52,506,793	48,754,657
Azerbaijan	108%	10,120,105	9,397,279
Romania	107%	23,400,000	21,904,551
United States	106%	331,600,000	311,591,917
Ireland	105%	4,906,352	4,670,976
Latvia	105%	2,309,000	2,204,708
Venezuela	104%	28781999	27,635,743
Kyrgyzstan	104%	5,653,000	5,450,776
Jamaica	104%	2,974,715	2,868,380
Albania	104%	3,100,000	2,994,667
Colombia	103%	46,200,421	44,725,543
Ecuador	102%	15,332,715	15,007,343
Japan	102%	129,868,418	127,469,543
Greenland	102%	58,742	57,670
Egypt	102%	83,425,145	82,079,636
France	102%	66,300,000	65,296,094
Liechtenstein	102%	36,970	36,422
Paraguay	101%	6,529,053	6,459,058
Mauritania	100%	3,283,371	3,281,634

*Population numbers are from U.S. Census Bureau 2011.

*Mobile figures from Aruba, Bermuda, British Virgin Islands, Faroe Islands, Grenada, Kuwait, Montenegro, Netherlands, St. Kitts and Nevis, and Vanuatu are from 2010.

*Mobile Subscribers numbers are from the International Communications Union.

*Mobile penetration found from Mobile Subscribers/Population.

*106 countries in 2011 have mobile penetration of 100% or greater.

NOTES

INTRODUCTION

1. Deloitte Digital, "The Dawn of Mobile Influence; Discovering the Value of Mobile in Retail," 2012, www.deloitte.com/assets/Dcom-UnitedStates/Local%20Assets/Documents/RetailDistribution/us_retail_Mobile-Influence-Factor_062712.pdf.
2. Strategy Analytics, "Wireless Smartphone Strategies (WSS)," October 2012, strategyanalytics.com.
3. IDC Research, "Worldwide and U.S. Mobile Advertising 2012-2016 Forecast Update: Year-End Review," January 2013, www.idc.com.
4. Cisco, "Cisco Visual Networking Index: Global Mobile Data Traffic Forecast Update, 2011-2016," 2012, www.cisco.com.
5. Strategy Analytics, "Wireless Smartphone Strategies (WSS)," October 2012, www.strategyanalytics.com.
6. Distimo, "Emerging App Markets: Russia, Brazil, Mexico and Turkey," 2012, www.distimo.com
7. Jane Yu, vice president and general manager of iWeekly, interview with the author, 2012.
8. National Retail Federation, "Retailers, Industry Experts, and NRF Partner to Launch Integrated Mobile Initiative," August 9, 2012, www.nrf.com/modules.php?name=News&op=viewlive&sp_id=1415.
9. Deloitte Digital, "The Dawn of Mobile Influence; Discovering the Value of Mobile in Retail," 2012, www.deloitte.com/assets/Dcom-UnitedStates/Local%20Assets/Documents/RetailDistribution/us_retail_Mobile-Influence-Factor_062712.pdf.
10. Juniper Research, "Mobile Search & Discovery: Web, Local, AR & Discovery Markets 2012-2017," September 12, 2012, www.juniperresearch.com.
11. M&C Saatchi Mobile, data collected between April and October, October 18, 2012.
12. InMobi and Mobext of Havas Digital, "The Role of Tablets in the Consumer Sales Journey," May 10, 2012, www.inmobi.com.

CHAPTER 1: THE RISE OF THE MOBILE SHOPPER

1. Cisco, "Cisco Visual Networking Index: Global Mobile Data Traffic Forecast Update, 2011-2016," 2012, www.cisco.com.

2. Deloitte Digital, "The Dawn of Mobile Influence; Discovering the Value of Mobile in Retail," 2012, www.deloitte.com/assets/Dcom-UnitedStates/Local%20Assets /Documents/RetailDistribution/us_retail_Mobile-Influence-Factor_062712.pdf.

3. Empathica, "Study: One in 10 Smartphone Owners Have Written a Review on a Website or Social Media Platform While In-Store," July 17, 2012, www.empathica .com/press-release/study-one-in-10-smartphone-owners-have-written-a -review-on-a-website-or-social-media-platform-while-in-store/.

4. Juniper Research, "Buy Now, Pay Mobile," October 9, 2012, www.juniperresearch .com.

5. Juniper Research, "Mobile Ticketing Evolution: NCF, Forecasts and Markets," April 11, 2012, www.juniperresearch.com.

6. Bonin Bough, vice president of global media and consumer engagement at Mondelez International, interview with the author, 2012.

7. Greg Stuart, CEO of the Mobile Marketing Association, statement, 2012.

8. GfK, "Own The Future of Shopping" June 25, 2012.

9. comScore, Inc. "Mobile Metrix 2.0 service," September 2012, www.comscore.com/.

10. The author tested the app in advance at Best Buy on both Android devices and iPhones and appeared at the media launch as a mobile expert on behalf of Citi.

11. Angel Anderson, experience director at CP+B, interview with the author, 2012.

12. Andrew Koven, incoming vice president of e-commerce at Guess, interview with the author, 2012.

13. International Telecommunications Union (ITU), 2012, www.itu.com.

14. Infonetics Research, "2G, 3G, 4G Services and Subscribers: Voice, SMM/MMS," July 16, 2012.

CHAPTER 2: THE SETUP

1. MarketLive, "2012 Consumer Shopping Survey," 2012, www.marketlive.com.

2. Mobile Marketing Association, "MXS," August 29, 2012, www.mmaglobal.com /research/MXS.

3. PQ Media, "U.S. Mobile and Social Media Forecast 2012-2016," 2012, www.pq-media.com.

4. International Data Corporation (IDC), "Worldwide New Media Market Model," October 2012.

5. BIA/Kelsey, "U.S. Local Media Forecast," July 16, 2012, www.biakelsey.com/.

6. Mark Zuckerberg, founder and CEO of Facebook, statements made to Mobile Marketer Analysts, October 24, 2012.

7. Adfonic, "Global AdMetrics Report 2012," 2012, www.adfonic.com.

8. Accenture, "Mobile Web Watch 2012," 2012, www.accenture.com.

9. Accenture, "Mobile Web Watch 2012," 2012, www.accenture.com.

10. Knotice, "Mobile Email Opens Report," 2012, www.knotice.com.

11. John Putman, director of lending business systems at CUNA Mutual Group, interview with the author, 2012.

12. Jeff Ulrich, senior manager of emerging technology at United Airlines, interview with the author, 2012.

13. Tom Weisend, vice president of user experience at Rue La La, interview with the author, 2012.

CHAPTER 3: THE MOVE

1. Deloitte Digital, "The Dawn of Mobile Influence; Discovering the Value of Mobile in Retail," 2012, www.deloitte.com/assets/Dcom-UnitedStates/Local%20

Assets/Documents/RetailDistribution/us_retail_Mobile-Influence-Factor_0627
12.pdf.

2. Juniper Research, "Mobile Coupons Update: Ecosystems Analysis and Marketing Channel Strategy," 2012, www.juniperresearch.com.

3. BJ Emerson, vice president of technology at Tasti D-Lite and Planet Smoothie, interview with the author, 2012.

4. Jeremy Wacksman, vice president of consumer marketing and mobile at Zillow, interview with the author, 2012.

5. John Donahoe, CEO of eBay, public comments, 2012.

6. eBay, "eBay SellerSphere," January 22, 2013, www.ebay.com.

7. Jason Toews, cofounder of GasBuddy, interview with the author, 2012.

8. Curtis Kopf, managing director of e-commerce and innovation at Alaska Airlines, interview with the author, 2012.

CHAPTER 4: THE PUSH

1. Chief Marketing Officer (CMO) Council, "Engage at Every Stage," 2012, www.cmocouncil.org.

2. Deloitte Digital, "The Dawn of Mobile Influence; Discovering the Value of Mobile in Retail," 2012, www.deloitte.com/assets/Dcom-UnitedStates/Local%20Assets/Documents/RetailDistribution/us_retail_Mobile-Influence-Factor_062712.pdf.

3. MarketLive, "2012 Consumer Shopping Survey," 2012, www.marketlive.com.

4. Research Now, "The Vibes Mobile Consumer Report," 2012, www.researchnow.com.

5. Jack Philbin, cofounder, president, and CEO of Vibes, interview with the author, 2012.

6. GroupM Next, "Showrooming and the Price of Keeping Buyers In-Store," 2012, www.groupmnext.com/.

7. Dearrick Knupp, founder and chief product officer at Shop My Label, interview with the author, 2012.

8. U.S. Census Bureau, 2012, www.census.gov/; International Telecommunications Union (ITU), 2012, www.itu.int.

9. Brent Van Rossem, brands director at V&D, interview with the author, 2012.

10. Noël Manning, manager of e-commerce at V&D, interview with the author, 2012.

11. Molly Garris, Digital Strategy Director and mobile practice lead at Leo Burnett and Arc Worldwide, interview with the author, 2012.

12. Pew Internet, "Teens, Smartphones & Texting," 2012, www.pewinternet.org/Reports/2012/Teens-and-smartphones/Summary-of-findings/Overview.aspx.

13. Canadian Wireless Telecommunications Association, 2012, www.cwta.ca.

14. ExactTarget, "Channel Preference Survey," 2012, www.exacttarget.com.

15. Juniper Research, "Mobile Advertising: Messaging, In-App and Mobile Internet Strategies 2012-2017," 2012, www.juniperresearch.com.

16. Juniper Research, "Mobile Messaging Markets," 2012, www.juniperresearch.com.

17. Informa Telecoms & Media, "The Mobile Content and Services Forecast," 2012, informatandm.com.

18. Jeff Hasen, chief marketing officer of Hipcricket, interview with the author, 2012.

19. Amit Shah, vice president of online mobile and social at 1-800-Flowers.com, interview with the author, 2012.

CHAPTER 5: THE PLAY

1. Wrigley Corporation, "Wrigley Heritage Timeline," 2012, www.wrigley.com.

2. Alex Muse, CEO of ShopSavvy, at the MediaPost Mobile Insider Summit, 2012.

3. David Javitch, vice president of marketing at Scanbuy, Inc., interview with the author, 2012.

4. Jane McPherson, chief marketing officer of SpyderLynk, interview with the author, 2012.

5. Dirk Groten, chief technology officer of Layar, interview with the author, 2013.

6. Quintin Schevernels, chief executive officer of Layar, interview with the author, 2013.

7. Maarten Lens-FitzGerald, co-founder of Layar, interview with the author, 2013.

8. Starbucks Corporation, "Starbucks Handbook," January 22, 2013, www.star bucks.com.

9. Edward Lake, attorney at Gacovino and Lake Attorneys in New York, interview with the author, 2012.

10. Target spokesperson, interview with the author, 2012.

11. Macy's spokesperson, interview with the author, 2012.

12. Sears spokesperson, interview with the author, 2012.

13. Best Buy spokesperson, interview with the author, 2012.

14. Walmart spokesperson, interview with the author, 2012.

15. Staples spokesperson, interview with the author, 2012.

16. BJ Emerson, vice president of technology at Tasti D-Lite and Planet Smoothie, interview with the author, 2012.

17. United Airlines spokesperson, interview with the author, 2012.

18. American Airlines spokesperson, interview with the author, 2012.

19. JetBlue spokesperson, interview with the author, 2012.

20. Delta Airlines spokesperson, interview with the author, 2012.

21. John Caron, vice president of marketing at Catalina Marketing Corporation, interview with the author, 2012.

22. John Caron, vice president of marketing at Catalina Marketing Corporation, shopping visit at a Stop & Shop with the author, 2012.

23. Michael Stromer, vice president of customer connections marketing at JetBlue, interview with the author, 2012.

24. Prat Vemana, director of mobile and e-commerce acceleration at Staples, interview with the author, 2012.

CHAPTER 6: THE WRAP

1. Assurant Solutions, "Adoption of Mobile Transactions by the Global Consumer: Does Protection Matter?" 2012, www.assurantsolutions.com.

2. Richard Hartzell, president of MasterCard in Latin America and Caribbean region, official statement, February 23, 2012.

3. Richard Hartzell, president of MasterCard in Latin America and Caribbean region, and Ajay Banga, worldwide president and CEO of MasterCard, interview with the author, 2012.

4. Pew Research Study, "Pew Research Center's Internet and American Life Project," 2012, www.pweinternet.org.

5. Bert Insight, "Handset Connectivity Technologies–3rd Edition," www. bertinsight.com.

6. SXSW Interactive Conference in Austin, Texas, attended by the author, 2012, www.sxsw.com

7. Ryan Hughes, chief marketing officer of Isis, interview with the author and public comments in the Isis panel presentation at SXSW, 2012.

8. Marc Warshawsky, senior vice president and mobile solutions executive at Bank of America, interview with the author, 2012.

9. Julio Alejandro Arango, representative of Arango Software, interview with the author, 2012.

10. Accenture, "Mobile Web Watch," 2012, http://www.accenture.com/SiteCollection-Documents/PDF/Accenture-Mobile-Web-Watch-Internet-Usage-Survey-2012.pdf.

11. Mung Ki Woo, group executive of mobile at MasterCard Worldwide, interview with the author, 2012.

12. IDC, "IDC Financial Insight's Consumer Payments Survey," 2012, idc.com.

13. IDC, "IDC Financial Insight's Consumer Payments Survey," 2012, idc.com.

14. Juniper Research, "Mobile Ticket Evolution: NFC, Forecasts and Markets," 2012, www.juniperresearch.com.

15. Jeff Sellinger, cofounder and chief product officer of shopkick, interview with the author, 2012.

CHAPTER 7: THE TAKEAWAY

1. Cisco, "Cisco Visual Networking Index Global Mobile Data Traffic Forecast," February 14, 2012, http://www.cisco.com/en/US/solutions/collateral/ns341/ns525/ns537/ns705/ns827/white_paper_c11-520862.html.

2. James Citron, founder and chief executive officer of Mogreet, interview with the author, 2012.

3. Eric Friedman, director of sales and revenue operations at Foursquare, interview with the author, 2012.

4. Steven Carpenter, founder and CEO of Endorse, interview with an author, 2012.

5. Kimberley Gardiner, national digital marketing and social media manager at Toyota Motor Sales USA, interview with the author, 2012.

CHAPTER 8: MARKETING THROUGHOUT THE MOBILE SHOPPING LIFE CYCLE

1. Brian Tilzer, senior vice president of global e-commerce at Staples at the time of the interview, interview with the author, 2012.

2. Prat Vemana, director of Velocity Lab and mobile strategy at Staples, interview with the author, 2012.

3. ForeSee, "ForeSee Mobile Satisfaction Report, Retail Edition," September 13, 2012, www.foresee.com.

4. ForeSee, "ForeSee Mobile Satisfaction Report, Retail Edition," September 13, 2012, www.foresee.com.

5. Larry Freed, president and CEO of ForeSee, interview with the author, 2012.

6. Donna Pahel, senior manager of interactive and online marketing customer relationship marketing at Giant Eagle, Inc., interview with the author, 2012.

INDEX